QUEASY:

a wannabe writer's bumpy journey through
England in the 70s

QUEASY

**A WANNABE WRITER'S BUMPY JOURNEY
THROUGH ENGLAND IN THE '70S**

MADELINE SONIK

ANVIL PRESS PUBLISHERS // VANCOUVER

Library and Archives Canada Cataloguing in Publication

Title: Queasy : a wannabe writer's bumpy journey through England in the '70s : a memoir / by Madeline Sonik.
Names: Sonik, Madeline, 1960- author.
Description: 1st edition.
Identifiers: Canadiana 2022016780X | ISBN 9781772141894 (softcover)
Subjects: LCSH: Sonik, Madeline, 1960- | LCSH: Sonik, Madeline, 1960-
   —Childhood and youth. | LCSH:
Sonik, Madeline, 1960—Travel—England. | LCSH: England—Social
conditions—20th century. | CSH:
   Authors, Canadian (English)—21st century—Biography. | LCGFT:
Autobiographies.
Classification: LCC PS8587.O558 Z46 2022 | DDC C818/.5403—dc23

Cover design: Dave Barnes
Interior layout: HeimatHouse
Represented in Canada by Publishers Group Canada
Distributed by Raincoast Books

The publisher gratefully acknowledges the financial assistance of the Canada Council for the Arts, the Canada Book Fund, and the Province of British Columbia through the B.C. Arts Council and the Book Publishing Tax Credit.

Disclaimer: While *Queasy* is a work of nonfiction, many names have been changed to protect identities.

Anvil Press Publishers Inc.
P.O. Box 3008, Station Terminal
Vancouver, B.C. V6B 3X5 Canada
www.anvilpress.com

PRINTED AND BOUND IN CANADA

This book is dedicated to all the strong, positive, female role models who've encouraged me to follow my dreams.

CONTENTS

CRIMINALS

THERE WAS A SAWED-OFF SHOTGUN. It was pointed at my face, and although I aspired to become a writer, I was fortunately ignorant of Anton Chekhov and the distillation of his prescriptive advice: If a loaded gun appears in Act One, it should be fired in Act Two.

A chilly March day succumbing to evening found me loitering by the Projects, smoking cigarette butts and swinging on the worn band swings in a nearby park. Someone called my name and then more quietly said, "Come here a minute."

I recall I was wearing my friend Karen's smock top. She'd made it herself using a Simplicity pattern and a few yards of bargain basement calico with a cornflower print. I wore the top open at the neck, even though it exposed more of my flesh to the cold, and once I'd made my way to the door of the townhouse to which I'd been summoned and saw the weapon taking aim, realized that my uncovered flesh was also exposed to the scrutiny of the gunman.

It was springtime in the 1970s, the world was busy spitting out dramas, translucent strands of human detritus, that time, as always, would harden to history. I'd seen the famous pictures of Patty Hearst, the submachine gun in her hands. She was only nineteen, only five years my senior when kidnapped and converted to terrorism. Soon, she would be arrested and brought to trial — the trial of the century, as some reporters would dub it — though they had no crystal ball to scry, no system to forecast the future trials of serial killer Ted Bundy, or O.J. Simpson, or president Bill Clinton, for that matter, who would earn the nickname Slick Willie for his troubles.

Hearst joined the Symbionese Liberation Army after fifty-seven days of captivity, in which she was blindfolded, kept in a closet, and raped. One of the terrorists who raped her, Willie Wolfe, gave her a rope pendant featuring an Olmec monkey charm. The charm, he told her, was twenty-five hundred years old and his "most treasured possession." She still had the charm when brought to trial, a fact which the prosecution claimed undermined her testimony, for surely any moral woman would dispose of such an object, no matter what its archeological significance, no matter what its value.

Seven women and five men would compose her jury. When interviewed afterwards, according to newspapers, finding Hearst guilty of bank robbery and the felonious use of a weapon was the most difficult decision of their lives. More difficult, apparently, than getting married, changing jobs, having children — a decision fraught with such emotional strain that some jurors wept uncontrollably; some even vomited.

But the sort of emotional strain experienced by having a gun poised to blow you away, as I did this particular March evening, and as Patty Hearst did by her kidnappers, is of a different kind, for even while the knees weaken and the plaintive stomach growls, such bodily affect is nothing compared to the psychological event. For me, it remains vivid in memory decades afterwards. It was as if the earth's rotation abruptly slowed, as if some flashing strobe had hijacked the sun. My arms moved yet lingered in the susurration of a moment, all haste spent, while consciousness expanded outward, taking in nuances like a sharp cognizant pleat. It was more than just experiencing the world in slow motion, more than just the odd lack of symmetry in time. This phenomenon, called *time dilation*, is a documented response to terror.

The man behind the gun, who I'd seen only once before, had an icy intensity in his blood-brown eyes. He was the father of a friend, a friend who like me felt alienated from the common herd and perched longingly on its periphery. Neither of us wished to commit ourselves. Neither of us believed we would wholly find acceptance anywhere. Both of us were oddballs and refused, or simply had no way of knowing how, to rid ourselves of our debilitating oddness. The insularity of adolescence made it impossible to entertain a time when we would no longer feel this way. I responded with calculated madness; my friend, Stan, responded with crime.

I thought of Stan as a cross between Henry Winkler and Al Pacino, a cool, funny sort of guy who could act tough but was really very sensitive. In the recent past he'd taken to wearing a gold lettered necklace that spelled out his birth name, Ibrahim. The jewellery was a gift from his wealthy Saudi Arabian grandfather who shared the name, though Stan found using an English pseudonym made life easier in our subdivision. My knowledge of the world was pitifully lacking in spite of having access to the *National Geographic* at home. When I thought of Saudi Arabia, the only image I could conjure was Barbara Eden in her pink harem pantaloons. My brother referred to Stan as a *camel jockey*. I didn't understand what it meant or know it was an ethnic slur. Stan pretended he thought it was funny.

He robbed a variety store at age seventeen, vanished from the neighbourhood, served some small time, and was released back into the world. Later, he amused us — the outcast students of his Grade 10 English class — recounting his trial in graphic detail; doing impressions of the frightened shrew of a variety store clerk and his wily lawyer; painting a picture of the courtroom and the mysterious black box he called *Exhibit A* that looked to the untrained eye like a weapon's container, but was actually a clarinet case.

"Was this what you saw the defendant, Stan Naji, carry into the store the night of the robbery?" he asked, with a booming comic voice.

"Yes. Oh, yes," he trilled, aping the store clerk, fluttering his eyes, laying his hand across his forehead as if he might faint. "That brown man over there was going to kill me."

"Mr. Naji, would you please approach the bench?" he said gruffly.

"Dear God, No! No! Put him back in his cage!" he screeched.

We outcasts were in hysterics watching and listening.

"Does this case belong to you?" the lawyer asked.

Stan nodded his head meekly.

"Would you please open it?"

He nodded his head again.

"Somebody stop him!" the clerk hysterically wailed.

"Would you mind assembling your weapon?"

He mimicked the clerk sobbing piteously.

"And now, would you mind playing a few bars?"

All the stories Stan told about his illegal exploits were funny: getaway cars that refused to start, bumbling partners blinded by ski masks.

"I have a plan," Stan said one day after everyone but me had vacated our classroom. He moved to a blackboard and started drawing as if he were a football coach rendering a play diagram.

"This is the bank," he said, drawing an oblong shape on the board, "and this is the banker's house," he said, drawing another smaller box. "And this," he said, drawing a slightly bigger box at the other end of the board, "is the safe house. It's where we keep the banker's wife tied up while we get *him* to give us the ransom money."

"That's not even funny," I said.

"Yeah, I know!" he responded, pulling an eraser through his chalk diagram, "*back* to the drawing board...very slowly," he added, turning towards me, lifting his arms in the air as if he were under attack, as if I had drawn a gun on him.

My arms instinctively did the same as I faced his gun-wielding father that March evening. In what must have been a split second, scenes from black-and-white cowboy movies flashed through my mind. *Gunsmoke* and *The Wild Wild West* theme music played on a continuous loop. I'd always hated those programs, the way they exuded a macho maleness and marginalized women, though I hadn't identified this as the problem then.

Hands up! Reach for the sky! The phrases came into my thoughts unbidden, the diminutive moustachioed Looney Tunes character Yosemite Sam appeared, shouting: *"Keep reachin' for the ceiling, a-till ya reach it, varmint!"* Strangely, I didn't think about Stan, but of his mother, for she'd been the one who'd called me to the door and to Mr. Naji's gun.

"It doesn't please me," she'd once said, "when you stay out so late in the park with my son." She didn't approve because I was a girl and Stan was a boy, and while staying out late at night was an okay practice for a boy, it was "shameful" for a girl, especially when she kept company with a boy. "It means you are not a good girl," she told me.

I wondered if this gun aimed at my face by her husband might have something to do with that — the perception I was bad. My defences suddenly kicked in. Every fibre in my body ached to grab the door frame and swing making monkey noises, or to leap at her, catch her in my arms and plant a wet sloppy kiss on her forehead, then stutter like Porky Pig, *Th-th that's all folks!* and run down the road laughing maniacally. Bursts of insane behaviour like these were my trademark and the way I handled stressful situations. But instead of doing any of these things, I just stood there, paralyzed.

This was all taking place in the city of Windsor, in the province of

Ontario, in the country of Canada. It was taking place in a subdivision called Fontainebleau, in a geared-to-income housing project some thirty driving minutes, or two and half walking hours, from Detroit, Michigan, U.S.A.

Detroit had recently garnered the title *Murder Capital of the World*. Windsor's nickname, on the other hand, was the *City of Roses*. Unlike our American neighbour to the North, shooting deaths rarely occurred here. But crimes, furtive crimes, had always flowered.

I myself am a petty criminal, though I don't see it this way. Although legally underage and forbidden to drink alcohol, I drink it whenever I can get it and have twice possessed and smoked marijuana cigarettes. I've stolen from the five and dime three pairs of fishhook earrings ornamented, respectively, with Snoopy, Woodstock, and Holly Hobbie. They are earrings that I'll never wear. I stole them only because I was unhappy and believed that theft was a sin. I stole them because in the twisted reasoning of the self-destructive, I'd hoped to inflict an indelible wound to my soul that would compromise my standing with God. But I've also stolen for other reasons. After the earrings, I stole from my high school's library *Some Day You'll Write* and *The Creative Writer*. I wanted to be an author, but wasn't a fast reader and figured it would probably take me a few years to get through these thin books. I also regularly steal cigarettes from my mother to feed my burgeoning tobacco addiction and cookies from the tins she hides under her bed. I feel entitled to both.

The most daring crimes, however, are the ones I and a coterie of outcasts are involved in at the behest of Elizabeth Felix, the most popular girl in school. We're happy to be her acolytes because her attentions legitimize our sorry existences, and so we agree to partner her in a variety of return fraud schemes. Elizabeth is a blond, blue-eyed, straight A+ student, who is a year younger than me, but looks as if she's in her twenties. No one would ever suspect her of doing anything untoward. She has exquisite, light piano-playing fingers and laughs adorably when revealing the haul she's accumulated from an afternoon of shoplifting, then judiciously determines which one of us will go back into the stores and ask for refunds. While a cut of ill-gotten gains might be nice and I would like for Elizabeth to find me indispensable, this kind of scam is far too nerve-wracking for someone as anxious as me, especially when Elizabeth begins stealing larger and more expensive items. When she selects me to return things, I inevitably fail. I don't mind lying to her, telling her that the store detectives are on to us, that the police have been called, that we need to leave. Occasionally, in these instances, she'll give me something she's stolen: a blouse, a piece of jewellery, an item that doesn't suit her.

Although Stan has never participated in these rituals, he, like most young men, is attracted to Elizabeth. He used to seek out opportunities to be alone with her, to lead her away from her acolytes, to ply her with alcohol. One day, when I go to call on Elizabeth, her father answers the door and tells me never to come there again. He shouts that I'm a bad influence, that I and my ilk, meaning I presume Elizabeth's acolytes, should all be in reform school, although from the tone of his voice, I think he really means we all should be dead. I'm afraid to ask what's happened. I wonder if Elizabeth's thefts have been discovered, if police have dragged her away, but the drama is far more covert.

It is Stan who finally explains because Stan is implicated. Elizabeth, he said, was drinking and got so shit-faced that she puked all over her good blue dress. He took her into a gas station washroom and tried, he said, to clean her up. Several hours later, he delivered her home: still drunk, only semi-conscious, and immodestly dishevelled. Mr. Felix was irate. If he'd possessed a gun, he might have turned it on Stan, might have pulled the trigger, might have put an end to Stan's eventful, tragic, uncertain life, but to my knowledge he didn't own a gun; there was no glass weapons case in the living room, no wooden rifle racks hanging on the wall. Elizabeth regularly rummaged through her parents' belongings for money and cigarettes and chewing gum. If there'd been a gun, undoubtedly she'd have found it, and on the day Stan delivered her home, looking as if she'd been taken advantage of, if there'd been a gun, the whole subdivision would have known.

Stan has a younger sister, Jannah, who everyone calls Jan. She, like Elizabeth, is both beautiful and physically mature for her age, so Stan can understand why Elizabeth's father was so angry. If some guy brought Jan home drunk and bedraggled, Stan says, he'd be angry too. He'd probably beat the shit out of the guy, or, haha, hit him over the head with a clarinet.

Guns do not play a large role in our neighbourhood. Few residents appear to harbour them. When, occasionally, one does materialize, it and, more pointedly, the story it's attached to, becomes epic. For example, there's the story of Larry Koziak, a boy who lives at the end of my street. He ventured into a nearby field to ride a farmer's timid horse. The farmer, fed up with the pranks of youth, loaded a gun with birdshot and rock salt, and then, at close range, blasted Larry in the rear end. "It was like being knocked down by a bulldozer," Larry said, and the excruciating stinging that followed had him running naked through the streets as the fabled Archimedes, though Larry was heading for a bath rather than away from one, and screaming *my ass is on fire*, rather than *Eureka*.

The stories we tell about guns are funny ones. There are none of accidental disasters, of unintentional maiming or heartrending deaths. Toddlers do not find handguns in our neighbourhood, teens do not take them to their classrooms. This is only because they're not prevalent here, for what teen could resist taking something so forbidden to school?

The households that contain guns are usually inhabited by police officers and soldiers and hunting enthusiasts. A few years hence, after I've moved away to England and left my old Barbie dolls temporarily in a friend's care, her eighteen-year-old brother who hunts pheasants with a pellet gun will string my dolls along a clothes line and, using his rifle, perform a mass execution.

But as the world slowly turns, as my knees wobble like jelly, as infinite seconds break into infinite nanoseconds, and as Stan's father, Mr. Naji, points a gun at my face, I can't imagine a future, especially one where the news of my dolls will feel like a bullet piercing my heart.

There has been no Columbine High School Massacre, no Sandy Hook Elementary School Shooting. Colin Thatcher is the Liberal MLA for Thunder Creek, Saskatchewan, not the murderer of his ex-wife, and it's still business as usual for Helmuth Buxbaum, the multimillionaire nursing home owner, and his spouse, Hanna, who has not yet been torn from the family car by a hitman and, at Helmuth's directive, shot in the head. The phrase "going postal" has not yet found its way into English usage because Patrick Sherrill, the ex-marine who will kill fourteen co-workers at the Edmond, Oklahoma, post office, has not yet become a harassed and vengeful letter carrier. So much looms in the future, while my mind and body are shackled in the here and now, looking into the stubby bore of Stan's father's gun.

But I will survive this moment. Time will swiftly move on for me. Traumatic events, in general, have a tendency to recede like barrel-bodied mole crabs, burrowing on the beach. They remain imperceptible until, by choice or accident, we unearth them, and I have discovered as the years have passed and I've attained my childhood career goal, that writing has a great deal in common with sifting living creatures from clammy sand.

There are near death experiences where people have reported life flashing before their eyes — time completely vanishing and details from their past playing out like movies on a screen. In some instances, they sit in judgement, observing with clarity all the mistakes they've made. But on the night Stan's father levels his gun at me, I'm not near death, only frightened, the mistakes I've made remain unseen. My *life review*, as the phenomenon is called, will not take place until decades later, and not in this quick conventional way. Rather, it will occur slowly and laboriously as an ongoing project once I'm cognizant of my own mortality. The act of writing will become my portal to a past where I will observe myself hell-bent on the future. Hell-bent on growing up, getting a driver's licence, legally buying my beer in a bar. Hell-bent on escaping childhood, the torture of which is so unspeakable it must be repressed until adolescence when, if one is fortunate, amnesia will set in, as it does for most adults who never have to think back to a time of being so powerless and at the mercy of a child-hating world.

When I consciously dig down into the recesses of my memory, the images of Stan and I that are most marked depict vulnerability rather than wrongdoing, dread rather than rage. I see us sitting on a toboggan hill on a cold wintery evening. It's the evening that Stan's sister arrives home late, argues with her father, and is hanged by the neck from a metal beam in the basement for her insubordination.

At this time there are gallows on the third floor of our city's antiquated, dirty Brock Street jail. Capital punishment is alive and well in Canada, even though no one has been legally hanged in the country since the early '60s, and not in Windsor since 1943.

Stan will take a knife, cut his sister down from the beam before she strangles, and have the forethought to pack a duffle bag for himself before he flees. "Where's Jan?" I ask when he tells me what's happened.

He doesn't know, it isn't his problem.

"Where will you go?" I ask. We're both shivering. The night is oppressive.

"Some place," he says. "Some place. Don't worry."

When the newspaper reports Stan's arrest at a house on Howard Avenue, it will cite neighbours as saying that he and another man had lived there for close to a year. Perhaps he had gone there every day without my knowing, perhaps his exodus had long been planned. There were many things, obviously, that Stan didn't tell me, but the one thing he did say that night on the toboggan hill, and that I failed to believe, was that he intended to rob a bank.

Police don't contact me when he's arrested. They do, however, speak to others in our neighbourhood. I wonder if it's considered a crime if I don't contact them — if I fail or neglect to tell them about Jan and what happened the night before, explain why Stan needed money, why he had to get away. In my teenaged manner of reasoning, with my heart and not my head, mitigating circumstances will always trump law.

A newspaper story of the robbery makes clear that Stan didn't use his clarinet, but a weapon resembling a machine gun, a sawed-off .303 carbine. It makes clear that another man, a man in his 60s, was Stan's accomplice, though Stan, alone, went into the bank; he, alone, brandished the gun. The accomplice, Warren Simon, a career criminal with a terminal illness, waited outside in the getaway car. A bystander at the bank jotted down his licence number, and Stan and Simon were picked up fifteen minutes after the robbery.

At the Brock Street jail, I become Stan's only visitor. Never having been incarcerated, I can't understand his nonchalance, his outward indifference. One day he appears at our visit time shorn of his long wavy hair, shaved completely bald, gashes on his scalp. He makes jokes, as usual, says he did this defacing thing to himself. "You think this is bad?" he points at his head. "You should see what the razor looks like." I don't believe him, not for a second, not that *he* cut off his hair, not that he doesn't care it's gone.

He asks if I'll wear his golden necklace. He can't keep it in prison, and although I'd rather not be responsible for something he values, I relent when he adds: "It's a superstitious kind of thing." My life, like his, is ruled by omens, by the occurrence of arbitrary events — *if a traffic light changes to green before I get to the corner, if a leaf falls from a tree, if the next person I see is female, then the thing I most dread won't come to pass.* This kind of forecasting is the result of uncertainty, the consequence of disempowerment, and so I agree to wear Stan's neckless, hoping it will bring him peace.

I sign for the necklace on my way out. It spills from a white paper envelope. It's heavier than it looked on Stan's neck. Heavier, I will discover, than I ever could imagine. I rub the letters between my fingers, read the exotic name, then unfurl the chain, clasp it behind my neck and allow myself to forget.

I know nothing of *world religions,* though I attend a class in high school that spuriously goes by that all-encompassing name. The teacher is a man who is obsessed with India. He lectures about Brahmins and Untouchables. He wears a black turtleneck sweater and a tweed jacket and one day takes us on a field trip to the only Indian restaurant in the city. Besides Hinduism, we don't discuss any other religions. If I've ever heard the term Muslim (or Moslem as the papers of the day spell it) I'm not sure who it applies to. The only holy book I've ever seen is a Bible, and during a childhood stint in the Baptist church when I was nine learned through a hymn that it was "the only book that God had giv'n."

I therefore know nothing about the Quran, or the great importance conferred upon Ibrahim (Abraham in English), the prophet who is considered the father of the Arab people. I know nothing of his war against paganism, or the many stories of his trickster antics, the way, for example, he smashes all but the largest idol that his father manufactures and places in its hands a stick. When asked later how this destruction occurred, he cheekily claims the largest idol did it. His purpose was not only to destroy what he considers sacrilege, but to show how ridiculous it is to see lifeless things as worthy of worship.

I wear Stan's keepsake, unconscious of the fact I wear it, and the night I'm summoned to the Naji's house and the gun is pointed at my face only gradually realize that it's this, the golden necklace, that Stan's father demands.

Symbolic jewellery is on the rise this decade, and according to an article in the *Ottawa Journal*, most of it comes from subcultures which either through legitimate threat or paranoia feel their messages must be guarded. For example, the eleventh letter of the Greek alphabet, the lambda, is worn on medallions as representation of gay and lesbian rights while a pictograph pendent of the planet Venus, a circle with a cross beneath, is a strong feminist symbol and even stronger when the circle contains a fist. Another popular jewellery emblem in this era of *vasectomania* (a term coined by researchers David and Helen Wolfers) is that of Mars, typically depicted as a circle with a projecting arrow. In this instance, however, the circle is broken, letting interested female parties know that the man who sports it is sterile.

Jewellery, throughout history, has been imbued with special powers: powers to communicate, powers to heal. In ancient Egypt, amulets were frequently buried with the dead to preserve the soul and expedite entry to the afterlife. For the living, amulets could ward off evil, eviscerate poison or attract love. Even in this decade, as I face Stan's father's gun, certain kinds of jewellery are said to be lucky, and though the scientifically minded, like the Montreal Canadians defenseman Serge Savard, might say they don't believe, when push comes to shove, when, for example, an admiring fan sends a lucky medallion, Savard won't dispose of it, but hangs it in the team's dressing room until the end of the final series of the year's Stanley Cup playoffs.

Because I'm young and my life is so uncertain. Because I live by omens, I know from experience that things which purport to bestow good fortune are not to be relied upon. They can sour quickly, turn afflicted, become cursed, and when Mr. Naji demands Stan's necklace, I have no qualms about surrendering it. I'm happy to remove it, happy to lay it in his hand, happy to escape a terrifying situation that will vanish from my thinking for many years until I reel it back and find the memory still quivering, even in the context of a different world.

As a teenager, I'm not yet aware of the relentlessness of time which moves onward, ever onward, like an impatient mother dragging her offspring home. I haven't yet felt the way days merge to weeks, weeks to years, years to decades, or how with this temporal passing, we pass too, into different people, different lives.

Shortly after this spring night, Stan will be transferred to Kingston Penitentiary, and I'll move away from Windsor. Although we'll correspond for a while, eventually the glaring discrepancies in our lived experience will starve communication. Jan and Mrs. Naji will return, for a time, to her homeland. Mr. Naji will die of cancer and Patty Hearst, after serving almost two years in jail, will have her sentence commuted, then marry her body guard, a San Francisco police officer, and live an extraordinarily, ordinary life. She'll do some acting, write some books, volunteer for worthy organizations, have children and grandchildren and be, as President Jimmy Carter said, "a model citizen in every way."

READING WUTHERING HEIGHTS

BEFORE WE GO TO ENGLAND, I spend hours in my yellow room, hours trying to read the novel *Wuthering Heights*, while I listen to the radio and think of my old boyfriend, while I examine my hands and smoke cigarettes. Dr. Luther Terry, U.S. surgeon-general, first reported on the hazards of smoking thirteen years ago, but I blithely puff away, take toxic smoke into my teenaged lungs, and push it out again, often in the form of shapely rings.

I read and re-read Emily Bronte's opening lines:

1801. — I have just returned from a visit to my landlord — the solitary neighbour that I shall be troubled with. This is certainly a beautiful country! In all England, I do not believe that I could have fixed on a situation so completely removed from the stir of society. A perfect misanthropist's heaven.

I admonish myself for my ignorance. No matter how many times I read it, I can't understand what it means. I put the book down, jot the word "misanthropist," which I then look up in a dictionary, but deciphering a single word doesn't make the passage any more comprehensible.

David Bowie sings *"Rock 'n' Roll Suicide"* on the radio. T-shirts and denim jackets sometimes brandish its title. *"Time takes a cigarette, puts it in your mouth. You pull on your finger, then another finger, then your cigarette."* These lyrics are cryptic words as well, but unlike Emily Bronte's, at least they make me conscious of my *nico-teen* ennui.

I examine my right hand. The index and middle fingers are stained yellow-brown. I deliberate over their shape and size, the crossings on the palms, the sweep of lines, the swirl of circles. I became an amateur prophet after finding my mother's Dell purse book on palmistry, and check and recheck my evolving fate. It's as if I've been propelled through time. As if my hand were a computer screen and I can't stop myself from surfing the net. But I'm a captive of the '70s. Tim Berners-Lee, the man who will invent the World Wide Web, hasn't yet graduated from Queen's College, Oxford, and I, a neophyte palmist, could never imagine the way technology will impact the future.

"You're too old to lose it, too young to choose it." Bowie's enigmatic words persist, and I think of destiny. I think of free-will. I have no conception of philosophical debate, yet feel completely hamstrung by my lack of agency. I pick the novel up again, light another cigarette, and wade through the lumbering prose.

Whenever I earn enough babysitting money to buy a new pack of smokes, I always turn the first one I touch upside down. It's a cigarette to wish on when all the others are gone. Right now, as my eyes skim over these unassimilated words, I'm wishing I could go out with my old boyfriend, wishing he'd call, wishing I were smarter, prettier, better; that I could read this novel straight the way through, without stumbling, or daydreaming, or feeling sorry for myself.

Since my mother sold our house and said we're moving, I've been unable to focus, unable to sleep. I find myself picking the flesh off my thumbs. When I finally do pass out, my dreams are filled with vehicles careening out of control. My mother is always meant to be driving, and I'm always aware of the real-life fact she never learned how. I don't have a driver's license either. Besides being too young to drive, my mother is dead set against "Drivers' Education" for girls. "Giving a teenaged girl a driver's license is like giving a baby a gun," she once said.

It's illegal for me to take the wheel, illegal for me to rescue us. When I wake, heart thumping, senses wired, my mind indiscriminately parades all the portents of misfortune that we ignored: a white owl that kept circling and landing on our roof, a sparrow that broke its neck after slamming into our living room window, a casserole dish that exploded in the kitchen for no apparent reason, and two red front doors. The first was in Chicago. My mother painted it red thinking it was lucky, and then my father lost his job. When we had to move to Windsor, Ontario, she made the same mistake again, and my father died. At his funeral, she blamed me for his death, said that with all my "back chat" and "defiance" I worried him into cancer, but I knew it wasn't my fault. I knew it had to do with bad energy.

Although my mother is a walking annal of superstitious lore, although she's taught me everything I know — like not to put my shoes on tables, not to put my hat on beds, not to whistle in the house, or walk under ladders, or sing Christmas songs until December first — she doesn't always get it right. Sometimes objects reputed to be lucky aren't, sometimes people and situations change them, sometimes what's lucky for most people isn't lucky for everyone, sometimes it's just a load of BS.

If you want to know what's really lucky, you've got to pay attention. How many stars were there in the sky? Which way was the wind blowing? Did good things start happening after you picked up a leaf? A twig? A quarter? But once you've identified it, don't think it will last. Luck is like gasoline. It evaporates quickly and has the potential to murderously explode.

Wuthering Heights is the name of Mr. Heathcliff's dwelling. 'Wuthering' being a significant provincial adjective, descriptive of the atmospheric tumult to which its station is exposed in stormy weather. Pure, bracing ventilation they must have up there at all times.

I persevere with my reading, persevere with attempts to understand. I jot down and look up the word "tumult" then suck my "little tube of delight" — a euphemism for a cigarette not yet coined by British dramatist Dennis Potter.

I put the book down and examine my palms. The left is said to reveal the lot one is born with, while the right foretells one's future destiny. I search for the certainty of better times, study the minutiae of the heart line, hoping to find my old boyfriend there. I've noticed that the marks and lines in both palms change, but I'm not put off by contradictions. Already I know my life's in flux. I examine my palms for outcomes. "What will the future bring?" I take a hit off my cigarette, lift Emily Brontë's book and read:

...the power of the north wind blowing over the edge.

I hitchhike to the public library, find a book on magic, and copy out a love potion before we move to England. I concoct it in my mother's kitchen, stirring water, cloves, honey, and cinnamon in her good stainless-steel pot. I need some rose petals, but it's winter and I can't buy them from a florist because I've spent the last of my babysitting money on cigarettes. I improvise with banana peel, with the rind of an orange, with a teaspoon of canned peas left over from yesterday's dinner, and with a few grains of tobacco, which I shake from the bottom of an empty Du Maurier packet. I retrieve *Wuthering Heights* from my bedroom, then light up my latest wish cigarette, hoping it will reinforce the spell. As I puff out grey halos the size of onion rings and stir, I continue my reading. The juggling of numerous activities will one day be called "multitasking," but I call it "killing a whole bunch of birds with buckshot" — which sounds more productive than simply "killing two birds with one stone."

I'll show you how far I've progressed in the Black Art: I shall soon be competent to make a clear house of it. The red cow didn't die by chance.

The novel is beginning to make a little more sense to me; I'm beginning to get a feel for the idiomatic eccentricities and the befuddling construction of sentences. In grade nine, before I dropped out, we studied *The Merchant of Venice.* I should realize that language and its composition are constantly evolving — that the world is constantly changing — that Bronte's English isn't my English, but I don't.

Oh wicked, wicked.

I imagine my ex-boyfriend.

. . . gasped the elder.

I take a toke from my cigarette.

May the Lord deliver us from evil.

In the 1970s, sorcery is a staple of popular culture. There's a whole slew of good witches who have nothing whatsoever to do with the devil. I've seen the 1958 romantic comedy *Bell Book and Candle* at least three times and have watched countless episodes of *Bewitched.* Still, I wouldn't want anyone to know that I've been driven to magic, that magic seems the only way I might get what I want. I stir the mess in the pot and say, *Spirits of the earth, spirits of the sea, bring my lover back to me.* I think of my ex-boyfriend and hope the magic will take. I don't question the ethics of trying to bind a person against his will. It will be years before I learn the inappropriateness of my action, years before a Wiccan priestess will tell me the considered negative consequences and long-term complications of such a spell.

I read *Wuthering Heights* and wait for my potion to boil. When it cools, it's more the consistency of tar than liquid. I transfer some into a white cosmetic jar. It's meant to be furtively poured into something my ex-boyfriend will consume, but I know this is impossible. Even though I still see his sister, and frequently get invited to the family home, I never have meals there and virtually never see him. His sister tells me all about the girls he dates. It's torturous to hear, but I always ask for more details. It's torturous, but I never stop the conversation. I never say, "I have to go home."

Some nights, I prowl the streets in front of his house. Some nights, I squeeze myself under his wooden back porch. I live with the hope of seeing him and fantasize that he hopes to see me. Yet when his foot touches the wooden porch stair, my heart races and I freeze.

In the 1970s, we don't call this kind of behaviour *stalking*. *Criminal harassment* — section 264 of the Criminal Code — does not yet exist. In our neighbourhood, *stalking*, as it will come to be called, is considered a part of courtship, though it's unusual for a girl to stalk a boy.

In most instances, a girl who is harassed by an amorous tormentor will rarely complain. She already knows her grievance will be dismissed, that she will be told she is making a mountain from a mole hill. She will be told: "Ignore him and he'll go away," or, "You should feel flattered." She will never be told, "Call the police."

We live in an era where musicals like *Seven Brides for Seven Brothers* are still nostalgically shown, where males kidnapping females, in replication of *The Rape of the Sabine Women*, is found charming by audiences, where song lyrics claim that abducted females may *act angry and annoyed but secretly are overjoyed*. I probably should already know that such sentiments aren't meant to apply equally to men, but I don't. I believe that once I win my former boyfriend back, he'll be grateful for my efforts.

The slogan *"No means no"* is unknown in my neighbourhood. It will appear, in the not too distant future, on T-shirts at a summer fair sponsored by Toronto's Rape Crisis Centre. However, there will be "no horror stories," "no discussions of rape." Such unpleasantness, while conducive to raising consciousness, isn't conducive to raising cash, and the Crisis Centre, as always, will be in crisis. Instead, there will be clowns and games, crafts for sale, a tarot reader and a palmist on hand.

While my Windsor neighbourhood is only 206 miles away from Toronto, it's light years away from "no means no." I'm just one of many of the resident teens here who don't understand the creepiness of inflicting unwanted attention. *No* doesn't mean *no* in my neighbourhood. It means, keep trying. It means, the person you're obsessing over is *playing hard to get*. It means, use alcohol or, in my case, magic.

I slide my potion into my coat pocket and put *Wuthering Heights* away. It's cold and icy and the gloomy sun looks as if it's not long for this short day. Although I can't see it, the Detroit River is crusted. In some spots, there are sheets of ice thirty inches thick. Water proceeds through this blocked and slushy strait, as I proceed through the frozen streets of Windsor. When I arrive at my former boyfriend's back door, my whole body is shaking. I stealthily scan the area, then ring the doorbell to make certain no one's home. The key to the door is hidden above the frame. My ex-boyfriend showed me. I retrieve it now, open the door, and trembling, enter.

In future years, I'll wonder what possessed me, astonished by my shocking actions, amazed by my inconceivable impudence. But there is no self-reflection as I conduct this trespass. I make my way to my ex-boyfriend's room and as quickly as I can, using my fingers, smudge clumps of tarry potion all over his walls and furniture. I rub it in well so he'll never see it unless he looks closely, and when I hear a noise that sounds like a car pulling up the icy gravel driveway, I bolt.

I'm aware of nothing as I exit, not the creaking wooden stairs or the rotting fence I bypass. I notice nothing of my surroundings as I hurry home, only that it's cold, too cold to light a cigarette.

Before we move to England, I make a self-improvements list. My hope is to overcome ugliness and stupidity, to erase all imperfection, to at last become a being worthy of love. Besides losing weight and getting my teeth fixed, I want to learn a new language and become knowledgeable of current events. I want to increase my vocabulary, make journal entries every day, and read a book a week. This last, I already know is impossible.

I light a smoke and crack open *Wuthering Heights*, which I'm certain will take me months to finish. My cigarette burns unevenly. I count until the ember smooths. According to superstition, the number, when converted to a letter, reveals the first initial of your *true love's* name. I always contrive to reach the number ten because my ex-boyfriend's name is Jack. I want to believe he's thinking of me, that one day he'll come back.

I love the ground under his feet, and the air over his head, and everything he touches, and every word he says. I love all his looks, and all his actions, and him entirely and altogether.

My eyes skim words as I consider what action I might take. I turn the radio on. I'm too obsessed with my own destructive passions to recognize the thematic parallels that exist in the book.

I might shape a prophecy, and foresee a fearful catastrophe.

Before we move to England, my nicotine-stained fingers rest upon the plastic planchette of a Ouija board. It belongs to Jack's sister, Joan, and whenever I visit she pulls the talking board from her bedroom closet and lights a candle.

I ask the board questions silently. "Will I see Jack again before I move? Will I be able to tell him that I love him?" I need Joan's board, but I don't want her interference. The planchette flies to "yes" and "yes," and for the rest of the evening I'm happy. For the rest of the evening I'm content to hear Joan's questions about rock stars and concerts and boys she has yet to meet, content to ignore Joan's planchette pushing.

I'm content, right up until the moment I hear Jack. He slams the back door, slams the door to his bedroom. His presence in the house is palpable and unnerves me. "It's getting late," Joan says. "Just one more question, then you better go."

I'm expecting her to continue: *rock stars, concerts, handsome strangers*, but she doesn't. Instead, she says she wants to ask a question for me. She wants to know when I'll find romance. It's an odd question. It makes me uncomfortable. And although I can't explain it at the time, her asking feels like a violation. Still, I allow my fingers to rest lightly on the planchette. I allow them to be led letter by letter until the word "tonight" is disclosed.

Jack's bedroom door opens and shuts, the back door opens and shuts.

"You better go now," Joan says, and starts packing the board away.

I light a cigarette as I leave and crunch down the gravel driveway wondering why Joan asked that final question, wondering if she'd made the planchette spell "tonight," but before I can seriously consider this, Jack's car is idling up the road and he's asking me if I want a ride.

Before we move to England, Jack and I make out in the parking lot of the Catholic school, and he promises he'll phone. I write his name and put it under my pillow. For luck, I wear my nightdress inside out. Day after day, I wait for his call. I smoke cigarettes I've stolen from my mother, and wait for his call, pick the skin off my fingers, and wait for his call, try to read *Wuthering Heights*, and wait for his call, consult the lines on my palms. I try to make excuses for why he doesn't phone, try to imagine obstacles that stand in his way, but eventually I exhaust every possibility, eventually I must concede that I just don't understand.

When I'm able to crawl from under my despair, I turn the radio on and light a cigarette. It takes seven seconds for nicotine to reach the brain, seven seconds for the heart to start revving and the blood pressure to rise, seven seconds to begin feeling a little less hopeless, a little more determined, and a little more in control. I open *Wuthering Heights* and read:

She kept wandering to and fro, from the gate to the door, in a state of agitation which permitted no repose; and at length took up a permanent situation on one side of the wall, near the road.

I trudge through knee-deep drifts and slide on the slick icy roads before we move to England. Outside Jack's place I linger red-faced and uncertain. Through the front window, I glimpse his parents and Joan and the illuminations of the television set. It always looks so warm inside, and I always wish I were among them. I walk back and forth in front of the house, back and forth, a spectral presence, no longer caring if anyone sees. The future unfurls hazily before me, like the landmasses I soon will be flying over, obscured by oceans of white rippling clouds. I take my gloves off and look at my palms. I light a cigarette and make one perfect smoke ring, which immediately dissipates into frosty air.

QUEASY

MY LITTLE BROTHER SLEEPS and drools beside me, exhausted and reeking of vomit. He threw up when the plane landed, then passed out as soon as we got in the car. I know it's a sacrifice for my uncle to drive us. It's over a six-hour journey from his house in Ilfracombe to Heathrow Airport, and over six hours back again. He'd wanted my mother to take a coach or a train. He wanted not to be inconvenienced, but if he's even mildly annoyed, there's nothing in his demeanour that shows it.

From the back seat of my uncle's Mini Clubman, a car that seems half the size of those driven in Canada, I can't always hear the front seat conversation, but I know that my uncle and mother are talking. I can see their lips, which are rarely still. My uncle is saying something about his journey and my mother, who is buzzing and effervescent, is saying something about herself. She's lost weight, bought a new wardrobe, dyed her hair an auburn red. "I look good! I feel good!" she tells my uncle smiling with two plates of impeccably straight and whitened dentures, which she seems to be wearing all of the time. It's a new beginning, a new start: she's cast off the shackles of Canada, buried her dead husband, burned, sold, or given away every trace of that awful life. "I made a mistake!" I see her lips move and know this is what she's saying because I've heard her say it a hundred times. "I made a mistake, and I want to come home."

My uncle has encouraged my mother's return to England. As a young man, he lived in various cities in North America and for a short while in Cape Town, South Africa. He's a well-travelled man, having visited all the European capitals, gone to Egypt, Cyprus, and Bombay, and he can tell my mother in his windy, weighty, public school way, without the slightest quaver of uncertainty in his voice, that England is a place second to none, that as far as beauty and atmosphere and pace of life go, it has no rivals. In short, England is, and always has been, the very best place on earth to live.

My mother is certain that my uncle is right. She can no longer abide the hideous bright orange margarine we're subject to buy in Ontario, she can no longer look at obscene plastic bags filled with milk. In England, she's told me, milk containers are still made properly, of glass; and margarine doesn't need to be a different colour because even the youngest British schoolchild can distinguish the difference in taste. She's railed against the Canadian postal service, because unlike England, there's only one delivery each day, and bilingual food packaging is "such a bloody stupid thing" it makes her apoplectic. At the drop of a hat, she can delineate all of the miseries of life in Ontario, including the fact that it's so "bloody cold" in the winter and so "hellishly hot" in the summer that it takes practically everything she has to crawl out of bed in the morning and turn on the TV.

I can see my mother's lips move, and imagine she is listing all of Canada's shortcomings. She is certain she was a fool to leave her homeland, though, at some point, she will remind my uncle that she and their mother did so at his bidding. It was after the war, the year tea rationing came to an end. My uncle had a bar in Detroit. He was married to Peggy and in-between marriages to Lena. My mother was single, and the war had left England with a serious deficit of men.

She regurgitates stories of her young life, as if their substance was too rich, and even when the front-seat voices disintegrate beneath the engine's thrum again, I hear the stories dizzily repeat. She extracts a long white cigarette from a golden cardboard Benson and Hedges package; there's a royal seal on the lid, and although both she and my uncle agree that the royal family consists of "a bunch of layabout hangers-on," these are her cigarettes of choice and she smokes them like a queen. In times to come, the seal will be revoked, taking away the phrase "by royal appointment," terminating a one hundred and twenty-two year agreement that this cigarette manufacturer maintained with the royals. The Queen's father, grandfather, and great-grandfather smoked. They all choked, and retched, and spat up phlegm; they all died from smoke-related illnesses, but my mother, who has no intention of dying in such an unattractive and torturous way, has devised a sensible precaution. Instead of smoking the entire cigarette, she smokes only half, leaving the bulk of tar and carcinogenetic chemicals untouched in a waste storage area in front of the filter. My father's life insurance money has made her extravagant, but even when my father controlled the purse strings, my mother still smoked her cigarettes in this lavish way.

I'm thankful for my mother's lavishness because when I'm short on funds, which is often, I can scrounge her leavings and with neat, white rolling papers create my own cigarettes. Fortunately, today there's no need for this. Travelling has made her generous and she leans from the front seat to the back, offering me her golden package and a flick of her plastic butane lighter.

As we motor along, the smell of vomit and smoke intermingle, and my uncle and mother discuss various plans. My uncle owns a twelve-room guest house, though no paying guests lodge there anymore. It's just my aunt and uncle and their two Pekinese dogs, Chan and Chloe, who all live mostly on the first two floors. There's a small shop attached to the house where my aunt and uncle once ran a café and later an antique store. Now they let it to a middle-aged widow who sells wool and knitting needles.

The small sitting room where my aunt and uncle take their meals and watch the news, where my uncle with his heavy magnifying glass scrutinizes bags of stamps for his collection and my aunt clips newspaper articles, connects to the shop through a serving hatch. It also connects, in the opposite direction, to a seventeenth-century cottage which in the early 1900s was converted into a kitchen, and has remained the only kitchen in the house.

I can't hear what they say in the front seat, but I can see that my uncle is enthusiastic. "Would you like that?" my mother asks. She strains to turn. The words are meant for me. "Your uncle wants to show you the deeds of his house when we get there."

I'm not sure why he wants to do this, but I'd rather appear agreeable than apprehensive. "Sure." I nod. I take a long drag off my cigarette, feel the nicotine surge, and try to follow the front seat conversation, just in case another question is volleyed my way.

The plan is that we'll live in my uncle's house while my mother is searching for one of her own. I know she wants something modern and pristine, with wall-to-wall carpeting and central heating. She's told me that she detests old houses like my uncle's; she hates their smells of kerosene and coal, the way they mildew and crumble, the way they never look clean and always feel cold. It's the 1970s, and she's determined not to live in England's past. She doesn't want to endure the discomforts of a bygone time. What she wants is to move forward into her life with as much ease and modern luxury as her finances will allow.

"I don't think I could manage the upkeep of a character home," her lips politely say, but my uncle isn't listening, he doesn't seem to care, and by the same token, she doesn't seem to care about Ilfracombe's past — all the facts he's collected, all the stories he longs to share, about the Celts and hill forts of the Iron Age, about pirates, and smugglers, and shipwrecks.

He raises his voice for my benefit. "I was out digging in my garden and damn me if the earth all around the blackberry bushes didn't start caving in. I didn't want to investigate too closely and disturb things, but I expect it's an old smuggler's passage we've got back there."

I know my mother's expressions, her frozen, courteous veneer, the mask that conceals a solipsistic disregard, the same mask my uncle wears when she speaks about her resurrection. They look very much alike, even though they're only half-siblings, even though he's sixteen years older than she. An invisible wall stands between them, in part because they've lived such very different lives.

My uncle was born a month before the flamboyant King Edward died, whose appetites of all kinds set a liberal precedent that defied the austere prudishness of his mother's, Queen Victoria's, reign. Known as the prince of pleasure, the playboy prince, and Edward the Caresser, his visits to brothels and gaming houses created scandal, yet kept him close to the common man. Though he came to the throne at age fifty-nine and his sovereignty was short, its stain like full-bodied wine bled into the fibres of my uncle's life. The pleasure-seeking bon vivant would forever be my uncle's calling; yet fused with this was a quiet practicality, a modest reserve, and a sense of conservation that often showed itself as miserly constraint.

Though he'd amassed a small fortune through a variety of business ventures, most having to do with buying items people believed useless and selling them at ten times what he paid, my uncle never bought a new article of clothing or a new piece of furniture or a new pot or pan. He never paid for a haircut or an envelope or a restaurant meal. When his second-hand socks grew worn, my aunt would retrieve an old skein of darning cotton. Instead of a daily shower, in order to save money, he washed himself with a face cloth in a sink and once a month took a bath in the same water my aunt had used. Although he wasn't particularly handy when it came to home repairs, he often was ingenious, using tar for countless holes and cracks as mildew repellent and wood stain. Both he and my aunt kept a small garden which they moistened with dirty dish water. They made juice and wine from the rhubarb and berries they grew and once got very sick when they cooked up a vat of rhubarb with its lovely green leaves because they didn't know they were poisonous, and it seemed such a shame to waste them.

My uncle survived two world wars and was an adult during the Great Depression. The gilded edge of his otherwise Edwardian self has long lost its lustre. He still enjoys high living and consumption on the largest scale, but all of this is tempered by expenditure — expenditure of time and money and energy, expenditure of stress. Instead of going out in the world, he finds it so much more pleasant to lounge in his faded armchair watching John Wayne movies and Coronation Street. It's so much nicer drinking port in the leisure and comfort of his home than in some smoky little pub, and so much more serene feasting on the roly-poly pudding and Battenberg cake my aunt serves, just the way he likes.

At home he can eat and drink as much as he wishes. He can play his organ or invite some neighbours over for a game of bridge. At night before he falls asleep, he says he relives all his romantic adventures: younger women, older women, women he seduced, married women who hid him from their husbands in their wardrobes where the smell of mothballs burned his nose, women he propositioned, women who propositioned him, one-night stands, two-night stands, dirty weekends, women he lived with, women he knocked up. He plays with these memories, embellishes them, turns them into defining tales: "I really was a bit of a lad." He can relive all of it knowing its outcome, extracting all its misery, molding what is left to farce. This kind of adventuring is so much more delightful than living everything fresh with danger and uncertainty, with responsibility and consequence.

My mother stops even pretending to listen when my uncle alludes to his playboy past. It's not that she disapproves; in fact, it seems she takes pride in it. Her brother was once handsome and seemingly irresistible to women, a real man with manly appetites and inclinations, she's said, but it seems this long journey has off-balanced her and what she really needs is to talk about herself — her hopes and dreams about life to be, everything she's chucked away in Canada — how she misses none of it, and how if a man were to come "crawling to her door, his hands dripping in diamonds," begging her to marry, she'd slam the door right in his face. "There'll be no more marriages for me!" she says. I see her expression in the rear-view mirror, see the familiar shake of her head, and although I can't hear what she's saying, I know this is what she's said.

She was born in 1926, the same year as the present queen. Some have dubbed her generation "silent," but if you were to ask her opinion, she'd vociferously disagree. Some have suggested that the *weltanschauung* of her era (closing at the end of World War II) is characterized by compliance and convention, that women of her generation felt duty bound in whatever role or occupation they pursued. Marriage and motherhood were important, and although during this era over three million marriages legally terminated in the United States alone, divorce was still frowned upon. Some writers have proclaimed that morals are conflicted for women of this era, that as a generation they seem to have lost their faith; they are solemn and pessimistic with few expectations, for they perceive life, by and large, as a rather disappointing affair.

"My problem is I expect too much from people," my mother says, and her confession wafts above the front seat with an exhalation of smoke. "I expect too much, and people are always letting me down." She stabs her partially cremated cigarette into the car's tiny ash receptacle and continues a diatribe of which I can only catch the occasional word. It is of course an outburst against my father, a dead man whom she now bitterly resents: his alcoholism, his disrespect of her, his stupid arrogance. Her face is hard and she spits out invectives, creamy memories that have all turned to curd.

In 1955 when my uncle owned his Detroit bar, he told my mother not to worry; he told her she could make a choice. She didn't have to marry. She wasn't the first woman with a belly full of trouble and she certainly wouldn't be the last. He had the name of a reputable doctor if she wanted to go that route and abortions weren't half as dangerous as they used to be. For one hundred and twenty-five dollars she could be rid of it; or if she'd rather, she could have the child, put it up for adoption or even keep it if she liked. He suggested that she and their mother could live with him, that their mother could look after the child while she worked. Things weren't like they used to be — nothing like before the war, when abortion and childbirth posed serious risks to women. Antibiotics and blood transfusions weren't readily available and death by puerperal sepsis, an infection of the genital tract, was responsible for five maternal deaths in every thousand births. Before the war, poverty was rampant, birth control for most young women was a mystery, and attempts at home abortion by the unwed not at all uncommon. Knitting needles and hat pins were the implements of choice, or syringes full of soapy water. There were purgatives and pills, herbal concoctions made from juniper berries, hot salt baths and gin. Before the war, unwed pregnant women who didn't marry quickly would most likely lose their jobs if they were employed, and get thrown out of their familial homes. They would most likely be spurned by their community and forced to seek shelter in places where the blot on their moral character was unknown. They would have no help, no familial support, in bringing an illegitimate child into the world. They would not have the means to care for it, and unless they were willing to lie about their past, there were no chances of them ever making a respectable marriage in the future.

But even though World War II was over and things had changed, in 1955 my mother did agree to marry, though she also tried salt baths and gin, stumbling down the stairs, lifting the heaviest pieces of furniture in the apartment that she and her mother shared. She'd always feared doctors and medical procedures, and wanted to take care of things herself, but there was no taking care of things; the child in her womb would not comply.

Often when she reminisced, she would say how sick she'd felt every day of her pregnancy, how she would vomit at the drop of a hat. She couldn't eat anything but the blandest foods, plain saltine crackers, cantaloupe melon, cottage cheese. Even the thought of pungent smelling spices would have her rushing to the nearest toilet.

My father's parents kept finding excuses for why the wedding should be postponed, and all the while, she recalled growing bigger and bigger, having to let out the waist of her ivory wedding dress, cursing my father and his family for humiliating her.

At least a decade after this journey to Ilfracombe, when my mother and I are both again living in Canada, a photograph of her will surface, young and sexy, leaning against a wall at Niagara Falls. She will explain, teary-eyed, that it was taken by her lover, not my father, shortly before she married, though the implications of this confession, like the name of her lover, will never be stated.

However, as we journey down the motorway to my uncle's house, I'm fortunate not to have to consider this. I steal the last hit off my cigarette, careful not to drag too hard and ignite the acrid filter. My little brother stirs, but nods off to sleep again. The road extends for miles and miles with nothing to look at but scrub and signs and other cars, which appear all remarkably alike.

Five years before my parents wed, Britain dominated the world automotive market; five years later, things had drastically changed. Because I'm a teenager, no one would expect me to know this, and because I come from Canada, no one would expect me to have any familiarity with the name British Leyland, and the current problems this car manufacturer is suffering. I can't speculate about its poor management, how competition was underestimated, how forceful trade unions played a role. I've never heard the word "nationalization." I didn't know it was possible for a government to bail a company out, or how such an act of charity must ultimately be paid for. Because I'm young, I've not yet personally experienced the way problems left unsolved creep into the future, although I know this to be the case. I've watched it happen often enough.

My mother's voice hits an emotional pitch, which my ears have been trained to perceive. "I should have left him, Geoff. I should have done it when I had the chance." She is still denigrating my father, and although my uncle's reply is muffled, I can tell by his bewildered movement that he can't fathom why she's carrying on. I imagine all the things he probably wants to say: "He's dead, for God's sake!" and "Don't you see, your chance is now?" He's probably thinking that she talks as if she's still stuck with him. He doesn't realize yet that she is, that she somehow has ingested him and that this harping and moaning is really just a reflexive gag. She needs to purge herself of the man she married and every memory of their toxic life. It's impossible for her to stop this nauseating droning, until she throws him up completely, until she discerns the borders of her own life. Everything she's done since his death, including moving here, has been an ongoing effort to separate, to rid him from her core. If only someone would invent a stomach pump for the psyche or locate its throat so she could shove her finger down. If only there was a pill, or draft, or rhubarb leaf to force him out of her, to set her free.

It doesn't matter that this nausea has only been prevalent since his death, that previously, my mother's faith and expectations kept all the sick-making toxins at bay. My father wasn't the total monster she describes; their life wasn't a total hell. It will take me years to understand that he was part of her and that she hates him because he died. My uncle, who has left many women, will probably never understand this. What he might understand, however, if only my mother could articulate

it, is the way we blame the dead for their departures as if they themselves have had some hand in their demise.

If my mother could give voice to this instead of an endless litany
of gripes, my uncle would most probably think of his father, a man
who died when he was very young. In pictures I've seen, his father is
gangly-bodied and smooth-faced, appearing far too young for puberty
let alone the possibility of fatherhood. I imagine my uncle recalling
his father's flat white cap, the anchor on the sleeve of his jacket, the
way he lifted and twirled him in the air until the world was spinning
and the breakfast porridge he'd eaten, threatened to return. I imagine
how my uncle would see him, chuckling, as he set him down. "It'll take
a while to get your sea legs, ole mate," he'd say, and be surprised my
uncle didn't find this as amusing as he did.

"Who's that man?" my uncle is reputed to have asked his mother,
being too young to remember her patient explanations of a father
duty-bound to the sea and then, when he finally grasped the concept,
couldn't stop calling every man he saw in a sailor's uniform "father,"
much to his mother's dismay.

If my uncle were inclined to think of his father, he would probably
also recall his mother's giddy pleasure when his father returned home
on leave, the way she dressed with extra care in clothes she kept especially for these occasions. She too was young then, but she went on
aging long, long after his father died.

My uncle was only eight when the Q ship Willow Branch, the ship
on which his father was a petty officer, was demolished by two German submarines. Most of the crew abandoned the ship for lifeboats.
The third officer was taken prisoner and a few men drowned. My
uncle was told that his father had drifted for days under the blistering
sun with no fresh water to drink. He was told that eleven of the men
were so desperate that even though they knew they shouldn't, they
swallowed sea water, and went mad.

My uncle once confessed that often in his childhood he'd consider thirst and sometimes go an entire day without a drink of any kind. He'd wanted to know what his father experienced, wanted to share this suffering, and usually by nightfall could bear it no longer.

Once when he and his mother went on a widows' and orphans' seaside picnic excursion, after he'd eaten more than his share of the jam sandwiches and tarts, he drank an entire tumbler of brine just to see what would happen. Within minutes he'd expelled the contents of his stomach with such violence that he was certain he'd die. His mother, who coddled him and had become even more solicitous since his father's passing, feared he'd had too much sun. All that night he waited for madness and was a little sorry when it didn't come.

Later, as a young man, he met a seaman acquainted with the Willow Branch sinking who told him that his father didn't drink the ocean's water, nor did he go mad. Poseidon did not whip the ocean into a frenzy of deadly waves, and the sweltering sun, though it might have been fatal, didn't have time to do its damnedest. His father had been sacrificed, according to the stranger. His flesh had been devoured and his blood imbibed. What else could explain two survivors after nine days on the open sea?

This report came so long after his father's death that my uncle said he felt guilty he wasn't enraged, guilty that his first thoughts were selfish and macabre — it was a story *to dine out on*, as the saying goes.

My mother drums her manicured fingers on her lap as we reach a stretch of undulating road. Although she's trying to maintain her cordial veneer, I can see, when she turns, that her eyes are glinting. She will never acquire the taste or aptitude for the kind of tailored history my uncle savours. She will never be able to recall a place, time, or person who has touched her, without some emotional keel. My uncle's reminiscences seem to be a tedious collection of reruns to her. I watch the back of her head as she fights to get a word in edgewise, as she struggles, busting, to talk about herself.

"I don't care how handsome, how gracious, how well off," she blasts. Although I attempt to create an imaginative barrier between us, a line where her fulmination can't pass, her words swell as they reach my ears, and glut them. "You can torture me, starve me, lock me up." My little brother stirs with a fresh waft of stale vomit, my stomach lurches, the road twists. "I'll never marry again! Never!" she continues.

Before I heave, I try to signal my uncle, try to get him to pull over to the side of the road. His mouth is moving, just like my mother's, words avalanching over words avalanching over words.

STRANGE CUSTOMS

THE LANDSCAPE WE left behind in Windsor, Ontario, was vast and flat; distance existed in every deliberation — even in our cut-rate subdivision where cheap houses were constructed with capacious borders and the local convenience store was over two miles away. The roads in this world didn't undulate. There were no feminine curves, no steep inclines, no sudden descents, no call to contemplate what might lie beyond. Our destination, however, presents an opposing layout, and so I will find myself speculating at every turn.

It's a place celebrated as *the land of hope and glory*, the progenitor of pork scratching and *Lorna Doone*, of the Royal family and steak and kidney pie, and the shocking Jimmy Savile cover up, which *Time* magazine will report upon some thirty-seven years in the future. It's personified as female, known to its inhabitants as "the motherland" and is, as well, the country of my mother's origin. The place she left, yet still calls home.

It circulates through her every day, sticks to her like flesh on bone.

It influences all she does, the way she cooks and calls my name. I covet the smoothness of her consonants, the arc of her vowels, and have wished, for as long as I can remember, that I'd been born in England too. "To be English was to have won the first prize in the lottery of life," Cecil Rhodes is frequently quoted to have said, and although I knew nothing of the politician or what had been attributed to him, because of my mother I shared these sentiments.

As a tot, I'd been swept away by Beatlemania, as I witnessed the Fab Four on *The Ed Sullivan Show* bring teenage girls to tears. A few years later, it was *The Monkees*, and the Manchester born Davy Jones who won my six-year-old heart. But on the day we leave Canada, it's the British rock stars David Bowie, Ian Hunter, and Marc Bolen who I dream about.

It's raining when we arrive in Ilfracombe and ascend the steep road towards my uncle's dwelling. The sidewalk is slick with moss. Perhaps it's the greyness of the sky that makes the town seem drab. The air is thin and smells of burning coal and salt, the raucous cries of seagulls bounce and echo off the antique buildings that adhere to one another in a row from the harbour. Some are simple dwellings, others shops, others guest houses, like my uncle's. His is close to the top of the road which forks into the High Street, the town's major thoroughfare. The door of his house is Kelly green. Above it sits a plaque printed in an old English script: "Seaview House, 1600."

The date, I will discover, is deceptive. The main part of the house, in which the twelve guest rooms exist, had been built in the late Victorian era. An earlier construction that endures below was built as a miller's cottage in the 1600s, revamped into a kitchen two hundred years later, and has remained, with minor renovations, the only kitchen this guest house has ever known.

My uncle points to a door inlaid with frosted glass. "The WC if you need it," he tells us. I don't know what a WC is. I look inside. There's nothing but a toilet with a wooden seat, a tank raised high, close to the ceiling, and a chain with a wooden handle that hangs like some kind of emergency cord. I suspect the chain is a flusher, but I'm uncertain. My common sense isn't calibrated for England, it doesn't function as it did at home. It will take some time.

The bathtub, I discover, occupies a completely different room. I assume that the toilet and bath are separate so people needing one don't interfere with those needing the other. It seems logical, practical. The separation, however, I will eventually learn has nothing to do with pragmatism, but with puritanical and classist Victorian demarcations between cleansing and purging. It was considered both "objectionable" and "vulgar" to bathe in a room where one excreted waste.

The Italian writer Beppe Severgnini, who in the 1970s has not yet begun his journalistic career, regularly visits Great Britain as a student. He comes to learn the language, enjoying "Alice Cooper songs in cavernous discos with French names" and attending concerts "at the Rainbow Theatre, where a sassy David Bowie strut[s] his stuff." Perhaps it's in these halcyon days of language acquisition that he first becomes aware of the "disconcerting relationship" (one might even suggest neurotic) the British have with their bathrooms.

As far back as the Middle Ages, he'll note, the British used an assortment of euphemisms to evade using the "T" word. "Necessarium" was employed by clergy and nobility, and "cloakrooms" were not originally places people hung their cloaks. These primitive WCs jutted from exterior walls of "finer homes and castles." Waste discharged directly below. "Many of the 'secret rooms' and 'private chapels' that tour guides show," Severgnini will one day write, "are actually latrines." But I've not yet taken any such tours, nor heard the many euphemisms (including *bog*, *loo*, and *lav*) that will rapidly become part of my new working vocabulary. If my mother had ever used these terms, she'd done so before I was old enough to mimic her. "Bathroom" was the only word we used at home. It made sense, because the room that housed the toilet also housed the bath. But ask to use a bathroom here, as the Tower of London's Ravenmaster Christopher Skaife will some decades in the future explain, and be prepared for ridicule. "Why? Are you dirty? Do you need to take a bath?"

Euphemisms for the body and its functions abound in Britain. Direct and literal terms appear unseemly. To be "up the Duff," is to be pregnant; to be "on the pull," means you're looking for sex. If you're "wanking," you're in danger of going blind. Therefore, a boy should stay clear of his "meat and veg" as a girl should avoid her "fanny," or, in Cockney rhyming slang (the progenitor of so many euphemisms), her Auntie Annie, or her Jack and Danny.

I'll soon learn that having "to spend a penny" is a delicate way of saying (as we did in North America) "I need to pee." I'll find this euphemism particularly confusing, as the monetary idiom I'm most familiar with is "a penny for your thoughts." Is it because with nothing else to do, one cogitates while on the toilet? The image of Rodin's "The Thinker," which as a child I first saw in reruns of the short-lived American show, *Dobie Gillis*, will flash in my mind wherever pennies in England are spent. I always believed Rodin's figure was on a toilet suffering the agonies of constipation. "Where's the *ex-lax*?" he might have been thinking, or "Prune juice! Where can I buy prune juice?"

It will be my aunt who finally clarifies the British "penny" phrase. It originates, like so many things, from Victorian times when the cost of using a public toilet, for women, was a penny. "Over the years, of course," she will say, "the cost of public toilets has risen." The phrase "to spend a penny," like so much of Great Britain I will learn, is simply an appendage to the past, a cultural and linguistic vestigiality, that despite historical developments can't quite bring itself to vanish.

The penny itself as a unit of currency is still alive and well in Ilfracombe, with no threat of demonetization, though as of 1971, Great Britain's plunge into monetary decimalization has changed its ancient character by making it smaller and engendering the signifier "new." And just in case the populace might forget this, the penny, along with two other recently decimalized copper coins (the half-penny and the 2 pence piece) will be branded with this adjective on their reverse sides. It's a word suggesting something fresh and better, though Britons, unlike North Americans, generally distrust it.

"New money" means one hundred pence in a pound, as opposed to two hundred and forty. It means ten 10 p pieces make a pound, instead of 20 shillings. Gone are the guineas, half crowns, and florins that my aunt and uncle still refer to when calculating the ever-rising cost of living. As a North American newcomer, I don't give currency decimalization a second thought. It's what I'm used to, what I know, as it would be for most immigrants the world over. It seems common sense to me, but even forty years after its inception, there will be many, like author Dominic Sandbrook, who will maintain its introduction "the thin edge of the wedge" in eroding Britain's unique character.

During the years I live in England, the talk about "new money" is not about the loss of national character as much as hidden costs. "The Government did a Tommy Cooper on the nation," a shopkeeper, Les Bober, will say in a *Daily Mail* article. "They took 140 pennies out of the pound — and told the public it wouldn't make any difference. The quickness of the hand deceived the eye, but six years later we know the truth. It was all a colossal confidence trick." His sentiments are echoed by the disgruntled throughout the land.

My lack of cultural literacy would have prevented me from fully grasping Bober's complaint. Tommy Cooper, a popular British comic-magician who, in future years will die of a heart attack on live TV, is a complete unknown to me. Unfamiliar too is the way proper nouns frequently transform to generic ones. My learning about the quirks and characters of this country will not come quickly. I seldom watch television, and although I've set my sights on becoming a print journalist, I never read newspapers. In fact, I consider these daily chronicles conveyers of gloom and avoid them at all costs. It's not the news itself I find gloomy. My aversion is a classically conditioned response dating back to grade school and Monday morning current events class. Tasked with finding interesting news stories — preferably ones my peers wouldn't choose — I'd procrastinate all week worrying about the quality of my potential selections. Finally, Sunday night I'd feverishly paw through old papers, convincing myself all the good stories must be gone and inevitably settling on something subpar. I'd dash off a synopsis, while my mother's beautiful English voice yelled in the background that it was too late to be doing *bloody* homework. In the morning, sleep deprived, groggy, anxious, and embarrassed, I'd have to present my synopsis to the class. But here in Ilfracombe, all my old school days are thankfully behind me. I'm a teenaged high school dropout, and defensive blindness to the broadsheet and tabloid spares me, at least at first, from even noticing the number of newspapers that overrun the land.

In my former home, *The Globe and Mail*, which called itself "Canada's National Paper," and the regional *Windsor Star* were the only objects of my aversion. Here, there is such a plethora of print, and my aunt and uncle such journalism junkies, that in less than a week, I'll be forced to conclude, as *The Times* reporter Alan Hamilton makes plain, "the English are among the world's most avid newspaper readers."

Several years after our arrival, *Yes, Prime Minister* (allegedly the favorite sitcom of Margaret Thatcher) will précis the press with both droll and discerning precision. It will find its way into popular culture, repeated and repeated, with copious variations sounding something like this: "*The Daily Mirror* is read by people who think they run the country, *The Guardian* by those who think they ought to, *The Times* by those who do, *The Daily Mail*, by their wives, *The Financial Times* by those who own the country, *The Morning Star* by those who think the country ought to be run by another country, *The Daily Telegraph* by those who are convinced it is, and *The Sun*, by those who don't give a damn who runs the country as long as she's got big tits."

In 1969, "Going Topless in The Sun" in Britain meant taking a summer ride in a convertible. The wealthy might drive a Mercedes-Benz 280SE or a Rolls-Royce Mulliner, writes Maxwell Boyd of *The Sunday Times*. The "family man," on the other hand, could take his pick from three much less expensive British Leyland vehicles.

But in November 1970, a year after media tycoon Rupert Murdoch took possession, *The Sun* newspaper both increased in circulation and gained notoriety for the topless "Page Three Girls" it began to regularly feature. According to biographer Rodney Tiffen, Murdoch had a formula: He wasn't going to have any "up-market shit" in his paper and there would be an emphasis on sex.

"The paper looked for any opportunity to be risqué, such as having Pussy Week, which was about cats." The British public, by and large, especially men, lapped it up. Circulation rose from 1.5 million to 2.1 million in a year. "*The Sun* was saucy, even naughty, but it was all good clean fun. The sex material was informative and amusing and, unlike porn, was not designed to induce the 'leer and the snigger,'" Tiffen quotes. But to a teenaged North American girl, the word "tits" when uttered by an adult was shocking enough. When a pair were actually staring up at you from a newspaper that your uncle was perusing — a sexagenarian, who you could not even imagine being connected to the word "sex" — it made you "red all over," like the 19th-century riddle "*what's black and white and...*"

Boobs are two of the many bodily parts the British call "naughty bits" in the '70s. They like to laugh about them, and besides all the North American euphemisms they use that I'm familiar with, the British have a wealth of expressions all their own. *Baps* and *Strawberry Creams* are two with foodie themes. *Bristols*, *Thr'pennys*, and *Earthas* couple with cities, bits, and Kitts, for the Cockney rhyming variants. There are *Jugs* and *Melons* and *Belisha Beacons*, *Easts* and *Carpets* and

Faintings. Alexander Pope and later Jonathan Swift humorously labeled the curvy female, much euphemized, milk-giving appendages *Fore-Buttocks*, and while I never hear this term used, I don't doubt that at least a few inhabitants of this ancient land probably make reference to breasts in this way.

Breasts, knockers, Page Threes, appear to be funniest to Britons when wholly or virtually naked, when extremely large and sexually arousing, and when there's an implicit pretense of an observer to ignore them. It is a standard comic routine. Comedians leer at big-breasted women. They frequently use double entendre and other wordplay to allude to them.

"You are a pair of Tweets," the beautiful, blonde, large-breasted Diana Darvey says with a Spanish accent to comic Benny Hill and his side kick, Jackie Right. To call the costume Darvey wears on the *Benny Hill Show* skimpy is akin to saying the American, lollipop-sucking, shiny-headed detective Kojak is "a little thin on top." Only two sparkling sashes cover Darvey's nipples, nothing else about her breasts are left to the imagination. "Tweets?" Benny asks, to the audience's enjoyment. Darvey then spells Twits, poking Benny on the chest as she pronounces every letter, and then, repeating "tweets," she rubs both hands over his breasts. After a moment of ecstatic shaking and preparation for retaliation in kind, he says: "You know what you are? You're supercalifragilisticexpialidocious."

Benny Hill was called "the least predictable of the droll" by journalist Ivor Brown in 1958. But well over a decade, when my mother and I take up residence at her half-brother's ancient seaside abode, "Britain's King Leer," as Hill comes to be called, and his "knicker and knocker" humour are still going strong. In fact, he now holds the number one spot in British television. At the height of the show's popularity, "more Britons tuned in to laugh at [his] antics," according to *Sunday Express* reporter Adrian Lee, "than watched the moon landing."

A limited number of Benny Hill programs were imported to my former homeland in 1972, though I'd never seen them. Neither had I read *The Globe and Mail's* review by Blaik Kirby: "Last night the CBC premiered what may be the most heavy-handed bladder-and-slapstick comedy show on record, a British effort which is going to give a rich opportunity to all the people who used to complain about indecency on the air."

But here in England in the 1970s, no one seems to be complaining. *The Benny Hill Show* broadcasts into my aunt and uncle's home, as it does into the homes of most who have television sets, with nary an eyebrow raise. Perhaps this is because there's currently so much else to find fault with in the country, or maybe it's because the protesting voices are all being muffled under the belly-laughs of Hill's fans.

When I first see the show, my aunt will relieve my discomfort by explaining Hill's bawdy humour as particularly "British," though she doesn't explain that his salacious wordplay and songs harken back to the music halls of Victorian times and that these provided the most popular and affordable entertainment for the masses. I'll become less squeamish as the weeks progress. Many British comedians make lewd jokes, emphasize the sexual, and leer at half naked women, I'll discover. "It's just a bit of fun," as my uncle says.

I won't be living in England when the hue and cry begins, when moral crusader Mary Whitehouse reaches out to Benny Hill's sponsors through a letter writing campaign. Originally she was brushed off as a fanatic and crank, but her success over the years in inspiring activism and winning court cases means she's not easily dismissed. In 1981, it will be her mission to alert Hill's advertisers about the smut they're funding. She'll find, according to the *Daily Mail*, that writing directly to them, as opposed to the *Independent Broadcasting Authority* (which is the UK's regulatory body for commercial TV) a much more effective strategy. The *IBA* treats her complaints "like water off a duck's back," she'll be quoted as saying.

"If we thought the Benny Hill show was leading the way to pornography then we would not allow the programme to be broadcast," an *IBA* spokesman will say in response to Whitehouse's complaints. The show "represents a very old tradition of broad humour which is particularly British," though some viewers "might not find it to their taste."

Thames Television spokesman in response to Whitehouse will say the show has "traditionally balanced on the knife-edge between the bawdy and the obscene." It "has served *ITV* and its advertisers, consistently well," and they don't "believe it falls on the wrong side of the knife."

But wrong side of the knife or not, as Dominic Sandbrook says of monetary decimalization and British culture, complaints like Whitehouse's are "the thin edge of the wedge." Before long, many salacious comedy routines will come under fire, and not only by moral crusaders. The "climate of criticism," as it comes to be called, will be fueled by entertainers as well — most notoriously, in Benny Hill's case, by comedian Ben Elton who will say in a 1987 talk show that he finds it worrying "when a comedian can end every program tearing off a woman's clothes and chasing her around a park in her underwear . . . in a world where women can't even walk safe in a park." Benny Hill's Thames Television contract will be cancelled in 1989, two years after Elton's interview, and a year after the Broadcasting Standards Council, according to *The Telegraph*, excoriate the show as "increasingly offensive." Hill will be found dead and decomposing in his spartan flat in 1992. His brand of "British humour," so much a part of the culture of the 70s, will become "deeply embarrassing" to the British, according to writer Jemima Lewis in a 2006 column.

But there is no embarrassment when I and my mother arrive in Britain, and sexual titillation, with an emphasis on "tit" is everywhere. My uncle routinely skims page three of *The Sun*, drinks tea and flexes the comfortable leather-look slippers that warm his feet. If there's talk of a newspaper mastectomy, it's not talk my uncle engages in. Like most Britons who read the paper, my uncle sees the voluptuous (mostly teenage) models as "nothing to get one's knickers in a twist over." It's years before Clare Short, Labour MP, suggests that "degrading images of women" should no longer appear in mainstream tabloids, and brings the "Indecent Displays (Newspapers) Bill" into the House of Commons. Conservative MP Robert Adley will say the bill deserves a "booby prize." Conservative MP Eric Forth will also be inclined to dismiss Short's concerns. "Young ladies, who [choose] to display whatever assets they [possess] for profit [are] successfully exploiting the male population," *The Times* will quote him as saying.

In the *Daily Mail*, Miranda Ingram will write that Clare Short's Bill, intended to outlaw The *Sun*'s Page Three Girls, "drove the red-blooded Real Men brigade of the Commons into a positive frenzy of innuendo." Even female Conservative MP Edwina Currie "threw in her halfpenny worth," saying "'I wish I had a figure like them.'" Short's jealousy will be at the root of her Page Three Girl problems, her detractors will declare. She will be harassed and belittled, derided and mocked, for daring to take on the bawdy tabloid photos, considered by some "as British as bangers and mash."

The Sun will retaliate against the "killjoy," Short, with its S.O.S. — "Save our Sizzlers" — campaign, according to the *National Post*. And the *News of the World*, the tabloid's sister paper, will "publish misleading and inaccurate material" about her, a Press Complaints Commission will find. *The Times* will report on these findings in 1991 and quote Short as saying, "[The] paper … crawled over the whole of my adult life," even asking her first husband, whom she'd divorced twenty years before, "if he had any 'naughty photos' of her."

But all of this lies in the future. Clare Short is not an MP, but the director of *All Faiths for One Race*, a charitable organization "defending the rights of the victims of poverty and discrimination." She can't foresee the future or know the ridicule and harassment she'll endure even after her Bill fails, after she grows disillusioned with the Labour government, after she leaves her government post.

In a 2003 newspaper column, she'll recount how after telling a woman journalist she was still against nudity in mainstream press, "busloads" of tabloid models arrived at her house. They were hoping to set up "embarrassing photos, and mock-up pictures of me as a very fat Page Three Girl." Some people hid in cars and, when they spotted her, chased her down the street. A double-decker bus "plastered with *Sun* posters" sat vigil outside her front door.

But in the year I first see *The Sun*, there's little call for such elaborate defences. Perhaps it's because of the systemic decay, the low standard of living, and the precarious economy that the sight of large youthful breasts bring comfort to the British. They cleave to the cleavage, naturally, unselfconsciously, like nursing infants in times of stress. It's the beautiful young "good mother" who bares her ample, reassuring, life-giving breasts to her needy little ones, and the ugly wicked hag with withered dugs who seeks to disallow this nurture.

Margaret Thatcher who, according to historian Robert Tombs, will become "the only deeply admired and genuinely hated Prime Minister since 1940," is already the Leader of the Opposition, and my Aunt's and Uncle's favourite politician. She is, to many, already "the dauntless Boadicea" fighting against "national decline," while at the same time the "malignant harpy" harping against socialism.

In 1971, as Conservative Education Secretary, she incited the slogan "Thatcher, Thatcher, Milk Snatcher," when she cut the government-funded milk program for schoolchildren over seven. The program, originally introduced in 1946 by the first female Education Minister, a former Communist, (Red) Ellen Wilkinson, came about in the aftermath of World War II.

Author historian Raynes Minns recounts that dairy herds were slaughtered in 1940 to free up land for "vital food crops." The National Milk Scheme arrived to ensure that the *life-giving fluid* — "a perfect food for infants" as Nestles advertisements boasted — be made available to a nutritionally weakened population. Milk, with all its mammary connotation and symbolism, had been strictly limited in the war years, and food rationing continued until 1954. But in the year we arrive in England, with rationing long over, milk is available in every grocery store and *The Daily Mail* reports, "nearly every home in England and Wales has a doorstep delivery of milk."

Because I don't read the newspapers, I miss the elaborate Milk Board advertising features that disguise themselves as news. They regale the heroic caring milkman, who really "gets to know his customers" and "by prompt actions" has saved lives. "Dairy companies throughout the country operate a 'Milkman's Care Code' with stickers on the delivery vehicle to remind" him of his duties, which go beyond the simple delivering of a "pinta."

If I'd read the newspaper, I would have discovered that the retail price of milk had just recently gone up "by Government order." I would have been baffled by the bureaucratic jargon explaining that the price increase "will ensure that the food subsidy expenditure" (whatever that is) "will not exceed the provisions for the current financial year" (whatever that is) "in accordance with the Government's policy on public expenditure" (whatever that is). And instead of feeling disgusted by this story's lack of concrete detail and clarity, I would, if I'd read the paper, have felt that it was all my fault because I was stupid and unable to grasp what must be simple and apparent facts. It never would have occurred to me that such bafflegab, like lactose, is not generally easy to digest. I know nothing of the history of food controls in this country. Nothing of prices boards and commissions or of the 1973 Counter Inflation Act.

What I do know is that milk in England isn't usually drunk on its own, but splashed in tea, hidden in desserts, or added to powdery malt mixtures at bedtime, such as Horlick's, which displays a busty, young, dark-haired milk maid on its label. Unlike North Americans, who seem to genuinely like its flavour and knock back a tumbler or two of milk at most meals, a general distaste for the substance prevails in England where it's treated as something akin to medicine. For decades, various British governments have lauded its health benefits: "It supplies the proteins that are essential for the growth and repair of the body. Fats and carbohydrates for the body's energy and warmth. Minerals, especially calcium, for the building of bone structures and teeth." Children, particularly, are encouraged to drink it, even when they sense their parents' hereditary ambivalence and shut their little mouths, grit their little teeth, and refuse to partake of the liquescent whiteness.

My grandmother, who detested the beverage, would make rice puddings to get the much-loathed substance into her children, my mother once explained. And likewise, even though she'd moved to a milk-friendly country, my mother continued to dislike the bovine fluid, yet felt it her duty to make me drink it. She'd lace the milk in my baby bottle (I wasn't breast fed) with substantial quantities of sugar and vats of well-brewed tea. "I knew babies needed milk, but I just couldn't bring myself to feed you something that on its own tasted so unpleasant," she'd said.

Unlike my young peers in the United States, milk was not a beverage I ever learned to drink at home. When, occasionally, I was invited to a friend's birthday party and a glass of the white liquid was served with cake, I felt a traitor to my mother if I drank it. If I happened to ask for tea instead, I faced the disbelief and suspicion of adults. "You're far too young to be drinking tea," a well-meaning mother once said, and then turning to her child, the birthday girl, declared me in the land of make-believe. "What child drinks tea?" she asked. Another mother warned me that drinking caffeinated beverages before I'd reached the age of majority would stunt my growth. Another announced I was only vying for attention. "If I gave you tea," she assured me, "you wouldn't like it. It's very bitter."

I was ten when we moved to Ontario and happy to discover that some Canadian children drank the British-favoured brew. Few, however, did so as prolifically as me, for even in this Commonwealth country, overseen by the Queen, tumblers of milk frequently accompanied meals. It was only those of us with English parents who knew what it was to be tea outcasts, to live between the devil of tea guilt, and the deep white sea of North American milk orthodoxy.

Attitudes towards milk in England seemed to conform more to my mother's views than those I'd witnessed in North America. I didn't question this cultural disparity any more than I questioned separate toilet and bath rooms, tabloid breasts, or *The Benny Hill Show*. I could see no reason why the British might be disinclined to drink milk, and knowing so little of the past, wouldn't have been able to even hypothesize.

Having come from Canada, I've frequently heard the phrase "The Great White North," but the euphemism "The Great White Plague" will be, for decades, unknown to me. I know nothing of the bacterium *M. bovis*, or how cow's milk was able to spread TB. Between 1851 and 1910 some four million people died from tuberculosis in England and Wales. "This was 13 percent of the total mortality during these years," writes historian Helen Bynum, who also reveals the disease killed "a third of those aged 15 to 34."

According to *Daily Mail* Consumer Affairs Correspondent Sean Poulter, during the 1930s, "bovine TB infected more than 50,000 people," and every year of this decade, 2,500 died from the disease. And in 1966 *The Times'* medical correspondent wrote about Britain's "slowness in dealing with contaminated milk. Although for long recognized as a major cause of tuberculosis, especially in children, it is only within recent years that anything like a comprehensive programme has been undertaken to ensure an adequate supply of clean and safe milk for the nation."

He suggests that it's Britain's "innate conservatism" that prevents them acting more quickly where public health is concerned and is writing at a time when another bovine-related disease, *Brucellosis*, is spreading throughout the land before reticent government policy makers. In the United States, the government always appears to act more swiftly and decisively in preventing the spread of disease. As early as 1908 tuberculosis spreading cattle were identified and slaughtered and milk pasteurization became the norm. In Britain, however, killing herds of cows seemed extreme and milk pasteurization destroyed much of milk's nutritional goodness. In the 1920s British farmers could even sell infected milk, though not as 'Certified' or 'Grade A (tuberculin-tested.)'

According to writer Mark Kurlansky, "The more scientists investigated, the more milk-borne diseases they found. Serious intestinal diseases could be transmitted through milk from unclean udders. Farm workers with contagious diseases could transmit them through the milk pail. Scarlet fever, diphtheria, and typhoid were all traced to contaminated milk."

I know nothing of milk's unwholesome history as I happily slurp my tea in Ilfracombe, nothing of its "disconcerting relationship" with the British public (as Beppe Severgnini might say). Although old enough to remember, there is no one in my immediate circle who apprises me of this fact. I'm only told that my mother almost succumbed to scarlet fever as a child, that my Aunt's half-sisters both contracted tuberculosis. One of them died. There are many seniors who inhabitant Ilfracombe. Many who have suffered the ravages of milk-borne diseases and survived. Yet none who I speak with ever allude to milk's insalubrious past, nor do they project into its troubling future.

Here, in Ilfracombe, milk still comes in glass bottles. Cream still collects at the top. When I was five and living in Ohio, a friendly milkman dressed neatly in pressed whites, delivered similar containers to our door. If I could get to a bottle before my mother had a chance to shake it, I'd remove the glinting silver top and greedily extract the cream with a butter knife. While I'd already inculcated the British repugnance for milk, I did love the texture of cream: whipped or iced or straight up from the bottle. I barely noticed, however, when glass bottles, milkmen, and the cream I'd so loved became extinct, and when in Ontario, even plastic milk jugs gave way to plastic bags. It was a point of comparison my mother frequently used to support a move to her homeland. "In England," she'd say, "milk containers are still made properly." She found the breast-like, squishy, litre milk bags "totally obscene." But as we settle in at my Uncle's ancient guest house, she laughs at *The Benny Hill Show*, and doesn't seem to notice Page Three Girls.

For a few weeks, at least, she'll be content, grazing idyllic pastures of childhood, aided by the sights and sounds: the smells of burning coal, the tastes of scones and Lardy cake. She was "in love with love," as she liked to say. In love with everything, as a girl, that lifted her from the chaos and squalor of war-torn England and promised the succour of romance. How she jitterbugged with American soldiers. How she cheated the ration system and sewed herself some beautiful clothes. In her dreamy inventory, there is no talk of deprivation or disease. These will be the sweet untainted thoughts that stream from the udder of her memory and I'll drink them in, as I drink in all that is both old and new around me. I'll drink them in, oblivious to the fact there is nothing here, at my Aunt's and Uncle's ancient guesthouse, that promises the romance she recalls, nor is there anything in England, that promises the future life she dreams of.

ANY TIME IS TEA TIME NOW

MY AUNT AND UNCLE are long retired as purveyors of accommodation. Most of the space in their enormous ancient English seaside guesthouse is now terminally vacant and drab. When my mother, little brother, and I first relocate to North Devon from Windsor Ontario, we move in with them. We take our meals and refreshments in a room that is smaller and more ragged than the rest of the aging house. We sometimes watch television there in the daytime and huddle close to the fire because there is no central heating, and even in the summer months, houses in England are generally cold. The room smells strongly of coal from the fire, and it also smells of my aunt and uncle's Pekinese dogs. Chan, the male, shares my uncle's auburn hair colouring, his stocky build and his introversion, while Chloe, the female, is dark and lithe and extraverted like my aunt.

At age sixty, my aunt looks younger to me than when, at age four, I first met her in Detroit. There, I recall, she looked vaguely similar to Auntie Peggy, the woman whom my uncle was usually with. My parents had stopped breathing when, at dinner, I asked who she was. She, however, completely composed, patted her mouth with a serviette and said kindly, "I'm your new aunt," and I got a sense from how she said this that she was not only my new aunt but, like the British new penny was supposed to be in 1971, a greatly improved variation. "You can call me Auntie Lena," she said and smiled a charming smile. Then, because I was having trouble keeping my peas from rolling off my fork, she offered to teach me how to capture and squish them. After dinner she and my uncle took me out to the five and dime and said they'd buy me any toy I wanted. Ignorant that decorum called for self-abnegation, I selected the largest doll in the store. The doll was only a few inches shorter than me and was designed with loose legs so she could stride along beside me if I held her hand. My uncle raised some quiet objections, but my new aunt vetoed these and paid for the doll from her own black handbag. I called the doll "Lena" in her honour, although afterwards my mother made me change her name to "Elsie."

I didn't know then that my new aunt wasn't really all that new. She and my uncle had a long history. They'd met in Birmingham before the end of World War II, married, and even had a child. They divorced, and my uncle had emigrated and remarried, but despite this complication, they'd kept in touch and decided, in the early 1960s, that they'd try their luck again. They moved back to England shortly after my aunt bought me the doll, and I didn't see them again until I was a teenager and my father died. They came briefly to Windsor to console my mother, and me and my Auntie Lena hit it off, discovering we shared an obsessive love (in fact, an addiction) for tea. Auntie Lena's love for tea was so great that each night she'd take a thermos-full to bed. She had asthma and maintained tea a much better medicine than her puffer. Although German biologist Albrecht Kossel first extracted the broncho-dilating substance, Theophylline, from tea's caffeine in 1888, this is not generally known, and my aunt's assertion appears to many simply as an old-wives' claim.

But there's nothing old about my aunt in the 1970s. She's as fit and sharp and as wrinkle-free as a woman twenty years her junior. She's full of energy, full of ideas, full of political will and community action. Each morning, in her flattering forest green housecoat, she touches her toes and practices French. "Un, deux, trois," she enunciates, mirroring the precise Parisian voice that purrs from a tape recorder. "Comment allez-vous?" she asks, following the lead of her taped tutor, moving on to the next physical exercise in her callisthenics regimen, and in between times quaffing a mouthful of our favoured brew.

Tea had once been my mother's drink of choice as well, though she disparaged North American variations. It all tastes like "maid's water," she used to say. Eventually, she turned to coffee, but not until she'd fostered my dependency on Britain's national beverage. She had emigrated from England in 1952, the year tea rationing ended, and according to historian Erika Rappaport, Britain's Tea Bureau commissioned Petula Clark (who would gain international fame twelve years later with the hit "Downtown") to record the chirpy ditty "Anytime is Tea Time Now".

The song begins: "One o'clock, two o'clock, three o'clock, four o'clock, tea time." It's a bouncy, upbeat number that encourages listeners to partake "of the cup that cheers" "morning, noon, and night." I'd never heard this song, though perhaps my mother had before she'd become a coffee traitor and taken the tune to heart. My Auntie Lena most certainly would have heard it, and I imagine if she sang it would have added fifteen-minute intervals to the chorus.

Unlike my mother, my aunt would never become a coffee drinker. Even if tea were suddenly made unavailable, I'm sure she would have chosen a number of other beverages, before reverting to "a cup of Joe." There are very few coffee drinkers who cross my path in this English seaside village of Ilfracombe in the 1970s. Those who do, drink the chalky instant variety, not the automatic drip coffee-maker kind that my mother favoured in Canada. "Maid's water!" She'll revive the old phrase to describe a cup of instant English coffee. She'll take to drinking loose tea, but not as much as me and my aunt. Our consumption rivals that of Samuel Johnson and both the William Pitts, who according to the chairman of Horniman's Tea company, "drank anything from 40 to 70 cups a day."

Johnson referred to himself as "a hardened and shameless tea drinker" in the 1750s, "whose kettle has scarcely time to cool; who with tea amuses the evening, with tea solaces the midnight, and with tea welcomes the morning." The same is true of my aunt and me.

In North America, I'd always preferred a large mug, but my Auntie Lena only uses proper British tea cups, ones my uncle found at public auctions, ones she's paid for at jumble sales. On the first day my mother and I arrived in Ilfracombe, she had me pick a cup. I chose the most ostentatious, one of pink and gold, with roses and violets. I noticed that her cup was a plain no-nonsense Kelly green. We use the same cups all the time, refill after refill, and wash them at the end of each day, or when they become brown with tannin. Like board game markers, our tea cups identify us. They say something about our preferences and perhaps about our characters.

I delight in the fact that tea is the country's national drink. It is said to be the "cup which cheers but does not inebriate." For almost three hundred years, it's been part of the history, tradition, and culture of Britain.

"To the true Briton, tea is as oil to the engine. It keeps the wheels of our social and business lives running smoothly, and if other nations say that everything stops for tea here, we would reply that everything might slow down were it not for tea," a jubilant *Daily Mail* editorial declared when the limitations on the elixir lifted, and the bitter phrase "tea-ration" could finally be strained from everyday parlance.

Famous politicians like William Gladstone have extolled its many virtues: "If you are cold, tea will warm you. If you are too heated, it will cool you. If you are depressed, it will cheer you. If you are excited, it will calm you." Royals as notable as Queen Victoria and King George V have also endorsed the beneficent drink. During World War I, soldiers brewed up in the trenches and during World War II, writes Simon de Bruxelles of *The Times*, Churchill gave tea rations for the troops the same priority as ammunition. Tea, he realized was "crucial for morale" and "stockpiles" of the elixir "were kept at 500 secret locations."

My aunt prepares tea in the tiny kitchen, which in the 1600s had been a stand-alone dwelling (a miller's cottage) and had once housed an entire family. Parents and children alike would have slept on bed-rolls stuffed with straw here and spent their days grinding flour, baking bread, pickling and preserving. Tea, though greatly popular with the French aristocracy, wouldn't have been available to this family. "The cup that cheers" wouldn't have lifted their spirits and invigorated them through their days. Beer, instead, with its dulling qualities, was their staple. They brewed it in great vats, and because the process rendered it more sanitary than water, drank it as water's alternative.

The floor of the cottage still slopes with the original clay dispro-portions, though it's now tiled. Slate shingles have come to replace a thatched roof and electricity, plumbing, and a fireclay sink have all been brought into the dwelling as necessary modernizations. My aunt is enthusiastic about her most recent acquisition and current pride and joy: it's an electric water heater she calls "a geyser." It hangs on the wall above the sink and boils water for our tea in record time. It can also be drained directly into her plastic washing-up bowl. Prior to installing this ingenious contraption, she was forever boiling water in a kettle for regular domestic cleaning and dish washing.

Before coming to England, it would have been difficult for me to fathom what life must be like without an automatic dishwasher. Even in the smallest and least expensive homes in our former subdivision in Ontario, dishwashers were the norm. But in England, although these appliances have been available for decades, they've made no significant inroads and are, "surprisingly," according to Carol Bowen of the *Daily Mail*, "one of the least-owned kitchen appliances" even as late as 1980. Ten years later, only one in eight households have dishwashers, and a government survey five years after this reports that only seventeen percent of Britons possess this labour-saving device.

In the decade I move to England, "the British housewife" is said to spend approximately five hundred hours a year washing dishes. Yet, she is "reluctant" to get an automatic dishwasher, journalist Penny Radford reports in *The Times*. Two million dishwashers are sold each year in the United States, Radford writes, while British purchases are "both pathetic and apathetic." In fact, the appliance sold so dismally in 1969 (there were only 23,000 purchased) that appliance manufactures formed the "Dishwasher Development Council" to promote its use. When asked why the disparate appliance makers decided to band together rather than compete in a good old-fashioned capitalistic style, chairman Michael Colston (the managing director of Colston dishwashers) said: "There was simply no point in slitting each other's throats over a market which hardly exists."

Why the British prefer to wash their dishes by hand, no one seems able to explain. Even after a contest in which a "champion woman washer-up" pitted her skills of speed and cleanliness against the appliance and lost, dishwasher sales didn't budge. "The psychological depths behind this apathy have yet to be plumbed," Radford wrote in 1971, and even decades in the future, the mystery will remain unsolved.

The water boils in my aunt's new geyser. Its whistle, as piercing as an air raid siren, only gradually dissipates. Though I've made countless cups in North America, I've never analyzed the minutia of tea making, never considered the possibility of better practices. In Windsor, Ontario, my usual method was to toss a tea bag into a cup or pot, to douse it with hot water, to squish it with a spoon, and after either pouring the brew into my cup or removing the bag, whiten with milk, cream, or Coffee Mate. It was the quickest way to satisfy my craving, the fastest way to satiate my thirst.

But speed is not the British way in the 1970s. Not in the washing of dishes, and not in the making of tea. Under my aunt's meticulous tutelage, the doors of discernment will swing open and I'll learn when it comes to making tea, "there's more than one way to skin a cat" as the time-sensitive Americans sometimes say, or "there are more ways of killing a cat than choking it with cream," as the leisurely British are apt to put it.

But the English would never think to put cream (or any chemical whitener for that matter) in their tea. Milk has been the substance that's accompanied the brew in Britain since the middle of the eighteenth century. However, this consensus is not without controversy.

"Milk-firsters" of this land strongly believe the bovine substance should be poured in a cup before the tea. "Milk-lasters" maintain the opposite is true. Some suggest that the sequence in which milk is added has historically been indicative of social class. To call someone "MIF" (Milk in First) was (at least in Evelyn Waugh's day) a euphemistic way of pegging them to the lower rungs of the social ladder. This may have been, as he explains, because governesses and nannies prepared their tea this way. Or perhaps, as others argue "Milk in First" traditionally buffered the effects of heat on cheap, lower class crockery. Or maybe it had nothing to do with class at all. George Orwell, an opinionated Milk-laster, wrote an essay for the *London Evening Standard* in 1946 which dealt with the subject. He claimed his technique of colouring strong black Indian or Ceylonese tea after pouring it in a cup was the only sensible method. "By putting the tea in first and stirring as one pours, one can exactly regulate the amount of milk, whereas one is likely to put in too much milk if one does it the other way round." In 1934, the *Daily Mail* in its regular "Boys & Girls" section presented a series called "Tea-Time Talks." The series commenced with "Put the Milk in First, Please!" — a story in which Dad explains the unquestionable logic to his children. "[Tannin] is an acid which is always present in tea, and it is very bitter. Now milk is able to change that bitterness, provided you mix it well with the tea. If you put the milk in first, it has a better chance of blending with the tea and doing its work. If you add it after the cup is almost full … the milk doesn't mix so well — and therefore leaves more of the bitterness of the tannin."

But Orwell, although he'd moved back home with his parents, was a grown man of thirty when "Dad's" helpful advice appeared and so most likely he would not have read it. He also may have missed novelist Naomi Jacob's warning in the same paper three years earlier: "Never, never, never" tea before milk. At this time, he'd have been on his way to Kent with vagrant hop-pickers, drinking brew from large communal drums, whitening it with condensed milk, and taking notes about the impoverished for future reference.

Even if he'd been aware that The Royal Society of Chemistry itself came down firmly on the side of Milk-firsters, it's unlikely that he'd have changed his position. Chronic lung disease and tuberculosis may have made him weak, but almost as if in compensation, he was apparently obstinate and drank his tea incredibly strong. "Tea is meant to be bitter," he wrote. And he continually maintained, along with legions of like-minded quaffers, that milk is meant to be added last.

In the 1970s, my aunt would disagree, though there are a number of tea-making rules to which she and Orwell, and most other Britons, would subscribe. Like a great alchemist of old, my aunt invites me into this learning. It's best to make tea when the boiling water still bubbles, best first to "heat the pot," which is a procedure of swirling simmering water, not just in the belly of the vessel, but all the way through the spout, and over the lid. She explains the importance of using freshly boiled water to make the infusion. It's a tea-making tip many in North America would scoff at and tag as an "old wives' tale." But old wives, I will learn in England, are frequently ahead of their time. Through experience and observation, they determined their truths long before science had the means to test or explain them.

My aunt opens a decorative tin that contains loose tea. She adds a heaping spoonful for each of us and an extra one, she says, "for the pot." Before I came to England, I'd never seen loose tea. I'm not even sure if it's something you can buy in North America. When we lived in the United States, there were Lipton's bags that came in yellow packages. In Canada, the brand we used was Red Rose. Tea historian Gervas Huxley claims Canadian bags contained more tea than the ones made in America, but as a child, I wouldn't have even suspected a difference. Tea, wherever I drank it, was simply tea until I came to Britain and discovered the substance denuded of bags.

Those small square sachets were such a part of North American culture that even the fortune tellers I'd seen who practiced tasseography would slice them open to ply their trade. Before our move, I'd sought the guidance of a psychic. She'd torn open a Red Rose teabag, sprinkled its dusty contents into my cup. "You'll cross the ocean many times," she told me. "You'll make new friends." She said nothing of culture shock. Perhaps teabag tea couldn't make this forecast.

The old miller's cottage-cum-kitchen, where my aunt makes the brew, joins the everyday sitting room through a small, narrow doorway. It was once used by the people of the seventeenth-century, a time when men, on average, grew no taller than five foot seven, and women no more than five foot one. Malnutrition was a way of life. Dysentery and intestinal parasites flourished. The average life expectancy was thirty-five and children born to the original dwellers of this place were more likely to have died than lived. After tea became popular among the aristocracy in Britain, its use eventually spread to all segments of the population. The phenolics in tea contained natural antibacterial properties and could kill a host of deadly germs. Cholera, typhoid, and dysentery microbes all took a hit from tea. Life expectancy began to increase. Infant mortality began to wane. The old wives claimed tea was healthful, but it would take decades before science concurred.

Tea drinking in Britain, has always been intimately tied to class, though all the time I live there, I'm ignorant of this fact. Besides Milkfirsters being perceived by some as un-posh, so are those who sweeten their brew, according to culture writer Kate Fox. "Taking sugar in your tea is regarded by many as an infallible lower-class indicator: even one spoonful is a bit suspect (unless you were born before about 1955); more than one and you are lower-middle at best; more than two and you are definitely working class."

While socioeconomics never informed the way I guzzled tea in North America, ardour had. I'd relinquished sugar — a two and a half teaspoon per cup habit — to mimic the preferences of my first sweetheart, Jack. Although Canadian, he'd been born in England, and perhaps had lived there long enough to know one's class could be read in a cup of tea. Some cultural knowledge is unspoken. It diffuses in the ether and is quaffed without consciousness, frequently evading the newcomer. While other social mores are handed down, customs are taught, and like the tea-making ritual my aunt demonstrates, something I can study and practice.

As she places the full pot onto a tea tray and covers it with a woolen cozy, I mentally take note. She heats our cups with the still-steaming remains of water from the geyser and adds the milk. She tops up the milk ewer for future cups and sets it down beside the strainer on the tray, which she then lifts deftly and carries with youthful vigour to the everyday sitting room through the tiny kitchen door. "Tea time," she calls. And as the two of us delight in the brew, I'm cheered. Cheered, not just by the substance, or the fact that my Auntie Lena, friend and mentor of old, is back in my life again. But cheered also, with the knowledge that in England, despite its lack of modern conveniences, any time is tea time now.

PASSING

THEY CALLED IT "the dirty factory" or "the prison," but I wanted in. It was white and brown and many windowed, an assemblage of at least a dozen rectangular brick boxes. Some of the boxes extended lengthwise beneath the soulful sloping landscape of the North Devon countryside; others appeared to be propped on their ends. It wasn't hard for my baby brother to recreate this structure with his Lego blocks.

"Th-th-th-this," he stuttered, "is f-f-for you." He'd made the building like a voodoo priest murmuring a silent prayer over each piece and purposefully snapping the construction together. I noticed that he didn't stutter when he whispered; it only ever happened when he spoke out loud.

"Thanks," I said, and placed his creation on the table in my aunt and uncle's sitting room. "Now I'm going to go there and see if they'll let me in."

It was during the 1970s, around the time the British Prime Minister made a momentous speech at Ruskin College and the seeds of the "Great Debate" on British education were sown. I'd dropped out of high school in Windsor, Ontario, even though a rather outspoken guidance counsellor had tried to stop me. "It's foolhardy you quitting and your mother taking you to England. Doesn't she realize it will ruin your life?" Ironically, the counsellor, who was close enough to retirement not to care about getting on the wrong side of parents or administrators, was herself from England. "Is there no one here you can live with while you finish school?"

I told her bluntly and honestly that it was hopeless, that I was happy to be leaving, that I'd missed so much school since my father died, I'd never catch up. I told her that Alice Cooper's song, *School's Out*, was chronically playing in my head and that while it was nothing personal, I became euphoric at the thought of being rid of all the people who composed this school. "Besides, there is no one I can stay with, Miss Penny," I said. "I have to leave." I was equally frank when I spoke, for the opposite reasons, to her equivalent in England at the jarringly unattractive Ilfracombe comprehensive school in North Devon.

I'm not entirely sure when the desire to return to school had seized me. I'd started keeping a journal and doing a lot of reading shortly before I'd dropped out. I'd purchased half a dozen steno notepads and was gradually filling them with words — what I called a satire on my life. According to researchers, parent loss in childhood and early adolescence can stimulate artistic creativity. Whatever the cause for my first flourish of literary invention, professional writing as a career goal had materialized like a life preserver tossed on a vast and unpredictable sea. It would be years before I heard Joseph Campbell's edict "follow your bliss," but in those months before leaving school and immigrating to England, I'd discovered something that I loved doing and had enough of an instinct to pursue.

Although "scribblers" (as some called them in England) were held in low esteem, I told the woman whom I spoke with at the comprehensive school that I wanted to be a writer, that I'd like to write novels and short stories, but thought training as a journalist might be more practical. The woman had a tight blonde bob and an intimidating sternness. Her voice had undergone such a purging of the regional accent and was so precise that she sounded as if she were trying to do a comic impression of the queen. "Remarkable," she said, staring at me, blinking.

Politely, I attempted to lift the reins of the conversation again. I assured her that I knew there was no training program for journalism at her school but thought perhaps I might be able to start on my career path by getting a high school diploma.

"High school?" her voice pierced the air. "Isn't that an American phenomenon?"

I hadn't been living in England long but had already grown accustomed to the way people here conflated Canada and the US. I already knew that the majority of the English I spoke with had no conception of the size or shape or the international boundaries that distinguished the country I'd come from. What I didn't know yet, but was in the process of learning, was that the mores and institutions of England were so completely different from those I'd left behind that there would forever be places inaccessible to me, and that this school would be one of them.

I didn't bicker with the woman over national identity, or answer her question, which really wasn't a question at all. I simply repeated the words "high school diploma" and then tacked on "or equivalent?"

I knew nothing about education in England, that no method existed of equating Canadian and British secondary school qualifications. I'd never heard of "O levels" or "A levels," which were the principal educational standards, and I was ignorant of the fact that most students graduated at age seventeen, a year beyond what England's official leaving age had been five years ago.

I didn't know about England's class system, or how this long history of discrimination and privilege was embedded in the ethos of the nation and influenced all its institutions. In the early 1800s in England, there had been great controversy over making education available to "the masses" while in Canada, there had never been "the masses" to worry about. Education in England for the lower, labouring classes, it was felt, would only cause them to grow discontented, to question their place in society, to seek privilege beyond their station or, worse, attempt to wrestle it away from their betters. Eventually, the realization that resistance to educate the masses was hobbling the country brought reforms. But even when the government made stabs at egalitarianism, as they did with education over the decades and most recently had done in the '50s and '60s with the rise of the inclusive comprehensive school model, the elite educational system that Britain had maintained prior to World War II would not be surrendered. Postwar universities had been popping up like crocuses after a spring shower; however, they accepted only a few very privileged applicants. The comprehensive schools, while embracing the many, by necessity still had to maintain rigid and asymmetrical hierarchies, ones that a dropout from Canada in 1970s shouldn't even attempt to scale.

My honest confession that I knew nothing of British history or geography and had been allowed in my former high school to opt out of science brought forth, from my confessor, a series of gasps. She was genuinely sorry — sorry she couldn't help me, and sorry that I'd wasted my time, and sorry that she couldn't even point me in some productive direction. "If only when you came in you'd told me you were working on your 'O's" she said, then after a pause, "Is it possible you can go back to Canada and finish your education?"

"No, it's not possible," I said.

"Sorry," she said again, and on that note I left "the prison" having failed at becoming an inmate.

The comprehensive school cast monstrous square shadows that made it look twice as large as it actually was and that distorted the steep and curving path down to the town. Before me, the dark and restless ocean extended. Rugged green hills and red earth wound and dipped and made a patchwork of the distant land that rolled out and away from the sea. Gradually, the ancient houses and hotels of the town appeared like a mirage, completely subsuming the present-day and in the process extinguishing my angst. The comprehensive school, high on a hill behind me, became nothing more than a geometric anomaly, a place out of time hovering over this comfortable, albeit petrified, land.

When I got to my aunt's and uncle's place, my little brother was in their back garden with half a dozen snails lined in a row and the Lego comprehensive school he'd built for me serving as a snail holding tank. He'd plucked the snails from the stone wall that divided a tiny patch of earth from another that belonged to the neighbours. Three or four more snails were hiding in the tank. "R-r-r-reserves," my little brother told me. He warned me against letting them know they were inside a school. He was afraid if they knew, they'd want to escape. He pointed to the snails in the row, and then to a finish line he'd drawn in the soil with a rock. "Wh-wh-who d-d-do you th-th-think will w-w-win?" he asked.

I told him I couldn't even wager a guess, though there was one snail I was certain wouldn't win, a plump muddy-shelled giant who, unlike his timid and lethargic competitors, had briskly bolted from the starting gate, but in the opposite direction.

Inside, my aunt made me a cup of tea, and my uncle commiserated. When he was a boy, he told me, there was a scheme in place to help academically gifted, working-class children secure places in upper class grammar schools. He wrote a test and won a place and his mother, a widow at the time, enrolled him despite the fact they were living on nothing. Two years later, she remarried, and her new husband put his foot down. "It wasn't so much the cost of uniforms and supplies he objected to," my uncle explained, "he just didn't like the idea of anyone having an opportunity he didn't have." Consequently, my uncle, who'd never been any good with mechanical things, became for a short while an apprentice mechanic.

My mother had told me about her father years before. He wasn't that much older than my uncle when he married my grandmother and was crazily jealous, but this wasn't a topic she wanted to broach right now. Since we'd immigrated to England, it had become her prime objective to convince herself of the rightness of her move. Whenever the occasion arose to extol the superiority of England and denigrate Canada, she seized it, and although she knew nothing of the reforms in education that had occurred since she'd moved to North America two decades ago, she was certain that the British system of education still was the best in the world.

"Children knew all they needed to know by the time they left school at age fourteen," she said. "We could read and write and do mathematics. We were prepared for the world and ready to help our parents. In Ontario," she huffed, "education is interminable. It goes on and on — even after secondary school, everybody planned on university and," she added, "I've yet to come across any Canadian high school graduate who can spell and punctuate properly."

I didn't know who she was including in her informal survey of graduates, but I, who was not a graduate, was well aware of my own inferiorities with spelling and grammar and hoped to overcome them by going back to school.

"Not to worry," my Auntie Lena said to me between sips of tea. "You can go on the continent as a shorthand typist."

"But I don't know shorthand, Auntie Lena, and my typing isn't all that good."

"Makes no difference," she said. "You can bluff your way through!"

Both my aunt and uncle had, in their younger years, bluffed their ways into unlikely occupations. My aunt, a working-class girl from Birmingham with no experience or formal education, learned the Queen's English, told a few well-fashioned lies, and at my age became the manageress of a Peter Lord's shoe shop. "It didn't take long to grasp the job," she said. "When you put yourself in a situation like that, you become highly motivated to learn." My uncle's motivation to lie and learn arose through his efforts to avoid World War II conscription. After chucking in his apprenticeship, he'd embraced a wild playboy's life, earning his living as a sometimes dance instructor, sometimes organist, at a local ballroom dance school. When the draft was announced and he was called up, he surveyed a list of reserved occupations and pretended he was a tool and die maker. Knowing nothing of the trade, he was sent to a shop in Birmingham, where he was expected to practice it. "But it wasn't hard," he assured me. "I just watched what another man did, and did the same. It was easy really. Never could figure out what all the fuss was about — much more difficult to teach a giggling Gertie with two left feet to fox trot."

While to me the idea of bluffing seemed dubious and flew in the face of everything I'd ever learned about appropriate moral conduct, I had to consider that if I'd "bluffed" with the woman at the comprehensive school, I'd most probably be purchasing my school uniform at this very moment. My aunt and uncle were adamant that "bluffing" was an entirely acceptable strategy used frequently in England under a variety of circumstances.

There was, of course, a long tradition of bluffers in England: commoners passing as royals, imposter royals who vied for the throne, confidence men and women who assumed alternate identities for fun, profit, and sometimes revenge. Famous local bluffers included the likes of Mary Baker, a cobbler's daughter and failed servant, who in the 1800s pretended she was a Princess from a mythical island in the Indian Ocean. Although feigning a foreign language, she was able to communicate that she'd been abducted by pirates and had taken a tumble from their ship in the Bristol Channel. The nouveau middle class made much of her, curtseyed and bowed to her, celebrated her as a local celebrity. When the truth was revealed, she sailed to the

United States where she could carry on her deceptions. Eventually, she returned to England, married, and took up the lucrative business of selling leeches to the Bristol hospital.

Another notorious bluffer was "the noted Devonshire stroller and dog-stealer," Bampfylde Moore Carew, whose memoir as a confidence man became a bestseller in the late 1700s, when it was first published, and continued to sell well for the next hundred years. Carew was a master of disguises, posing at times as a shipwrecked sailor, a Quaker, a rat-catcher, and as the grieving mother of a child who had been burned to death in a fire.

The history of bluffing in England extends well beyond its myriad of colourful characters. The game of poker, as it has come to be played throughout the world, evolved from a popular British 16th-century bluffing game called "brag." The Q ships, first used in Britain to help defeat Germany in World War I, hid their weapons and masqueraded as passive merchant marine vessels in order to lure submarines to their doom. Pretence as a social mechanism is constantly affirmed in the British media with "how to pretend" articles that offer up summaries of films and literature so people might appear more urbane or "in the know" than they actually are, and there's even a series of bestselling books, notably called "Bluffer's Guides," that purport to school the disingenuous on a multitude of topics ranging from accountancy to women.

Canadians, on the other hand, are not natural bluffers. When we feel ignorant, we tend to call a spade a spade and consult the popular US book series, *The Complete Idiot's Guide*. The cartoon Mountie, Dudley Do Right, is a character who reflects our national spirit. When asked by his well-meaning sweetheart to bluff or deceive his way out of a life-threatening situation, he inevitably responds: "But that would be wrong." The contrasting British archetype is the Artful Dodger, who when brought to court for crimes he actually did commit puffs himself up like a blowfish and announces full of bluff and bluster:

"This ain't the shop for justice." Even though unquestionably in the wrong, he threatens that heads will roll when his influential attorney arrives and that the police who picked him up will "wish they'd never been born, or that they'd got their footmen to hang 'em up to their own hat-pegs, afore they let 'em come out this morning to try it on upon me."

My aunt insisted that it was no crime to "bluff" and believed a short-hand typist job on the continent was just the job for me. "You'd be able to see Europe, meet influential people, accumulate all sorts of writing fodder."

Even if I had been a crackerjack stenographer who could take dictation at the speed of light and type three hundred words a minute, I still wouldn't want to be a shorthand typist. I felt a little sad and almost guilty telling her, but she took it well.

"Not to worry, I expect we'll be able to find something else for you to do," she said, and within twenty-four hours she had.

Each morning after breakfast I accompanied my aunt down the High Street and assisted her in collecting the necessary provisions for the day. These usually included meat from the butcher, fruit and vegetables from the greengrocer, bread, cakes, and rolls from the baker, and four or five newspapers from the newsagent. My aunt was a staunch Tory and was a local town councillor and knew the concerns of every small business owner in Ilfracombe. "This is my niece from Canada," she'd introduce me proudly, and the shop owners, seemingly pleased to meet me, would inevitably allude to relatives or friends who'd immigrated to New York or California.

The morning following my interview at the comprehensive school, my aunt took me further up the High Street than was usual and told me she wanted us to nip in and visit her friend and fellow councillor, Eric Heath. Eric, as he insisted I call him, was a paunchy, dissipated man in his mid-forties, balding with a dark, Henry the VIII-type beard. His hotel, which shared the same Victorian design as most of the hotels in Ilfracombe, was of a moderate size and less well kept than most. His office, situated off the main common room, where a group of hearing-impaired senior citizens were readying themselves for a day excursion to Clovelly, was dark and dank and reeked of alcohol.

He complimented my aunt on how well she looked and told her he thought that I was a real stunner. He dropped his voice low, said something I imagine was lewd, and pinched my aunt's backside. She laughed charmingly, though I could tell that his antics didn't amuse her, and she gave his hand a swat. He winked at me and said, "Your aunt's a corker!"

Gradually, she got him lamenting over his business, how tax laws were destroying him, how the hotel had recently lost a star from its rating, because he just couldn't afford to do repairs and paint, "and the staff!" he moaned. My aunt skillfully drew him out here, and he explained how hard it was to find good help, how he had no choice but to hire rude fly-by-night yobs from the North Country — yobs, no sooner trained than tipping their hats and shouting Cheerio.

"It sounds as if we came along at the right time," my aunt said, breaking the rhythm of his rant. "My niece is looking for a job, and as you can see, she's quite respectable."

I could see a flicker of thought momentarily appear in Eric's heavy, dark-lidded eyes, and he surveyed me in a way he hadn't done at first. He was taking in my height and weight, looking at my arms to see if I had any muscle strength. I almost expected him to ask me to open my mouth so he could examine my teeth, but instead he asked: "Do you have any waitressing experience?"

My aunt was standing directly behind him and I could see her lips forming the word "bluff."

"I have a little," I lied.

"Oh, come now, no need to be modest," my aunt said, and then proceeded to give a detailed, yet entirely fictitious, inventory of my previous waitressing jobs.

Carl Jung, the Swiss psychoanalyst, once observed that Americans won't believe something if the content lacks authenticity, while the British won't believe something if there are violations of form. The form of my aunt's performance was flawless, and Eric was duly impressed.

My aunt congratulated me on getting the job as we headed back down the High Street together, past the old newsagent and the ancient shops and dwellings that had been part of this town for well over one hundred years. "I expect you'll meet lots of interesting people to write about and it won't take you long to learn the job," my aunt said positively, but I wasn't even thinking about these practical considerations. I was thinking about the comprehensive school, high on the hill behind us, casting fixed and resolute shadows in places I couldn't even see.

GROCKLES

I HAD NO IDEA that the pretty woman sitting with Eric Heath was his mistress, nor did I know that the scowling chambermaid who'd earned the nickname "Mean Noreen" was his wife.

Lilian, the ancient waitress who was supposed to be training me, nudged my ribs with her bird-beak elbow and whispered over the din of the noisy hotel kitchen that had erupted into manic activity that "the lady at the family table is the gaffer's bit of fluff. You mind you treat 'er respectful-like."

It was my first morning at The Molesworth Hotel, my first genuine experience of employment. I wasn't used to waking up at 5:00 a.m., and I wasn't used to life in England.

"Oi! Over 'ere!" Lilian called. She could have been eighty but was agile and flew around the kitchen like a finch. "This 'ere," she said, when I finally caught up with her, "is your server." It was a white towel, and she placed it over my palm and wrist. "Them dishes, when you pick 'em up from the hot plate are burning like incendiary bombs, so always cover them 'andy-Os, or you'll end up without fingerprints."

Behind the hotplate bustled the kitchen staff: a waifish, blue-eyed sous-chef called Lynne; Charlie, a petite and slight, grey-toothed dishwasher; a handsome culinary apprentice from a local trade college, whose name no one seemed to know; and a fat and griping chef, named Chris, whose hair was streaming with perspiration and whose white work jacket was stained black.

I'd already met Janice and George, who like me, were members of the wait staff. I hadn't yet met Elaine, a skinny, young blonde, who apparently was persistently late and who burst into the kitchen with smudged mascara and a wrinkled skirt and danced past us while Lilian was in the middle of explaining how to hold plates properly. Elaine collected six full breakfast dishes, then karate kicked the kitchen's swinging door so it opened wide enough for her to sail through.

"That Elaine," Lilian huffed, as she situated four blistering plates on my server: "She thinks she's the bloody queen of Sheba cuttin' it so close like that, but thems who won't swallow their pride end up chokin' on it and I don't doubt that's exactly what'll 'appen to 'er."

The waiter, George, hurried after Elaine with his six plates and made it through the still open door, and then Elaine returned through another swinging door, her empty hands drawing the next group of plates like magnets.

In what seemed less than five seconds, Lilian warmed, then filled, a china teapot with boiling water from a large steaming urn, buttered six slices of fresh toast, chopped them in half and expertly tossed them into a metal toast rack. I noticed her hands were covered in calluses.

"Now don't you mind what anyone else says or does, you understand? The gaffer says I'm to train you, no one else, so you listen only to me, right?"

I nodded and followed Lilian out through the swinging door into the busy dining room, cautiously carrying the four plates as she'd arranged them.

Lilian was the only waitress to remain in Eric Heath's employ season after season. Her husband had died leaving debts, and her only son, a grown man now, was off in London making his mark. Lilian rented a small flat on top of a laundromat and lived less than five minutes away from the hotel. She knew that Eric could hire younger, quicker wait staff and that most of the hotel proprietors in town wouldn't even doff their caps at her, so she was incredibly grateful for her job.

The family table, where Eric presided, was the first beyond the kitchen doors. He sat a little straighter in his chair, and his "bit of fluff" stopped fussing over his two squabbling children as I slowly and carefully set the plates before them.

"How's our new Canadian darling getting on, alright?" Eric asked Lilian. His porky fingers slid from the table and pinched her meatless thigh.

"Oh, Gov'nor!" she exclaimed, laughing, "you'll 'ave me in such a tizzy that I'll spill tea and wet meself."

"Wet yourself?" Eric teased. "We do have a staff loo, you know!"

"You're such a card, Gov!" she laughed.

"Well you know what they do with cards?" he rejoined.

Lilian assumed a wide-eyed dumbness.

"Play with them," he whispered lewdly, pointing towards his crotch.

"Oh, Gov'nor," Lilian laughed covering her cheeks with her calloused hands. "Av I gone red?" The "bit of fluff," whose name, Suzie Drude, I would learn later, swatted him playfully, and in a thick North Country accent said, "Do you want all the bleedin' guests to know you're a perv?"

The guests wouldn't know he was a perv, at least not from this transaction, because they wouldn't have heard him. The noise in the dining room was deafening. Chairs ground under tables and cutlery clanked and scraped across plates, and most of the guests, who were old and hard of hearing, were chatting with frenzied enthusiasm at full volume. They'd all come from Yorkshire by inexpensive coach tour and had made of fellow travellers on their journey friends for life, which judging from all their wrinkles and decrepitude, wouldn't be that long. I wondered if this perhaps explained the necessity of such frenetic and desperate communication. Like supernovas, they were exploding with a final burst of energy before ultimately fading from the galaxy.

Lilian introduced me to a table of her guests. "This 'ere is our new waitress, from Canadar," she announced, her thin-lipped smile shaking with exertion. "The gaffer's asked me to train 'er, so breakfast might be a bit late in comin', alright?"

"Oh, that's fine chuck, nowt to fuss on," an animated bald man at the table said, pronouncing his short u's like oo's. "We're chelpin and chin waggin, so tek ye time."

"From Canadar?" a plump, florid-faced woman called over him, "that's in 'Merica, int it?"

The Molesworth had come to be part of Ilfracombe's landscape in the late 1800s. Originally constructed as three distinct, four-storey board-ing houses, it only became a proper hotel in the early 1900s. The town, however, had been a popular spa and sea-bathing resort long before this. In 1819 a local businessman contracted hundreds of Welsh miners to hand carve six tunnels through rock cliffs to provide an entrance way to beach coves. Four of the tunnels were still func-tional, and sea bathing, although no longer vaunted as a miraculous cure for "want of stamina and general lack of tone," still remained a draw to thousands of tourists. Ilfracombe was "greatly enlarged by the addition of numerous commodious lodging houses and elegant ter-races" by 1832. "It had become a place of fashionable resort to the affluent and the valetudinarian…" the *North Devon Journal* reported.

The town had originally tried to establish itself, unlike gaudy Blackpool and resorts of that stripe, as a rather up-scale seaside town catering to the refined and decorous. Easy accessibility by channel steamer, however, allowed for the undesirable element — "trippers," as they were called, who'd come only for the day and generally take advantage of their anonymity to behave like boors.

The Molesworth, even at conception, had never been one of Ilfracombe's most fashionable establishments, and a century of few economic peaks and numerous troughs had left it worn of any little fashion it might once have possessed. It was Eric Heath's mandate to cram in as many busloads of holiday makers — or "grockles," as they were called by Ilfracombe locals — as he possibly could fit. "Cheap and cheerful accommodation" he offered, but it was obvious to anyone that The Molesworth tended to be top heavy with cheap and wanting in cheer.

"We serve a very good full breakfast," Eric would tell busloads of grockles on their arrival, and that was all he could boast. The rooms were cold, the beds old and lumpy, the sheets patched, some to the extent that they wouldn't lie flat. Plumbing and electrical problems frequently wreaked havoc, as did, according to the hotel manager, Arthur, a poltergeist that he occasionally communed with in the hotel's ballroom.

But most grockles didn't have lofty expectations for the prices they paid, and excluding the poltergeist, many were used to similar and worse conditions at home. They had come to Ilfracombe because it was a relatively inexpensive holiday and because at the seaside, with its myths and rituals and nostalgia, they could dip their toes in an invigorating symbol of life, feel merry and carefree for a moment, and remember all the joys of holidays past.

The "very good full breakfast" that Eric mentioned was of the old-fashioned Victorian variety and according to historical writer Joe Moran, despite being traditional, was on the wane in British hotels.

The surging costs of eggs and bacon in the 70s were to blame. Twenty per cent of hotels, the *Daily Mirror* is purported to have chronicled, had stopped offering the high calorie, high fat and high cholesterol fare.

Health-conscious individuals had not yet come to dub this national archetype "stroke on a plate." And while Robert Carrier, celebrity chef, food writer and American immigrant, may already have "declared war on the cooked English breakfast" calling it "stodge," he would never have been the sort of person Eric Heath would attract to his hotel.

Guests who flocked here looked forward to the choice of orange, grapefruit or tomato (pronounced "tomahto") juice to start. They looked forward to instant coffee and steamed milk or tea, to corn flakes or porridge, and for their main meal, sausage, bacon, eggs scrambled or fried, baked beans, fried mushrooms, stewed tomatoes, bubble and squeak and bread. Lots of bread. They could pick thick white tombstones of it or crisp brown toast, slathered with New Zealand butter and Robertson's Golden Shred marmalade. Doorstop wedges of glistening fried bread also adorned each morning table. And the grockles would consume this stupendous breakfast, as if they hadn't seen food for days. "Ah'm fair clemmed this mornin,'" they'd explain, or "Ooo, ah'm so 'uuungry ah could eat a scabby 'orse between bed rags." As they called for two or three additional racks of toast, someone at the table might say, "'e's got 'imself an 'ollow leg," or "'e could eat three more 'tatas thant pig," and they'd all wolf down whatever was set before them, and leave their tables reluctantly only when they saw the wait staff adjourn. Today I'd learn this, along with the practical procedures set in place for the timely dispensing, to such a voracious group, of what my co-workers referred to as "nosh."

There was a refrigerator on the wait-staff side of the hot plate where juice and milk and marmalade and butter were stored, and we were responsible for filling a variety of receptacles — glasses, jugs, pitchers, bowls — with these various substances. There was a huge, open

container of cornflakes that looked like a cardboard industrial drum
into which we'd stick our cereal bowls and scoop out a moderate
portion. Waitresses were forever losing bracelets and rings in the cereal,
and the waiter George once lost his watch. For guests who chose cooked
cereal, we'd thoroughly stir the large pot of congealed porridge on the
hot plate, and then ladle out enough to fill one-third of a bowl.

We'd shout numbers at the kitchen staff, "two fried with bacon, four
sausages with three scrambled and one fried," and miraculously, they'd
accommodate us, even though our words came quickly, and we never
took turns shouting.

Over time, I'd learn that a service was a performance, that there were
good ones and bad ones and ones in between. There were services in
which you could feel a kind of rhythm and everything hummed along
with a swift and flawless beat, services where early on you knew the
beat was missing, and it took a lot of effort from everyone to pull things
back into synch, and there were also services that were utterly hopeless
— ones that no one tried to salvage, but instead fueled with their own
personal discontent. I learned, over time, that bad moods could create
bad services, and that both kitchen and dining staff were sensitive to
a thing they called "atmosphere." A bad atmosphere was as oppressive
and searing as mustard gas and could hang around for an inordinately
long stretch. If a bad atmosphere got out of hand, as it had done at a
few hotels in Ilfracombe, it could create a mass exodus of staff. No one
wanted this at The Molesworth, not because (with the exception of
Lilian) they weren't capable of getting other jobs in town, but rather
because their prevailing feelings were that the devil you knew was
better than the one you didn't. There was also, of course, the
consideration of having to learn new routines and procedures. The
staff at The Molesworth shared the desire for an easy life.
Consequently, most everyone took pains to turn off their animosities
and frustrations for the duration of the service with the notable
exception of the chef, who bitched and whined and criticized, but

amazingly was tolerated and, for the most part, with gracious good humour.

As the grockles finished their various courses, we returned their dirty dishes and cutlery back to the kitchen. There were two plastic waist-high bins under a stainless-steel counter where we scraped and poured everything the grockles hadn't consumed: hard lumps of porridge, pools of cornflake-stained milk, overly crunchy egg whites, baked bean sauce, unbreakable fried bread crusts, rubbery sausage casings, tough tomato skins, and mountains upon mountains of bacon rind.

"Where does it all go?" I asked Lilian.

"A farmer pops in a few times a week for it."

"What does he do with it?" I asked.

"Paints the bloody walls of 'is castle, what do you think?" she snapped.

I was both shocked and appalled when Janice told me it was used to feed pigs.

"But there's bacon rind in there," I protested.

"Piggies are quite cannibalistic." The diminutive dishwasher's refined voice floated over the hotplate. He was the kind of person who could turn himself invisible at will, and no one ever noticed he'd been eavesdropping until he decided to join the conversation. "I've done a bit of pig farming in my time, and I've seen sows making meals of piglets. It's quite gruesome, really."

Charlie took our stacks of dirty plates once we'd scraped them and immersed them in scalding water in a large aluminum tank. The cutlery was supposed to be washed separately in a sink on our side of the hotplate. It was supposed to be done by a stillroom assistant; however, the hotel didn't currently have one. Apparently, according to Lilian, the former stillroom assistant "had words with the gaffer," so now it was "all 'ands to the pump."

But Elaine didn't wholly share Lilian's cooperative Dunkirk spirit. "It's not bloody right, us 'aving to wash cutlery! We're not getting paid to do stills. He could 'ave 'ired someone else by now, but 'e's on to a bloody good thing 'aving us do extra work for naught, the cheap sod!" Lilian's lips quivered again under the exertion of her "pay no heed" smile, and she showed me how to wash the cutlery.

There was a bottle of dark green industrial-strength washing-up liquid that smelled like a cross between sulfur and ammonia. Less than half a cap in a full sink of hot water would remove even the most persistent grime; more than half a cap would remove the cutlery's finish. Lilian showed me how to swish the cutlery around in the water and then plunk it into a draining bucket. Before the water turned grey with debris and lost its suds, bright white bubbles clung to the blades of knives and in-between fork tines.

"Wouldn't it be a good idea to rinse?" I asked Lilian.

"Don't 'ave time," Lilian responded. "We'll give'm a good wipe on their way back to the tables for the next set up."

Elaine, Janice and George whipped through the swinging doors, taking last rounds of hot buttered toast out and hauling dozens of dirty dishes back in. I was painfully conscious of my slowness and aware I was often under foot. My hands were sensitive to the washing up liquid and had begun to develop small slit-like wounds at the knuckles. Lilian gave me half a dozen dishes to scrape into the slop bucket. I was trying my best to do a proper job. I heard Elaine sigh behind me and tap her impatient foot. "I'll just be a second," I turned to tell her when the knife I'd been using to scrape the plates fell from my hand into the bin with a splash. The expression on Elaine's face was one of sheer delight. "Shhhh," she whispered, "don't say anything to the Dosser, as she called Lillian or she'll 'ave you wading through that muck."

I looked into the slop bin. I thought about the pigs. Surely, if the pigs ate the knife, it wouldn't do them any harm. Surely it was worse to eat your own kind than to eat metal. I reached for another knife and continued scraping.

When the service was over and all the grockles had cleared the dining room, the wait staff commandeered the largest table and we all gathered together to eat breakfast. George and I were the only ones to tuck into the hot breakfasts we were offered. Janice had a bowl of cornflakes, Lilian had toast, marmalade, and tea, and Elaine, denigrating all the food as slop, picked at a piece of toast before pushing it away and lighting a cigarette.

"You want to watch yourself wif vem breakfasts," Janice warned me.

"Wot's wrong with 'em?" Lilian asked defensively and then took a dainty bite of her toast.

"Well let's just say vay ain't the most slimming fings in the world," Janice responded. "You'll get as big as a 'ouse if you get in the 'abit of eating vem every day."

"Meals is part of our wages," Lilian said, buffing her lips with a napkin. "If she wants to eat breakfast and get 'er money's worth, who is you to tell 'er not to."

"I'm only sayin' if she don't want to look like va back end of a lorry, she ought to fink it froo. It ain't easy doin' fis sort a work if you're heavin' 'round a fat arse and blubber bags. I wish someone had said somfin to me."

Janice was thirty-five years old but looked fourteen, and while not as skinny as Lilian and Elaine, certainly wasn't heaving around a fat arse or blubber bags. She and her former husband had done seasonal work in hotels across Europe. She struggled with her weight for a time, but then took up smoking and cut out most cooked meals. The weight had been a problem for her, but by far the greater challenge of her adult life so far, she confessed, had been her husband. He'd had a nervous breakdown when they were waiting tables in Madrid and she just couldn't stick it.

"'E always was a bit peculiar, but I didn't fink 'e'd go balmy. If I fought 'ed go balmy, I never woulda hitched up wif 'im," she chuckled a bit.

Lilian, obviously bored with Janice's narrative, picked up a news-paper that one of the grockles had dropped. "Let's see wot the stars 'ave to say," she said.

I didn't know what she was talking about, and must have looked puzzled because she said, "Don't you read wot the stars 'ave to say in Canadar?"

"You mean, like the celebrities in *People Magazine?*" I asked.

"She means astrology," Elaine said contemptuously.

"Wot's wrong with it? The royals 'ave an astrologer," Lilian defended. I didn't want to confess that I also read my horoscope every day.

"Just 'cause the royals is a bleedin' bunch of nutters, doesn't mean every bleedin idiot in Britian 'as to be," Elaine snapped.

George, who until now seemed completely disengaged from the conversation, shouted, "Oi! Watch who you call a nutter. In the ole days, you'd 'a been 'anged for treason."

"Well it ain't the bleedin ole days," Elaine retorted, "though you'd never know it, 'round this dump, with 'is nibs acting like bleedin King 'enry the eighth, havin it off with Suzie Floosy right under 'is wife's nose."

Janice and George were Virgos, Lilian said, trying to diffuse the situation. This explained why they were always so critical, while Elaine was an Aries, "like Hitler," Lilian whispered *sotto voce*, "always looking for a row." Lilian herself was an Aquarius, which she liked to pronounce "queer arse" for the fun of it, while believing it to be the superior sign of the zodiac. "Us queer arses know how to muck along," she said lighting a cigarette. "Live and let live is our motto." Her tight smiling lips quivered before releasing a light fog of smoke.

"Bollocks!" Elaine barked.

"I wish you'd eat a bit a somethin'," Lilian said. "If you'd eat a bit a somethin', you wouldn't be 'arf so shirty."

"Bollocks!" Elaine repeated hoarsely, crushing her cigarette into a saucer.

Later, as we were setting up and Lilian was showing me how to turn the tablecloths so they'd look clean at lunch time, she told me in the strictest confidence that Elaine had "an attitude." Attitudes, she explained, if not checked, would detrimentally affect "the atmosphere." She only hoped that Elaine had the good sense to realize this, "and jack in the faffing."

But Elaine didn't seem to have the good sense to jack in the faffing. Once the tables were set, she hunted Arthur down in the ballroom and demanded that he get a stillroom assistant by lunchtime, or she, George and Janice were all going to walk.

"What is this, the bleedin' mutiny on the Bounty?" Arthur asked. Arthur was tall with natty gray hair. He'd been in Eric's employ for years, but there'd been lots of issues over staff lately, and he and Eric butted heads regularly over expenditures. Arthur wanted to hire a new stillroom assistant, but it was likely that Eric had told him to save the money and use his charm and diplomacy to jolly the wait staff along.

While Arthur tried to put on a stern front and act indignant over Elaine's insubordination, it was difficult for him to pull it off. "No need to get all hot and bothered," he relented. "I'll see what I can do," he promised, and at lunchtime he himself sashayed into the kitchen wearing an apron and took the vacant post at the sink.

For lunch there was a choice of mulligatawny or oxtail soup, both made from mixes with a bunch of leftover vegetables thrown in so the soup appeared homemade. Guests had the choice of a slice of ham or a slice of beef with a cold salad, or Quiche Lorraine with green beans. For dessert there was bread and butter pudding, which was actually stale pieces of bread cooked up with milk, eggs, and sugar, or there was reconstituted Bird's custard with fruit cocktail.

Lilian gave me two of her tables to practice on. She told me it was important I went solo because tomorrow three new busloads of grockles were coming in, and I'd have at least five tables to deal with on my own. I didn't relish these prospects at all. I still hadn't got the hang of carrying four plates in one hand, let alone six in two, and knew I was shamefully slow. I was still serving my two tables their soup, while the rest of the staff had finished serving their main courses.

"What the bleeding 'ell's wrong with you?" bellowed the red-faced chef, Chris, when I approached the hot plate. Ferocious mist from his angry words scattered the small sweating curls of my hair. I recoiled in terror. "Stir your stumps!" he commanded, pushing two plates of Quiche Lorraine at me and I took them, even though both tables wanted salad. "I don't know why we 'ave to put up with this," the chef ranted. "What do you do?" he shouted to Arthur at the sink, "put notices in the Labour Exchange, 'only the gormless need apply?'"

I could feel tears sting my eyes as the chef continued his diatribe and no one came to my rescue. All the staff, including Arthur, were silent.

"We just usually let 'im blow 'imself out," Janice whispered, once we were in the dining room. "Don't take it personal."

"'E's a cretin," Elaine whispered on her way past me, delivering salads to my tables, "take no notice."

I did my best to mask my upset and carry on, and by the end of the service, the chef had recomposed himself and vanished someplace, gladly, out of sight.

I was surprised that Elaine didn't seem particularly happy that Arthur had taken her gripe seriously and was washing the cutlery. "'Is nibs ought to be in 'ere, doing that," she grumbled, "but I guess 'e's on the job with Suzie Floozy bonking his brains out."

Lilian fluttered around Arthur, calling him "love," and saying how good it was of him to "grasp the nettle" and deal with the problem, but when he removed his hands from the foamy water, they looked as if he actually had been grasping nettles. They were red and swollen to three times their size and looked like claws because the inflammation prevented him from extending his fingers.

"Bloody 'ell," he said, "it's me bleedin' dermatitis."

"Not to worry," Lilian said, rolling up the sleeves of her white blouse. "All 'ands to the pump."

"Pump my arse," Elaine called.

"No need to be vulgar," Lilian said, but Elaine either paid no heed or didn't hear her. She was beyond the swinging door, collecting the dishes that the grockles had all but licked clean.

THE EXISTENCE
OF GHOSTS

SUN LIGHTS THE foggy sky as I hurry down the slick steep pavement. A cry, low and wild, like Jacob Marley's ghost in the 1951 film version of *A Christmas Carol*, keens from the floors above a butcher's shop. It bounces across the narrow streets of Ilfracombe and echoes in a pained and primal way that makes the fine hairs on my arms bristle. Once it fades, I bolt across the deserted road and run as fast I can to the safety of my workplace, the Molesworth Hotel.

"She must 'ave seen 'im. 'E must 'ave waved his willy at her." Lilian, my workmate speculates as I enter the stillroom looking distressed.

I'm a teenage high school drop out, a US citizen, formerly a Canadian landed immigrant, who has landed once again in a seaside resort, this time in North Devon, England. Thanks to my aunt, I've got this job, but the old world, as my new world, is discombobulating to say the least.

There's a local flasher, currently the scourge of the town. Three days before, he dropped his pants outside the hotel and gave a group of elderly female guests "the fright of their lives." One of them, it was rumoured, ended up in hospital.

But it wasn't the flasher who made the blood drain from my face and my heart pound like a jackhammer. I try to explain this while, with trembling hands, I light a cigarette.

"'E better not try it on me. I'll wrap 'is wots it round 'is wooz it and 'e'll be a very long time sortin' 'imself out," Lilian says, not hearing. She fishes a smoke from her purse.

The dishwasher, Charlie, arrives. I call him *Little Charlie* because although he's seven years my senior, he's eight inches shorter, and of a delicate build. "Good lord!" he exclaims, "You're as white as ash."

Sometimes, after breakfast, when I'm late setting up for the lunch service, I hang around the kitchen instead of walking home, and little Charlie and I chat. The new second chef, also named Charlie, is tall and of a larger build. I call him Big Charlie or B.C. He often joins us, and at the end of the day, the three of us stop at a nearby pub for a pint.

Recently, Little Charlie purchased an old Zephyr, so some nights instead of the pub, we buy scrumpy cider and drive to a precipice overlooking Hele Bay. I always look forward to our outings; forward to the opportunity to converse about the challenges of living in Ilfracombe and the upsets of the day, but right now, minutes before the guests we call "grockles" arrive into the dining room looking for food, Little Charlie is asking what happened and I have no intention of waiting until after the service to tell him.

I've been superstitious for as long as I can remember, but unlike my work mates, skeptical of the ghosts which are said to abound in Devon. Spectral star-crossed lovers wander a 14th century castle at Berry Pomeroy; spirits of hungry pigs squeal on Merripit Hill, and at Buckfastleigh, a headless rake, reputed to have sold his soul to the devil, is said to appear summer evenings with a pack of hell-hounds snapping at his heels. Even here, in Ilfracombe, there are spirits. *The George and Dragon* pub, for instance, has a drunken poltergeist who hales from the late 1300s, there are spirits of misanthropic pirates lying in wait for the unwary, and on every misty beach and cove some unregenerate smuggler, who doesn't realize he's dead, fruitlessly attempting to ply his trade.

Virtually every hotel in Ilfracombe boasts a resident phantom. The manager of the Molesworth claims he's on intimate terms with ours, but by far the most celebrated local ghost in our community lives at Chambercombe Manor, a small 11th century dwelling.

In the future, the old Manor will fill with ghosts almost in proportion to the decline of living tourists, who through economics, caprice, and the availability of cheaper air fares and better holidays on the continent, won't frequent the town as they once did. The paranormal reality show, *Most Haunted*, will feature the house in 2006 and report on a child ghost swinging in a cradle, two dead six-year-old playmates, and two phantom men who inhabit the same room, but in the 1970s when a gathering of ghosts would literally be "*overkill*," there is only ever mention of one ghost at the manor whom is referred to as "the lady in grey."

I doubt the wraithlike shriek I heard, ghostly or otherwise, was produced by any kind of "lady." I don't believe in ghosts, but Little Charlie and Lilian speculate.

"It's not impossible," Little Charlie says.

"I expect Arthur'll be very interested in this," Lilian adds, and seconds before the breakfast gong, Arthur is duly summoned from the ballroom and arrives carrying a bottle of brandy. "'Av a thimble full a this," he offers, pouring some of the golden liquid into a shot glass.

I down the shot, then down another, and feel the explosion of warmth knock colour back into my cheeks. "Do you 'av people 'oo might be tryin' to make contact?" Arthur asks. "I mean on the other side."

I knew that he wasn't talking about the other side of the Atlantic. "My father died recently," I tell him. This is the reason my mother moved us to Ilfracombe, which I don't tell him. "My Grandmother is dead too," I say. Coincidently she's buried in the cemetery behind our house, just up the hill. "Does physical proximity matter?" I ask.

"Could do," Arthur says sagely, "could do."

I float through the breakfast service in a swathe of brandy calm, though things at the Molesworth are far from serene. The owner recently decided to make his mistress, Suzy Drude, assistant manager, and her perfectionism along with what she calls "*a no-nonsense approach*" has everyone ready to lynch her.

"On the street Suzy came from in Blackpool," the chef says loud enough so everyone including Suzy hears, "there were either priests or prostitutes, and we all sure as hell know Suzy was never a priest."

The owner's wife, Noreen, with her perpetual ambiance of misery, is in the stillroom looking for a needle and thread to patch up a sheet. I notice the corners of her mouth lift and her lips form a tight thin line, which is as close to a smile as I've ever seen her come.

After I set up my tables for lunch, Arthur beckons me to the ballroom. I've heard of his ballroom spirit, a female ghost who enjoys a good laugh, performs the occasional trick, and responds to the music Arthur plays on the piano with various creaks and knocks.

"It's only the bleedin' plooooomin'!" Suzie Drude has insisted repeatedly, but Arthur maintains she's wrong.

The ballroom is long and wide with a parquet floor. There are framed photographs of dancing guests on every wall. Arthur closes the sliding doors and invites me to take a seat next to the piano bench. He looks like an older, nattier, Dick Van Dyke, in the role of Bert, Mary Poppins' chimney-sweep friend. "Spirits can manifest in many ways," he says *sotto voce*. "Sometimes they look just like people and sometimes they come upon yas in sound, and sometimes they ain't no more than little dots of twinklin' light, just like stars in 'eaven."

I nod my head, try to look like I'm absorbing what he says. He's a nice and thoughtful person and although I'm not entirely convinced ghosts exist, I don't want to hurt his feelings.

"In their sparkly-twinkly form, some people think they're fairies — call 'em willo-the-wisps — but there ain't no such thing as fairies." He guffaws at the absurdity. "People get confused. They expect visitors from the spirit world to look just like they did in life."

Arthur tells me that spirits usually make themselves known to people when they have an important message to convey and that rarely are spirits evil. "Occasionally, a bad 'en might try mischief," he says, and again, mentions willo-the-wisps, who are reputed to lead lost travellers over cliffs. "But I expect your ghost," he says, whispering again, "just wants a word or two. Nothin' to be scared of. Just ask what it wants, if you ever hear it again."

The ballroom door slides open and the tall, thin, moon-faced Suzy Drude stands at the threshold looking angry. "I need a word, Arthur, if you can puuul yourself away."

"Thanks for the advice, Arthur," I say. Suzy smiles in a wooden way, and I know that trouble is brewing.

Little Charlie is washing up breakfast dishes in the kitchen and the chef is smoking a cigarette and drinking a pint of beer. The radio plays in the background as it normally does, but there's a heaviness.

"What she wants," the chef is saying, "is a good dosing of strychnine."

"But then you'd hang, mate," Little Charlie replies.

"It might be worth it," the chef responds.

Before the end of the day, I know it's Suzy they're talking about, that Suzy is trying to re-organize and economize and "sort out this bloooody doooomp of an 'otel." Little Charlie tells me that she's reduced the amount the chef can spend on food, which really is a reduction in his wage, since he's allowed to keep everything he saves. Suzy also, apparently, has had words with Arthur about his managing. She wants staff to pay more for dish breakages, and she wants to force us to go through the slop bucket at the end of each service to retrieve missing cutlery. She says our still room needs to be tidier, and when she's in the process of "cleanin' the bleedin' moook ooop," Arthur seeks out Eric

Heath, the hotel's owner, and gives his notice. He says he'll leave after breakfast the following day. There's not a hint of malice in his voice.

After our dinner service, Little Charlie, Big Charlie, and I buy three flagons of scrumpy cider and drive up to the cliffs overlooking Hele Bay. Big Charlie has a wife and son in New Zealand, but says next to nothing about them. Little Charlie teases him, calls him "The Dago" because he looks Spanish, and because he wants to give him a pejorative name. Whenever Little Charlie and I go to the pub, we wear jeans and t-shirts, but when B.C. accompanies us, he always nips home for his three-piece suit. I've been to his flat a few times with Little Charlie. He strips off his clothes in front of us. Horrified, I always avert my eyes. Little Charlie once told me that B.C. never wears underwear. "Why should I?" B.C. mumbled, "Underwear would just mean more laundry."

Once I know this about B.C., my perception of him changes. His ostentatious three-piece suit, which I once considered merely eccentric, becomes tawdry, and although emotionally, he remains a friend who I care about, in my mind, he transforms from an endearingly odd man to the kind of man I wouldn't want to sit next to on a bus. I grapple with my feelings over this; ask myself, "What difference does underwear make?" I have never heard the term "socialization," never stopped to consider the reasons some things disgust me.

Because we're in Little Charlie's car and not at a pub, B.C. is wearing jeans instead of his suit. He confesses he only wears it to impress women, who he calls "birds." When B.C. first met me, he considered me a "bird" — but now that we work together, and I've laughed at all his corny pick-up lines, he's come to think of me as someone without sexuality... or feathers.

We drink our cider straight from the bottles. It's our drink of choice because it's less expensive than beer, more potent and better tasting. Little Charlie is a cider connoisseur and tells us this scrumpy is "the real stuff." It doesn't fizz, it isn't cloudy, it feels pulpy against the lips, and when you drink it, it's cool in the pit of your belly. "But don't be deceived" he warns, "it can do more damage than the hard stuff." I'm not deceived. I can feel the alcohol slowly working. In my case, it's loosening my tongue and making me ask questions. I'm not always so sociable when I drink other types of alcohol, and I know that B.C. and Little Charlie aren't either.

Little Charlie has resided in Devon most of his adult life. A few years before now, he'd been a pig farmer and lived just outside of Exeter with his girlfriend in a rusty caravan. "When she'd had enough and left me," he said once, "I chucked it in, came down here to Ilfracombe to work the season, then when the season ended went on the dole." Little Charlie likes it here. "A good place to lick your wounds," he says. "A good place for cider," and we swig from our bottles, and look out at the churning ocean and the sharp, jagged rocks beneath.

"Once upon a time," Little Charlie begins, and I think he's about to tell us the story of his life, but he doesn't; he says instead, "there were wreckers." I haven't been living in England very long, but it seems to me that most of the people I've met here eventually begin to tell stories.

"There were wreckers," he repeats, "and in the black of night they strapped lanterns to the tails of horses, and lead them back and forth, over those cliffs yonder," he points to the rocky overhangs above the ocean. "They did that so the ships would be fooled into thinking the GGs — the horsies — were other ships and that the ocean went on and on and then, having lost their bearings, they'd crash on the rocks."

I look out at the ocean and think of the ships. I think of the decoy lights on the horses' tails, sparkling and twinkling like stars in the heavens, or willo-the-wisps, or the spirits Arthur talks about, who just want to speak their truth. Then I think of that withering shriek over the butcher's shop that neither sparkled nor twinkled, and I feel a sudden chill.

The following day at the Molesworth, the chef alters the breakfast menu. The wait staff slink into the dining room carrying dishes denuded of the usual bacon, eggs and beans. There are only scoops of fried mushrooms, two stewed tomatoes, and a solitary slice of fried bread on each plate. I serve a table of four elderly guests, thinking how the stewed tomatoes, without benefit of protein's camouflage, dominate the china. I'm embarrassed. The tomatoes look to me like two blushing breasts. The three women at the table smile sweetly and cluck, "Well this is a change, looove," and "best not to eat too mooch meat foooods" and words to that effect, trying to put the best spin they possibly can on this unfortunate event. The man at the table, however, isn't so sweet. "Wot in bloody 'ell's this?" he shouts, picking up the piece of fried bread and dropping it on his plate again.

"Breakfast," I say, closing my eyes, scrunching my face. I don't want to look at the man. I scuttle back to the kitchen.

"This is plain 'umiliatin'" a new waitress, Ann says. "I wouldn't a come an' worked 'ere if I'd known the 'otel was so stingy. You can't serve up slop like this and expect tip money."

I inhale, then exhale, and collect four more plates. I'd like to put a blindfold on, or pull a brown paper bag over my head. I'd like to become a ghost and turn invisible. I can't look the guests in the eyes.

Gradually, as more guests are served, the quality of ambient discussion in the dining room shifts from curious anticipation to discontent. I feel like an actress, completely unprepared for this part, not knowing my lines, not even knowing the general gist of the play. When one of the guests asks: "May I please 'av bacon and eggs with this?" I'm not sure what to say. Finally, I sputter, "I'll go ask." All of the guests at the table nod at one another, like they've solved the riddle, or found the "open sesame" command that will put everything right.

"They want bacon and eggs," I tell the chef.

"They can go on bloody wantin'. Tell 'em to have a word with Miss Suzy Drude."

Before I can return to the dining room to deliver the message, Suzy is in the kitchen, swearing for all she's worth. The chef is swearing back, louder and more violently than I've ever heard him swear before. Their voices radiate into the dining room, and when I serve my next table, all the guests have stopped talking.

Arthur, still technically manager until the end of the service, tries to stop the fight. He knows things are way out of hand, that if this battle continues it's likely that the hotel will lose a portion of its guests, and even though he shouldn't care, he does.

"It's you 'oooov bloody poot 'im oop to this!" Suzy screams at Arthur.

The owner, Eric Heath, arrives and enters the fray. At first, it seems, he doesn't know whose side to take. He doesn't want to lose his chef. Good chefs are hard to find, but he doesn't want to lose Suzy either.

"Why you fancy that cow, is beyond me!" the chef bellows. "A bit a rumpy pumpy is one thing…by all means shag 'er till your todger drops off…but don't inflict your tart on the rest of us."

Eric's face collapses. If only the chef had just kept screaming at Suzy and Suzy had just kept screaming at him, but now Eric has to say something, no matter how insipid, and he does: "There's no need to be vulgar." The chef disagrees. He sees the need to be vulgar.

I and the rest of the wait staff continue to serve breakfast. We try to pretend we don't hear the din of obscenities emerging from the kitchen. The chef, Eric, and Suzy are all screaming at each other, while Arthur, even though he's only the manager for another twenty minutes, is trying to exert his authority and get everyone to calm down. But no one wants to listen; they're all too much in love with their rage and the fireworks continue until the all-encompassing grand finale. "I don't take shit from shit," the chef says dramatically, throwing a large white apron to the ground, then storming out the door and violently slamming it.

Many of the guests have left the dining room. A few have moved a little closer to the kitchen doors so they can enjoy being shocked and disgusted. Only a couple of people stay at their tables, stalwartly eating their tomatoes and trying to remain cheerful. When the service finally ends, we're all thankful. However, the tension doesn't dissipate.

"The gaffer'll 'av to temporarily close," Lilian says.

"You can't run a 'otel wifout a chef," another waitress, Janice, concurs.

"Wot about me wages?" Ann asks.

Our discussion is heated, but quiet. It's as if we fear our voices will rouse again those destructive energies that made our breakfast service a living hell.

"If you ask me," Ann says, "all of this is the work of Suzy Drude."

"She ain't wot you'd call very tactful," Lilian says.

"Turfin' poor Arthur out like that," Janice adds.

"She didn't actually turf 'im out," Lilian corrects.

"All but," Janice says.

Much to our surprise, Eric doesn't shut the hotel. Instead, he dons a large white chef apron himself, and relying heavily on B. C., tries to prepare lunch. First, he's got to orient himself to the kitchen, discover where everything is kept, examine the recipes. He's got to take stock of the food on hand, the leftovers, the dry stores, and the preserves. He continually mutters obscenities, but amazingly he does pull lunch off, and pulls dinner off, and again, in the morning, breakfast. It takes him much longer to cook a meal, and the food is somehow never as tasty even though he uses the same recipes. Still, he gets the job done, even though the job is obviously taking its toll.

Suzy tries to find a replacement chef, a substitute, a stand-in, but according to staff gossip, no one is willing to come to the hotel for the wage offered. "You're going to have to offer more. I can't keep this up," Eric is alleged to have told her.

"It's bloooody 'ighway robbery," she's alleged to have fumed.

We're all glad she's occupied looking for a sub. It means she's less likely to get on our backs. But too soon, she finds a temporary replacement: an older, calmer man, without much personality, named Frank. He's in between jobs and can only stay for two weeks. Janice claims he's paid almost double what Suzy was originally offering. He runs the kitchen so smoothly and quietly we hardly know he's there.

"Ghost chef," we joke, "we ought to introduce him to Arthur's old friend in the ballroom."

Our mirth is short lived. Suzy grumbles about the disheveled state of our stillroom and wants to impose fines on wait staff who neglect to clean their dirty cups and ashtrays. "It's disgooostin,'" she says. "Ya woooodn't treat yr 'omes that way."

We all know the room really isn't as messy as she makes out, but Suzy, at least since Eric made her assistant manager, has always needed some renovation project to swear about. She scrubs and cleans the stillroom from top to bottom while we're serving lunch. She uses black marker on white paper to write threatening signs: "Do Not Leave Dirty Ashtrays!" "Do Not Leave Dirty Cups!" "Do Not Forget Personal Items or They'll Be Thrown Away," "Leave this stillroom exactly as you find it or God Help You!"

In the future, when I'm studying psychology at Fanshawe College in Canada, I'll think of Suzy and her pathological desire to impose order and consider that perhaps it was some form of compensation. Perhaps it was because her own life seemed so completely out of her control, so unclean, so overwhelming. But I don't think this way at the time. I don't wonder how Suzy perceives her life, if she feels happy with her lot, good about herself. In fact, as a teen in the 1970s, I'm so devoid of compassion, that I don't think about Suzy at all. I take the black marker, which she's put neatly on a shelf, and I begin to illustrate her posters with swastikas and skulls and crossbones.

"Wooot do you blooooody well think your dooooin?" she asks.

"Adding pictures," I say, nonchalantly.

"Dooon't you get smart with me, or you'll be on your bleeedin' bike!"

"I don't have a bleedin' bike," I say, getting smart, "but if you mean that I won't have this job anymore, that's fine with me. As far as I'm concerned you can shove this job where the sun don't shine." Though I don't really say "where the sun don't shine" I say something worse. I finish the last vestige of my drawing, collect my jacket, purse and cigarettes, and leave through the kitchen door.

That same day, Little Charlie and B.C. walk out in solidarity, protesting Suzy's bullying of the wait and kitchen staff. That same day, rumor has it, there's an accident in the ballroom. Suzy was shouting at some musicians who had scraped the parquet floor. There was thumping and pounding in the walls. "Plooooooming," Suzy shouted, just before a framed photograph of guests dancing, hanging over the piano, slipped from a hook and crashed down on her head.

B.C, Little Charlie and I contemplate the existence of ghosts that evening. We swig scrumpy cider, look out over the rocky craggy inlets of Hele Bay, discuss wreckers and consider the potential anger of spirits. Though I'm skeptical about ghosts, I still offer up theories as to why spirits might inhabit places, why they might remain, long after their existence holds value, long after their presence seems anything more than a waste of time.

BLOWING SMOKE

"YOU'RE A LIGHT," SAID the man at the Ilfracombe labour exchange. As a former US citizen, and a recent Canadian expat, I was still trying to decipher an array of British idioms.

"Dole Hole," for example, is what the locals called this employment office, but for me the term evoked a pineapple slice with a perfect empty circle at its centre.

The man behind the desk, suited with a long black tie, repeated his curious phrase, and I wondered if it might be disparagement or acclamation. I'd walked out of my last job. For a short time, I'd been a waitress at a local Ilfracombe hotel, and now, after my dramatic leave-taking, was looking for something better.

To be a light is to be a beacon, to be a star, I thought. "Thank you," I was about to tell the inscrutable man. I noticed a cloud of smoke wafting from my handbag, a small leaping flame bounding from its lining. I'd snuffed my cigarette on a brick wall outside and then tossed it into my purse. A good two inches of tobacco remained, and enough satiating nicotine to inspire salvation. But some secreted ember must have been dissembling, for now the entire bag was ablaze.

I knew the British slang term "flaming," which meant to express annoyance, and could see that the Dole Hole man was beginning to figuratively ignite. I threw my bag on the floor and pounced. The reek of burning plastic filled the room. There were cracks and snaps and crunches as I churned the char beneath my shoe.

"Sorry," I exhaled, like a good Canadian, "So very, very, sorry."

It's over a decade before *The Furniture and Furnishings Fire Safety Regulations* set standards for less flammable materials and even longer before *The Smoke Detectors Act* insists that sensors become mandatory in all new British homes. Self-extinguishing cigarettes have been talked about for the past four decades, and in 1970, successfully made and test-marketed. However, the tobacco industry benefits by insisting consumers won't buy them. After all, as *Reader's Digest* pointed out in the 1950s, you'll go through a cigarette much faster if it continues to burn when you set it down.

But I know nothing of self-extinguishing cigarettes, nor, obviously, how difficult it is to snuff one of the ordinary kind, even though, so far, I've been smoking all of my adolescent life. I'm unaware that accidental cigarette fires are the leading cause of fire deaths in the Western world and will remain so for many years to come.

My purse is a broken smouldering heap of "rubbish," a word I've learned in England that translates to garbage, and my spirit is more than subdued.

"Take this," the expressionless Dole Hole man commands, thrusting a card towards me, which I gratefully seize before, in a haze of shame, I scrape my purse off the floor, carefully salvage some crushed cigarettes, and quickly scuttle away.

Is it a coincidence that my first encounter with Candar Hotel's head housekeeper, Mrs. Newall, should begin like this? With smoke and fire and cigarettes?

The card I clutched held her name and number, and because I was *skint* (a British term meaning impoverished, arising, apparently, from the medieval torture of flaying debtors), I phoned her without delay.

The tourist season was well in motion and good help was hard to find. Mrs. Newall, seated in the Candar's lounge in a red wing-back chair, smoking a Players No. 6, pointed to the seat across from hers. She was thin, skirted and smocked, shoulders stooping forward contemplatively, taking me in as she kissed the filter of her cigarette. One of her eyes held me fast with an intense gaze while the other seemed to drift away. Had my soul ever been scrutinized so closely? It was terrifying, but then she asked: "Like a fag?"

Though a relative newcomer to this country, I already knew her kind offer had nothing to do with homosexuality, that the term "fag" in England was not meant as an insult, that it did not intend to enforce the "patriarchal, heterosexual, hegemony" as its usage did in North American school rooms, according to sociologist George W. Smith.

Because I was skint, I'd ponced some Woodbines — cheap, harsh cigarettes, without filters — from a former hard-smoking workmate. They numbed my tongue and left my throat raw. Happily, I accepted Mrs. Newall's proffered fag, and in that moment realized I'd found not only an employer, but an intuitive and empathetic friend.

She was over forty years my senior, and although gifting me with the Players, confessed the harsher Woodbines were her cigarette of choice. She'd been born at the end of World War I, on the day King George and Queen Mary attended a St. Paul's Cathedral peace service. According to newspapers of the time, the Archbishop of Canterbury mounted the pulpit and declared this day "the greatest occasion in human history."

World War I — believed to be the War to End all Wars — had terminated and though battle worn and diminished, Britain survived. Jubilant crowds cheered outside the Cathedral, naive as newborn babes about the war soon to follow.

The reigning monarch of the 70s, Queen Elizabeth II, had not yet been conceived, and her father, Bertie II, had not yet assumed his father's name, and had no more notion of becoming king than, as the British sometimes say, fly 'round the moon.

Mrs. Newall was born on the fifty-first birthday of Edward the VII's daughter, Princess Victoria. She was born on the 26th wedding anniversary of George V and Mary of Teck. She was born on the day that R-34, nicknamed Tiny, a British Zeppelin, which measured 643 feet long and 79 feet wide, landed in Mineola, New York, setting a world's record. It was the first dirigible airship to make a trans-oceanic flight.

Mrs. Newall was born into a world of cigarettes, into a world of throat and mouth and lung cancer deaths, which were largely overlooked. "We may surely brush aside much prejudice against the use of tobacco when we consider what a source of comfort it is to the soldier and sailor engaged in a nerve-wracking campaign" were popular sentiments of the day.

World War II had transformed tobacco. The pipe had succumbed to the paper tube, and soldiers in the trenches with six-week life expectancies needed their smokes as much as they needed their patriotic convictions.

American General John Pershing cabled the War Department in 1917, telling them "tobacco as much as bullets" were needed to win the war. "[It's] as indispensable as the daily ration; we must have thousands of tons without delay," he demanded.

The stodgy old killjoy Queen Victoria, who had died eighteen years before Mrs. Newall's birth, deplored tobacco and had banned its smoking at court. However, the day her cigar-loving son, Edward, took the throne after a sumptuous royal banquet, he lifted the ban. "Gentlemen, you may smoke," he told the collection of male couriers who had assembled for after dinner libations. According to authors

Chris Harrald and Fletcher Watkins, "Where Edward VII went, the country followed: private homes, country houses, meeting halls, music halls, theatres." But still, it was not until the fateful war, the Great War, the War to End all Wars, that cigarettes became a staple for the aristocracy as well as for the common man.

King Edward died with chronic bronchitis and heart disease, his son and heir, King George V, also a tobacco aficionado, would suffer obstructive pulmonary disease and pleurisy. His son, George VI, another effusive smoker, would die of lung cancer, but on the day that Mrs. Newall is born, King George V still reigns, and tobacco, as the British sometimes say, "rules okay."

Over half a century later, Mrs. Newall and I puff on our fags. Her voice is high and crisp and queenly. She asks me only questions about my availability. It doesn't seem to matter to her that I've never done chambermaiding before. "You strike me as a bright girl," she says. "I'm sure you'll pick it up."

I don't want her to know the truth about me, that I'm really an idiot. That no matter how hard I practice, I still can't spell, still can't do multiplication tables, still can't be confident in my ability to tell time on an analogue clock, even though I'm in my teens.

I fill my lungs with smoke and cough a little as I exhale. She doesn't ask me why I left my last job. She doesn't ask me for a reference. I tell her I can start work right away, but she tells me to take a week. "Tie up loose ends," she says. "Get yourself a smock." Her eye surveys me head to foot. "And shoes!" she says, homing in on my platforms, "comfortable shoes. And a dowdy skirt...like mine," her laugh is refreshingly maniacal.

She tells me that she makes decisions about people very quickly and she's rarely wrong. "You'll fit in nicely," she says. "Arrive at 6:00 for breakfast." She stands. "And don't be late."

On the day Mrs. Newall was born, silent films that featured China were in vogue. "East is East and West is West and never the twain shall meet." This line, extracted from a Rudyard Kipling poem, was frequently found on the title cards of these movies. Yet the world was growing smaller and smaller, and the meeting of West and East, not to mention West and West, was becoming a reality that few could ignore.

The American Ambassador called this change in proximity the "drying-up of the Atlantic," and the British newspapers pointed out that even though only on "the threshold of the air-age," America was closer to Britain "than was Manchester or York to the London of a century ago."

The King sent a telegram, according to the *Times*, congratulating the R-34's crew on the "stupendous achievement" of their perilous crossing. The ship had encountered "fog and violent storms, and there was a moment when it seemed — after Canada has been reached — that it might run short of petrol … yet in the end … under her own power [attained] her goal."

Her mission was both practical and patriotic. It pressed past the limits of a bygone world. It chronicled, in microcosm, the metamorphosis which war had wrought, and with it, the ubiquitous cigarette, omnipresent even when absent.

The worst part of the voyage, according to meteorological officer and weather observer Lieutenant G. Harris, was the fact the airship was filled with hydrogen gas, which meant no one onboard could smoke. "That was the devil of it," he said. "It killed me, you know."

When I floated from the Candar Hotel after my interview with Mrs. Newall, like the airships of old, I was lighter than ether. I lit a Woody and began to skip, but soon was choking. Ilfracombe is notorious for its mountainous terrain, and I had to scale a steep hill to get home. I snuffed my fag carefully against a brick wall yet continued choking.

My platform shoes blistered my feet. Still, I remained buoyant, for soon I'd be gainfully employed and would no longer have to smoke "rubbish" cigarettes.

In the mid-seventies, Woodbines are the eighth most popular brand of cigarette in England. They differ from Player's No. 6, the top product, in possessing .6 milligrams more nicotine and 5 milligrams more tar. The Health Education Council placed a full-page ad in *The Daily Mail* asking: *Which Cigarettes Kill You the Quickest?* In 1974, there were 50,000 deaths in the UK attributed to smoking, but the addictions of hard-bitten puffers make them impervious to these facts. The Council, in an effort to present the "lesser of evils," lists tar and nicotine stats for all British brands. It encourages readers to smoke those which are less toxic and to hang on to this ad until cigarette manufacturers include this information on their packets. The Woodbines I imbibe are among the most murderous. I don't know this because I rarely read newspapers, and never saw this ad. If I had, however, it would have made little difference. The world I know as a teenager is a battleground heedless of health. Like the men in the trenches of World War I, I smoke whatever comes into my hands. The Woody is at least better than the homemade cigarettes I sometimes roll from the leavings of public ashtrays.

During World War I, army chaplain Geoffrey Studdert Kennedy won himself the nickname Woodbine Willie by gifting soldiers in the frontline trenches with copies of the New Testament and packet upon packet of Woodbine fags. I survey the crumpled meagre remains of my gaspers as I scale the arduous hill, and although I've never heard of him, wish for a cigarette Santa, like Geoffrey, who would understand my anguish and see me right with smokes, even if only "rubbish" brands.

I borrow money from my mother for a skirt and smock and comfortable shoes. I assure her these are necessary items and promise that I'll reimburse her on my very first payday. But when my remaining crumpled cigarettes have turned to ash, and I run out of rolling papers — when I can no longer forage my mother's generous Benson & Hedges leftovers — I go to the town and buy two packets of No. 6. I feel guilty, but the monkey on my back advises I find a jumble sale instead of going to a clothing store. I can get what I need for cheap and keep the remaining funds to supply my habit.

Although I've tried to quit, cigarettes inevitably call me back. They calm my nerves and align my thinking, give me comfort when I'm ailing and focus when I come unglued. I need them more than ever here in England. My future is precarious, and although I remain virtually oblivious to the economic turmoil in the country, it impacts my life in ways that I cannot yet fathom.

I haven't yet realized that England is a socialist country. I don't even know what that means. All I know is that when I work more hours than usual, I don't reap the expected greater rewards. Income Tax and its "little brother," National Insurance, suck it away, and as the British say, "I'm running to stand still."

But I'm young, and I don't mind running. I don't mind having few material possessions. I don't yet think realistically about my long-term future — if I'll ever be in a position to own a home or retire, or pay for special care if I become infirm.

According to the *Daily Mail*, "the typical British couple now pay more in tax and National Insurance contributions than they scrape together to spend on food." The weekly grocery bill, according to this pundit, comes to just over fifteen pounds, while tax and National Insurance equals almost seventeen.

The talented wealthy have been fleeing the country in droves. The Labour government's mission to "squeeze" the better-off "until the pips squeak" is proving extremely successful. "The top marginal rate of tax" stands at 98% on investment income and 83% on income earned, according to the *Times*. Nobel Prize winner Francis Crick has already fled England and laureate Max Ferdinand Perutz is currently considering a "leap across the pond."

Actor Michael Caine, who has, as he says, been "making lots of noises about taxes," according to the *Daily Mail*, is now planning to emigrate to America. He's "never made a tougher decision," he says. "It's been agonising." Yet his "industry has been destroyed in England," and he says he will "stay away until the policies of taxation change."

Many other entertainers, writers, and scientists have already found their homes in exile. "The class system on one side has led to resentment, [and] a real Socialist cloth-cap attitude," Caine explained. "On the other side, [the] class society ... has led working people from ... serf for the rich to ... serf for the Government."

While I may be a serf for the British government, I don't really mind my serfdom. I'm only a teenager and besides casual babysitting and sometimes ice cream selling for Dickie Dee in Canada, until my father died and my mother moved us to England, I never held a job. I'm too young and financially inexperienced to be jaded or indignant about a crippling tax system, too thrilled about actually earning a wage to question the fiscal mechanisms that take it away from me.

I spend my money mostly on books and records and cigarettes. I subscribe to *Melody Maker* and *New Musical Express*. I should know that many of my favourite rock stars have bolted from England due purely to taxation, but because my mind automatically shuts off when it encounters numbers and abstract financial words, I don't. In fact, I believe many who have relocated to the United States have always lived there.

I know nothing of Led Zeppelin's legendary farewell concert at London's Earls Court, nor how Robert Plant addressed the audience: "Somebody voted for someone and now everybody's on the run ... [Denis Healey, Chancellor of the Exchequer] must be Dazed and Confused." I'm unaware that my chances of seeing this British band in England, along with many others of my favourites, is remote; that, as

Plant told the Earls Court crowd, the tax laws are ensuring that "there'll be no artists [left] in the country anymore ... If you see Denis, tell him we've gone."

The mighty Zeppelin rock band crossed the Atlantic, as the British Zeppelin R-34 had done on the day that Mrs. Newall was born. Both events were significant, each capturing the vicissitudes of their time. Neither actors nor audiences could gaze beyond the present, nor realistically prepare for the unknowable circumstances yet to come. Future fortunes and disasters figured nowhere in these moments, and the world continued turning, with its hope and promise, its desolation and despair, while all around was smoke, rising like an undecipherable signal, wafting into the lives of generations yet to come. No one could imagine the tragedy or elation, the unthinkable acts, the joyous revelations. No one could foresee the zephyrs of change which defy our best efforts as time travellers to hold an even keel.

In the chambermaid's stillroom of the Candar, Mrs. Newall and I bond. We fill the space with cigarette exhaust. Day after day, we sit and gab and drink tea, clouds and clouds of billowing smoke rising from our breath, hanging above us like grey sheets, tainting the dish towels and dusters we've hand washed and slung upon a wooden drying rack. These breaks extend as the holiday season evaporates, as hotel guests diminish, as our conversations become longer and more personal. As we become friends.

"What do you plan to do with your life?" is one of Mrs. Newall's most constant refrains. "It's no good being rudderless or building sandcastles in the air." As a former World War II Wren, Mrs. Newall has learned the importance of realistic goal setting as well as the fact that anything less than honest and direct communication is a waste of time.

She approves of my ambition to be a writer and encourages me to make a realistic list of the necessary steps I'll need to take. In the meantime, she says I ought to find a job that pays more than 60 pence an hour, that I ought to consider having a Plan B, that education is important, and that I shouldn't discount the notion of going back to school, even though I'm a North American high school dropout and conventional routes of upgrading in England aren't open to me.

She puffs on her cigarette, legs crossed, and leans forward: "I don't doubt things will work out for you," she says. "You're obviously a bright girl, but you need some method in your madness. You need a strategic plan."

I don't want her to know the truth about me. I don't want her to see me as I see myself: stupid, inept, clumsy, hopeless. I inhale the smoke from my fag as I take in Mrs. Newall's words and feel a calming exhilaration. It's both uncomfortable and reassuring to have one's life under the scrutiny of a friend. I take her recommendations to heart. I promise her I'll become more methodical — that I'll try very hard to set realistic and attainable goals.

"Good lass," she says, butting her fag, which is the signal our break has come to an end.

As a teenager, realistic goal setting and methodical, incremental achievement is not something that comes easily to me. As I'm addicted to cigarettes, I'm also addicted to airy dreams and fantasies about my future life. As I make beds, clean toilets, and empty chamber pots, I imagine myself a famous writer, living in a blissful tropical setting, contentedly draped over a chaise longue drinking champagne. In some of these fantasies, I'm being interviewed by kind and admiring reporters; in others, my Canadian ex-boyfriend is there, seeking my autograph.

These daydreams buoy above me, seamless in their conception, luxurious, like smoke rings, almost too perfect to touch or rearrange.

They're inflated constructions of a future, a place unsullied by sweat and blood. A place of self-comfort, where the nitty-gritty diligence needed to actualize dreams never figures, and worries of unknowable days ahead vanish like stardust into the heavens.

SHRIEK

ONE DAY, I NOTICED that the shrieking had stopped and I missed that peculiar otherworldly cry. For weeks, I'd been hearing it in the early morning as I passed the butcher shop on the way to the Candar Hotel. Was it some acoustical aberration, the sound of the ocean, distorted and trapped between rows of buildings on the narrow street? In my ongoing efforts of literary self-improvement, I'd recently read *A Passage to India* and recalled the echoing caves at Marabar. But unlike that relentless murmur that Forster rendered, the shriek I heard was not profound — it was simply startling.

Gimmicky kids' clocks had been fashionable for a number of years. In fact, I awoke at the crack of dawn to one each morning. My Canadian clock wasn't compatible with the British electrical plugs, so I'd borrowed my little brother's wind-up Raggedy Ann and Andy alarm.

The shriek sounded nothing like my little brother's cheerful clock that would sweetly entreat me to "please get up, brush my teeth and start my happy day." I considered the child who might own a shrieking alarm, a child who liked to be terrified to wakefulness. The image of Wednesday Addams came immediately to mind, and then, for a while, I searched the town for such a child, looking through the crowded streets at day's end on my way home. I was certain that I would know her when I saw her, but I never saw the like in Ilfracombe.

There were only two children, excluding my brother, whom I saw and interacted with before I first heard the shrieking: Polly and Andrew Heath, the progeny of my first employer, Eric, and his wife, Noreen. They sat, chubby and demanding, every morning at either end of the family table flanking Eric and his mistress Suzy who, side by side, faced the hotel's dining room. If Noreen had once sat at that table, it had been long before I'd waitressed there. "Mean Noreen," as we called her, was head chambermaid and by the time her children and mate, and mate's concubine, were chowing down, she'd already been slogging it out for over an hour with dirty sheets and toilets and hairy bathroom floors.

Polly and Andrew, age five and seven, didn't seem to mind the fact their mother didn't eat with them. Suzy wasn't very maternal, but at a pinch could scold and correct if her attention happened to stray from Eric. "Uuuup straight, you two," she might command, if her wandering vision caught them slumping in their chairs, or "Stop your bleeedin muuuuckin about," if she noticed they were throwing cutlery at each other. Eric, for all the world, seemed oblivious to the children, bawdily joking with whichever waitress came to serve him. "Sometimes I wish I were this dining room table," he'd say to a new young woman, who hadn't yet learned not to ask why. "Because," he'd retort, "when breakfast was over, I could look forward to you laying me." He and Suzy would laugh loudly at his jokes, while the waitress would blush and the children, taking advantage of this raucous moment, would launch sugar cubes across the table at each other.

None of us liked serving this table for a number of reasons, not least of which, it never tipped, and so at the beginning of the day, the waitresses all drew lots. Frequently, I would be the one to select the stained butter knife — the inevitable harbinger of the dreaded task. In a very short time, I'd learned to turn a deaf ear to Eric, but what I seemed incapable of blocking out were the uncensored comments of the children. "Hey you! Hey what's it! Take the crusts off my toast. I don't like crusts ... actually," Polly once said.

"Please take the crusts off my toast?" I instructed between clenched teeth, but Polly wouldn't say "please." She just gazed at me with large defiant eyes, then swept her fat little arm across the table and knocked her bowl of dry cornflakes onto the floor.

"Wooopseeeeday!" she squealed, her round blubbery cheeks, which reminded me of Alfred Hitchcock's, jiggling with joy.

"Whooot in blooooody 'ell?" Suzy asked, attracted by the chaos.

"It was an accident ... actually," Polly said.

Andrew tended to be more sneaky than defiant, blowing dried peas at my legs through a pea shooter as I walked away from the table, or unobtrusively sticking a "kick me" sign on the back of my skirt. I was only a teenager, too young to consider what compelled these children to behave like beasts, too ignorant to offer compassion. I swept the cornflakes into a dustpan off the grimy hotel dining room carpet, carried them back into the kitchen towards the slop bin, and then, when no one was looking, picked out the few bits of red lint, and poured the cereal into a fresh bowl for Polly.

I hadn't yet heard the shrieking the day I came to work and found Polly with a sticky lollypop in her hand, skipping rope and blocking the gate to the kitchen. "My father owns this hotel ... actually," she said. "You're just a skivvy. So I don't have to move if I don't want to."

I felt the muscles in my ankles twitch. I automatically assessed the height of the gate. If I'd allowed my body to respond as it wanted, my strong hill-climbing, waitress-striding legs would have punted her into the empty garbage bins that rested just beyond the kitchen door. I took a deep breath and counted to thirty.

It was the 1970s, Roald Dahl's book *Charlie and the Chocolate Factory* in which he brilliantly rendered the four faces of the archetypal brat had been in print for many years, and I had just recently scratched it off my long "books to read" list. Polly reminded me of Veruca Salt the most, and I delighted in imagining her gruesome comeuppance. Even though Dahl had laid the blame with the parents, I never once considered this or the dynamics that had worked to engender such a brat as Polly.

"Move out of the way ... *sweetie*," I finally said, grabbing her defiant shoulders and trying to shift her from my path.

"I don't have to move ... actually," she said, pushing her sticky lollypop against my clean skirt.

Children born in the 1980s will earn themselves the moniker "the generation of excess," and although Polly was born before this, she typified the worst characteristics of the children of that future age. She'd been showered with material goods, deprived of realistic discipline and boundaries, and at age five already had formed such a narcissistic character that she perceived the world as her own exclusive oyster in which her voracious desires must be endlessly met.

In China, they will come to call it "The Little Emperor Syndrome," and perceive it as a direct result of the one-child family planning policy. In the Western world, however, it will simply be called "overindulgence," though such a benign word can't begin to do justice to the social maladies it breeds.

I removed Polly's lollypop from my skirt and crushed it under the heel of my shoe. The following day, when I first heard the shriek emanating from the butcher shop, I recalled Polly's feral cry. It was a shriek of undomesticated nature thwarted, and I saw Polly, morphing into Alfred Hitchcock, and then into an angry phantom with Hitchcock's cheeks, and I began to run.

Soon after that, I left my job and with it all the contempt I'd ever felt for Polly. I began working as a chambermaid at the Candar Hotel. This required me to traverse the same route, down the winding Marlborough road, down the plunging steep hill, past the butcher's shop and the chilling primal shriek, which over time had grown as physical to me as a landmark.

I noticed I was lonely after the shrieking stopped. I hoped that one day it would start again, but gradually even the memory of that thrilling sound began to fade, and because it had been so strange, I began to wonder if I'd really ever heard it at all.

There was only ever the occasional child at the Candar Hotel. An old couple owned it, and the holiday makers who stayed, for the most part, were senior citizens or middle-aged childless couples. Also, a band of marauding rock musicians and their groupies, all with hair down to their hips, annexed an entire wing of the building, at one point. They had come here accidentally — a wrong exit on the motorway — or perhaps they'd been given some indecipherable instructions — or maybe the instructions were fine, but the recreational drugs they were taking made it impossible to figure them out. At any rate, they ended up at the Candar and promptly plunged into a noisy orgy, which ended quickly with their eviction, though not before they'd made a considerable mess and damaged a mattress.

It was when this unruliness was still a fresh topic of gossip among the staff that we heard about another kind of wildness. It was occurring in a place called Exmoor, which extended from Devon to Somerset, and had become a national park in 1954. The total area of the park was roughly 160,000 acres. In the Middle Ages, a Royal Forest had been created there and sheep farming flourished. In the earlier medieval period, farms and villages formed, which remained over the centuries.

Now there were many farmers reporting the destruction of their sheep in this area, and because meticulous care seemed to have been taken in the skinning of these creatures, the farmers wondered if it was the work of some depraved delinquent. Juvenile crimes had been on the increase for years, and many believed this was occurring because the school leaving age had been raised in 1972 from age fifteen to sixteen, preventing bored scholars from finding meaningful employment, and leading them into the paths of truancy, mischief, and felony. The police were called in to investigate but said they could find nothing untoward. "Some local predator," they offered, "a fox, perhaps," but the farmers would have none of it. They knew the handiwork of a fox, and the remains of their livestock showed none of the hallmarks.

Much to the farmers' frustrations, animals continued being ravaged, and psychics in the area pulled out their Ouija boards to get to the bottom of this unprecedented assault. "The Beast" was the ominous soubriquet given, with all the connotation of a biblical antichrist. The wise women in the vicinity distributed boughs of ash and satchels of dried fennel and anise. They braided garlic and nailed it to wooden posts and cultivated houseleek wherever they believed it might grow, but the evil continued and wouldn't subside.

In the stillroom of the Candar, where I smoked and drank my tea, we chambermaids ruminated on the carnage. I recalled, for my colleagues, the face and fingernails of Satan, as depicted in the book *Rosemary's Baby*, another novel I'd read in my efforts toward literary self-improvement. This led us into all kinds of ponderings on how Rosemary must have felt in discovering she'd begat the child of Satan. Our needlewoman, Mrs. Murray, said she thought Rosemary had been lucky. "At least she knew what she was dealing with from the outset. It took me and Mr. Murray, God rest his soul, fifteen years before we had any idea about the little devil we'd spawned."

A young co-worker of ours, Mary, or Magpie, as we called her, because she was forever nicking pillowslips from our carts, launched into stories of vicious aliens, which led to a general discussion about UFOs and their sightings, and other strange and supernatural phenomena. When it was time to get back to work, we were all a little bit jumpy. In one of the rooms Magpie was cleaning, a breeze from the ocean transformed a curtain into a billowing ghost, and the door she'd propped open for security noisily smashed shut. I recall her deafening shriek, though it was nothing like the sound that had once emanated from the rooms above the butcher's shop.

It was at a pub one night a few weeks after this when I and some old work friends were playing darts that a man, who had lived two doors down from the butcher's shop, joined our table. I struck up a conversation with him and was dumbfounded to discover that not only had he heard the same strange shriek I'd heard emanating from the upper floors of the shop, but claimed he knew exactly what had made it. The butcher, he said, had had a black leopard. He'd bought it as a small cub in the hopes of raising a watch-cat. He fed it on the choicest cuts of meat, let it sleep in his bed, and took great pride and pleasure in acting *loco parentis* to this cuddly curious ball of fur. In less than two years, it weighed more than one hundred and forty pounds and from head to tail was over seven feet long. Its once endearing kitty-cat snarls became frightening; its once playful swats now threatened to seriously maim, but even more perilous became the leopard's sense of privilege, its presumptions of dominance, and its inability to be controlled. "There are no instruction manuals for bringing up leopards," the stranger said and then went on to explain how the butcher eventually had to chain the cat in a cage where it miserably met out its remaining days, until finally its wretched primordial shriek ceased.

"Did the butcher put the poor beast out of its misery?" the stranger asked for effect, "Or did he bake it in a pie?" People at our table speculated, but none of us, including me, suggested that the butcher's remedy for coping with his unruly pet may have been to abandon it. Having lived over four decades beyond this time and knowing what I know now about human beings and other animals, it's difficult for me to fathom why such a conclusion didn't offer itself then. It would be several years before the hypothesis of exotic animal dumping would be used to explain the strange and savage livestock killing on Exmoor, as well as in other parts of the country where similar events began to occur.

Harrods, the high-end department store and quintessential symbol of excess, had sold big cats and other trendy exotic pets to fashionable

Brits throughout the 1960s and early seventies, endeavouring always to be true to its motto *Omnia Omnibus Ubique* — *All Things for All People*. In the mid-seventies, the Dangerous Wild Animals Act came in to being, which was an attempt by the government to have a say in how certain exotic pets were housed, cared for, and bred. People owning potentially dangerous pets needed to buy a license — and could only hope to purchase one if they could demonstrate the animal posed no threat of injury or nuisance to neighbours and that provisions for the animal's accommodation were adequate. It's unlikely that the majority of British leopard owners would have been able to meet these demands. The animals would either need to be euthanized or relinquished to a zoo which, to a population influenced by the 1966 movie *Born Free*, was tantamount to the same thing.

Initial sightings of big cats running wild in Britain were dismissed by authorities, and while some have suggested a conspiracy of silence, others have suggested that wild cats out of control are so foreign to British self-perception that to recognize this strange phenomenon might be hazardous to collective identity. Over the years, however, evidence of the existence of big cats roaming the countryside has mounted. In 1980 a Scottish farmer set a trap using a sheep's head and caught a puma. In 1988, a Dartmoor farmer shot and killed a leopard that was harassing his ducks. According to the *Financial Times*, 1,077 big cat sightings were reported in 2002, and while The Department of Environment, Food and Rural affairs eventually granted the possibility that more than a few of these beasts may be out there, authorities didn't want to even entertain the notion they might be propagating.

But all of this awaits future speculation; right now it's only the absence of the shriek that I think of. I fill its void, not with unruly, rapacious offspring, but with the image of a solitary creature, safely contained in a cage in a room. I imagine it lithe and black, a sentinel, feeling every invisible detail of the silent morning, and puzzling over every unidentifiable sound.

CHAR

I KNEEL BEFORE a toilet, shake in some blue, bleachy crystals and plunge a rag deep inside with a nicotine tarnished fist. Flecks of digestive debris loosen, float, infinitesimal dark warships, unmoored from earthly anchors. I decimate this enemy fleet, then flush the scum to Kingdom Come.

More and more, I slide into metaphors of battle as I clean. I hold my plastic powder keg of blue explosive chemicals. I attack and bombard and rid the filth that threatens the toilet bowl's tranquil shores. I annihilate dirt, eliminate dust, and destroy untold colonies of noxious germs.

I've not always thought of cleaning this way. When I lived in Canada, before my father died and my mother moved us to England, before I needed to get a job and landed this one as chambermaid at the Candar Hotel, these necessary activities were to me anathemas of civilized life. I could see nothing but futility in such efforts. Everything cleaned immediately began to lose its lustre and soon would require energy and elbow grease once again. But here, at this seaside hotel in Ilfracombe, North Devon, I reconceptualize these pessimistic notions. Thanks to Mrs. Newall, my boss and strategic advisor, the task of cleaning has been recast in a radically different light.

I'm not sure when she told me she'd once been a Wren, that she'd joined the *Women's Royal Naval Service* to do her bit in World War II. As Head Housekeeper of the Candar, she conducts her watch with military discipline, yet also uses humour and rousing rhetoric, often purloined, to lead the maids under her command.

"We shall clean to the end, we shall dispose of muck in the bedroom, in the toilets, in the lounges, on the settees." To lessen the dreary arduousness of our burden, she often breaks into Winston Churchill: "We shall hoover in the hallways, hoover on the landings, no picture frame, nor lamp shade shall be spared the damp cloth of obliteration; we shall never surrender." Churchill, already middle-aged in the year that Mrs. Newall was born, already married to his beloved Clemmie, already the father of four, already "fallen," according to historian Richard Ollard, "from the height of power to the depths of ineffectiveness," had already been partially boosted back up again. He was unaware of the "political wilderness" he would face in the future, unaware that Britain's policy towards Germany would become appeasement. The Great Nation his rhetoric mythologized and extolled would make no immediate attempt to rearm itself. After all, the war that had ended was "The War to End all Wars." And while a handful of would-be prophets may have seen the dark clouds of looming dangers scudding in the distance, war talk was "sick making" — although this particular British term for the popular sentiment would not be coined until the 1930s by Evelyn Waugh.

In 1917, Lloyd George, the Wartime Coalition Prime Minister and Churchill's long-time friend, installed him as Munitions Minister, and in the year that Mrs. Newall was born, he was catapulted even higher as Secretary of State for War and Air. "[We have] emerged from [war] stronger than ever," he speechified, "with glories before which all the achievements of the past [are] forced to pale, and with a position gained and deeds done on which our most remote posterity will look back with reverence and with awe." If only he'd known.

Some ninety-three years in the future, a British poll will reveal that young adults know little about World War I. Fifty-four percent of those surveyed between the ages of sixteen and twenty-four couldn't say when it began. Two-thirds couldn't correctly guess when it ended. Twelve percent underestimated the number of British and Commonwealth military personnel who were killed in the conflict, guessing the number to be under 10,000, when in reality some 19,240 died on the first day of the Battle of the Somme.

And as far as Churchill himself is concerned, not only will he become an optional subject in the British school syllabus, but according to a survey Boris Johnson cites on this legendary leader, "most young people [in 2014 will] think that Churchill is the dog in a British insurance advertisement."

But it's the 1970s, and Churchill, though he's been dead for over a decade, still lives on and on in British memory. His picture hangs in several shops and pubs and on many-a-wall where the still patriotic recall the blitzes of World War II and food rationing as if it has only just occurred. Post Traumatic Stress Disorder has not yet been identified, nor the hallmarks of this strange psychological miasma that does odd things with one's sense of time. Could it be that Britain's inability to throw off the mantle of the past arises from this malady? There are still wartime tunes sung in the pubs, still talk of the "Hun" (a derogatory term for the people of Germany.) Germany itself is now a divided country. The Western portion has already outstripped Britain economically, and in the ensuing years will reunify, becoming intimately connected with its former foe by way of the European Union.

I'm a Canadian ex-patriot, who was born in the United States and lived there for only ten years. My traumas, as far as I know them, are not collective ones. I haven't learned how to be patriotically selfless, as Mrs. Newall's generation, which faced deprivations post-World War I and then, at the start of World War II, were forced to confront the rupture of peace, precarious mortality, and ongoing deprivations in the postwar years.

My mother, born in Manchester seven years after Mrs. Newall, moved to Canada in the early '50s. All her memories of war glistened with a rosy hue, with handsome America soldiers, with dances and music, and movies. With all the ways she ingeniously defied repressive government restrictions.

She was too young to face conscription, and her mother, who'd lost her first husband in World War I, far too old. Patriotism, though it blazed in England, never appeared to have ignited her carefree soul. But Mrs. Newall was different. She'd been old enough to answer the call. In 1941, she was twenty-two, and The National Service Act (No. 2) required her efforts and those of other single women aged twenty to thirty in beating the "Boche." It could have been she joined the WRENS before this directive of female recruitment. After all, the women's branch of the Royal Navy, which disbanded after Word War I had, as early as 1939, been revivified.

However, as a teenager, engaged in cleansing combat, chemically annihilating toilet intruders, unpacking the parachutes of parched sheets, I never think to ask her. As far as I'm concerned, World War II and her place in it seem irrelevant. It would only be in future years that I'd realize not only how it must have shaped her, but also how it rippled, like a raindrop in a pond, diffusing into the tributaries of my life.

Although I wouldn't have been able to articulate it at the time, I loved Mrs. Newall in a way I would never be able to love my own mother. I admired the qualities she demonstrated, her commitment to honest toil, and the imagination to see it as vital to survival as food and water. Unlike my mother, who'd spent the greater part of her adolescence dreaming about, and hunting for, a materially successful man, one who'd spare her from worldly work and offer a life of leisure, Mrs. Newall was different. Though she married, leisure was not her major life goal. She said that she'd always enjoyed working. And it was obvious that the work she did was important to her, and she made sure that those who worked under her knew its value.

Unlike my mother, who fled a troubled postwar England in the 1950s, Mrs. Newall heeded the words of Winston Churchill, who lamented that more than half a million Britons had applied to emigrate to more prosperous shores. "Stay here and fight it out," were the words he offered. "If we work together with brains and courage, as we did in days not long ago, we can make our country fit for all our people. Do not desert the old land."

His words, as Edward Rothstein puts it in The *New York Times*, were an "expression of a life force." His rhetorical accomplishment was "almost a musical one, in which [his] innate optimism provided [an] elevating promise even as he [tried] to map out the scope of cataclysm." He unified opposing government factions with the vision of cooperative strengths, brought together people of all classes in the struggle of a common goal, and harnessed teamwork in the service of a flagging world.

Mrs. Newall, too, marshalled words and an indomitable spirit, wit and the grandiloquence of a common purpose to unify her maids. She kept our morale high, indoctrinated a strong work ethic, and prevented the creeping laxity which so frequently undermines physical labour. An untucked sheet, a dirty skirting board, a smudged or speckled water glass, for example, were never tolerated. "Look here!" she'd command, her voice as crisp and neat and clean as a starched white pillow slip. "This will never do!" And then humorously warping some of Winston's words, she'd admonish: "Never allow yourself to slack, never allow yourself to weary. Brace yourself to your duties, my girl, let us to the task, to the battle and the toil."

In the year Mrs. Newall was born, ladies wore wide-brimmed hats and satin wraps and smart fur capes made from the pelts of skunk and opossum. They wore simple shirt blouses of crepe-de-chine and travelling coats in all-wool blanket cloth. According to the fashion reporter for the Daily Mail, "long gloves, even in cotton or silk," were an exorbitant price, and many women "objected to the quaint appearance of short gloves with short sleeves." But at the Candar Hotel, over half a century in the future, short gloves with short sleeves are exactly what Mrs. Newall wears.

She scrambles up a ladder, her soldier maids observe. She extends a blinding white finger, as quick as an incendiary bullet, towards a light fixture. If this manoeuvre turns up dust, there'll be a skirmish in the sky. Like a Spitfire, her pale yellow shammy is intent upon destroying hidden enemies in the clouds. Does she see some Luftwaffe aircraft over London? Does she flick her duster to bring them down? There is no great explosion, no screaming tortured crew, no blazing wreckage, no plumes of smoke, only the scent of furniture polish that falls like a fine mist of fog and burns my eyes.

It is only later in the stillroom that the atmosphere grows grey and dank. Where Mrs. Newall and I, unrepentant addicts in a spit and polish army, light cigarettes and pollute the air. Since the end of World War II until the mid 1970s, according to medical historian Rosemary Elizabeth Elliot, smoking among British women "hovered between 36 and 45 per cent" and began to decrease thereafter. But the females under Mrs. Newall's command, besides myself, have already quit or never seriously started. Economics more than health considerations have determined their decisions, and while both Mrs. Newall and I would rather keep our cash for the time being at least, we've quit trying to quit, and resigned ourselves to being the vassals of "the little white slaver," as Henry Ford once referred to our constant companions.

While we may speak of "addictive personalities" and imagine reductively that this is the reason some of us find it so hard to quit, it won't be until the 1980s that a clearer picture of nicotine's capacity to hijack the brain begins to form. For decades, the tobacco industry has denied the fact that cigarettes cause disease. They've rejected scientific findings, obstructed public policy, and knowingly, through a smoke screen of controversy, befogged the deadly reality that threatens every individual exposed to tobacco's noxious pus.

In 1946, the year Churchill as Leader of the Opposition used the term "iron curtain" in one of his most important speeches, the tobacco industry was erecting border defences of its own. Epidemiological evidence, according to researcher Allan M. Brandt, showed that lung cancer had tripled in the past three decades. This correlated profoundly with the enormous rise in cigarettes smoked. But the tobacco industry would have none of it. "Who's to say it's cigarettes?" they asked, exploiting the fact that statistical data alone was not conclusive evidence. By the 1960s, according to Brandt, they had created enough controversy to undermine the truth.

The Royal College of Physicians, the Medical Research Council of Great Britain, and the World Health Organization had all acknowledged the deadly link between smoking and ill health by 1962. "Diseases associated with smoking now cause so many deaths that they present one of the most challenging opportunities for preventative medicine today," stated the Royal College.

Yet in the stillroom of the Candar Hotel, Mrs. Newall and I puff away. We both have smoker's coughs. I suffer from chronic bronchitis. The other maids, who don't smoke, make no protests of our pastime. They cheerfully endure the tainted, sullied air. Non-smokers' rights are a thing of the future.

If asked, none of us could explain the difference between "mainstream" and "sidestream" smoke. None of us realized that "sidestream" smoke, the type that comes off a cigarette's burning tip, contains, in many instances, toxic substances proportionately higher than the smoke drawn into one's lungs.

"Live and let live" must be the motto of passive non-smokers, even when it's slowly killing them. To voice discontent would brand them as "zealots" and force them to incur the wrath of a world which still predominantly normalizes incremental self-destruction and murder by way of tobacco smoke.

Mrs. Newall and I puff away, ignorant of the fact we inflict harms on our co-workers, even though the phrase "second-hand smoke" has been around for ages. It's all a "tempest in a teapot" we addicts would like to believe, and while there's no longer any doubt that this habit is bad for our own health, the tobacco industry fuels our skepticism, and we're doubtful that it makes any negative impact on others.

We don't know about the Bell telephone worker in the United States, who allergic to cigarette exhaust, took the company to court and won the right to work in a smoke-free room. Nor do we realize that New York has banned smoking in public places and that the US Surgeon General has stated categorically, "an atmosphere contaminated with tobacco smoke...exerts complex pharmacologic, irritative and allergic effects."

At the Candar Hotel, as in all hotels in Ilfracombe, North Devon, these transatlantic happenings faze us not a bit. It will be over a decade before Joan Clay, a Bedfordshire civil servant, wins a momentous ruling and heroic status among British anti-smoking groups. Illness caused by toxic second-hand tobacco fumes is an industrial accident, a social security tribunal will conclude. But if our non-smoking comrades at the Candar suffer any pulmonary ill-effects from our weeds, they would be hard pressed to prove it.

Unlike the year that Mrs. Newall was born, there's an overwhelming array of synthetic cleaning chemicals on the market. At the Candar Hotel, we use *sodium hypochlorite, anionic surfactants*, and *ammonium hydroxide*, just to name a few. There's *parachlorometaxylenol* that we use in spray bottles, and powdery *sodium bisulfate* which we shake jauntily from plastic canisters, not to mention aerosol *Dimethicone* which lingers, sweetly, in the air. None of us use (nor even know) the proper names of these chemicals, which appear in small print on the cleansers' respective labels. *Vim, Dot, Pledge* are instead some of the easy-going, monosyllabic brand names we apply. Most of us have never read the product instructions, and those of us who have don't take them very seriously. Cleansers in the battles of cleaning are like armaments in the battles of war. A little does not go a long way. Heavy duty arsenals are required and, when vanquishing the enemy, must be liberally deployed, despite what bureaucrats might say.

"Apply small amount," "use in well ventilated room," "dilute with four parts water" are instructions obviously written by people with no knowledge of the realities of frontline purgation. There's no room for restraint or timidity when facing down a filthy foe, "No time to go wobbly" as Margret Thatcher will say to George Bush about Iraqi embargos in years to come.

As we brace to fight, we throw all caution to the wind. We steel ourselves to battle, selfless, focused solely on our task, disregarding anything that causes bodily distress. When we inhale thick clouds of toxic powders or scorch the mucosa of our noses, we continue our relentless toil, though we may wheeze, and cough, and sputter, though invisible acids may sear our eyes. Like the soldiers in the trenches, like triumphant British bombers over ashen skies, nothing can move us from our mission. Nothing can reduce our resolve. Nothing can force our hesitation.

Much that is unimaginable has happened since Mrs. Newall was born. The British Empire, the largest to ever have existed, ruling some 25% of the globe in 1922, is just a shadow of its former self and still declining. Once "banker to the world" — "lending [all nations] capital whenever wanted," Britain has incurred tremendous debt; it has incurred tremendous losses, and over the course of Mrs. Newall's life, through a combination of faultless circumstance, error, and foot-dragging, it has become so mired in economic setbacks that its future currently looks bleak.

But not to Mrs. Newall, nor others of her persevering stripe. "There'll be blue birds over, the white cliffs of Dover," and "the valley will bloom again," as the wartime singer Vera Lynne (the Forces' Sweetheart) still croons on television. Mrs. Newall and Vera Lynn and other women of their generation have survived the Spanish Flu pandemic, survived the General Strike of 1926, the stock market crash and the Depression. They've survived the abdication of a king and the shedding of British colonies, the turmoil and national shame of the crisis of the Suez Canal, the humiliating rejection of the UK's request to join the European Economic Community. In their lifetime, they have seen the emergence of the "Republic of Ireland," the civil rights march in Londonderry, the escalation of the "Troubles" and the start of Operation Banner (the deployment of soldiers to Northern Ireland).

They've lived through the Great London Fog of 1952, when an anticyclone centered over England resulted in a build up of chemical vapour. This lethal air-mass sat stagnant over thirty British miles for five days. It killed between 8,000 and 12,000 people. Although the frog in boiling water experiment had already occurred when this catastrophe materialized, the cautionary apocryphal fable had not yet become a popular metaphor and would not yet be used to explain this historic torpor in the face of rising peril.

Instead, a more vivid picture of the escalating calamity was painted in *The Times*. Just past noon, in Trafalgar Square "the figure at the top of Nelson's column was almost invisible from the ground. Lights on Christmas trees that decorated the facades of stores in the West End seemed to be suspended in mid-air." Shoppers, however, continued to shop. Incidents of "dense green-yellow fog," referred to with "gloomy affection," as the *Illustrated London News* explains, as "London Particular" were frequent enough in the city. The fog did not, at first, raise human alarm.

As the situation worsened, visibility decreased. The Automobile Association couldn't find members who phoned for help. "There was hardly half a mile of road in the centre of London where visibility was more than five yards." Car accidents were rampant, and vehicles were abandoned. Buses stopped running. Planes stopped flying. River traffic halted. Trains crashed. The football match, scheduled at Wembley, was postponed, as were all sporting events in the *fog belt*.

Yet the inhabitants of London, like languorous, mythical frogs ignorantly boiling in seething cauldrons, as some future historians will declare, covered their faces with scarves and continued with their Christmas shopping. Most stores "were fully illuminated through the day, and streetlights at road islands and on obstructions were switched on." Like ants intent upon pheromone trails, shoppers bustled from store to store, collecting consumer items, ignoring the rising threat of toxic air. However, such apparent unresponsiveness may have ascended through something more gritty than mindless Yuletide instincts.

"Business as Usual" became "the maxim of the British people," according to Churchill in 1914, and was the philosophy of the government in the early part of World War I. It continued to inform the British public, forging in the smoke and ashes of World War II the stolid "Blitzkrieg spirit" of defiance in the face of ruin.

As Syd Bailey, a former Birmingham police force clerk recounts in BBC's *WW2 People's War* archive, when air raids were occurring nightly, "we had to thread our way through shattered streets, past ruined buildings and over what seemed like miles of hoses where A.F.S. firemen still struggled to control fires and traffic skirted bomb craters." Bailey and his neighbours "crunched [their] way over glass from broken shop windows," and even though these German raids prevented sleep, "there was no thought of missing work." If it were impossible to drive or catch a bus, people walked. Shop owners swept up debris from their blown-out shops and posted witty notices: "We are still open — more open than usual." There was "a spirit of togetherness, a feeling of co-operation," Bailey recalls, who, equipped with a tin hat and accompanied by a group of fellow clerks, biked around the city extracting people from the rubble.

"K.B.O.," Churchill wrote at the end of his letters. "K.B.O.," he advised when times seemed particularly bleak. It was a humorous acronym which inspired persistence in the face of despair. "Keep Buggering On" was the phrase he illustrated by doing, inspiring many of the British people to do the same, even when, exhausted and war weary, they could barely bugger at all.

"Difficulties mastered are opportunities won," Churchill speechi-fied. "Bells will clash the peal of victory and hope and we will march forward together, encouraged and invigorated." Such may have been the spirit of the people when facing deadly fog in 1952. It certainly was the spirit of Mrs. Newall, and by example all the maids at the Can-dar Hotel.

When confronted with a chamber pot's excrement submersible, floating beneath a yellow urine sea, we rarely cowered, we rarely quaked. Our commander, Mrs. Newall, instructed in a pilfered parody of the war Prime Minister: "Arm yourselves with disinfectant, and be ye maids of valour." And as *maids of valour* there was little we would not endure: condoms glued to bed sheets, sanitary napkins wedged in toilets. Human waste and filth in all its manifestations were ours to combat, as was industrial grime and debris which collected in dark films everywhere it settled.

In the 1970s coal as a major energy source is in decline. However, uncertainties over the future of British fuels has ignited a will to breathe new life into this choking industry. Just as the popular prop-aganda song of World War I, "Keep the Home Fires Burning," was res-urrected in World War II, no one can say with surety that coal will not be sparked into a similar second coming in the years ahead. In Ilfra-combe, its pungent acrid scent mingles with the fishy breezes off the Atlantic. Its dark sooty particles, sulphur and nitrogen oxides, carbon dioxide, and mercury find their way onto picture frames and mantels, wardrobe tops, and into the cloth fibres of curtains and chairs.

With shammies, always in our pockets, furniture polish, always ready to deploy, we wipe out every small invader, every stalking speck. This nuisance, for which I've developed a microscopic vision, is nothing compared to the effluence that Mrs. Newall has seen, nothing to the smoke and debris that swirled over blitzed British cities in World War II, nothing compared to the brume that descended over London in 1952, and was called "fog" instead of "smog" because "smog" was such an ugly word.

The Director of the Electric Association for Women, Caroline Haslet, wrote to the *Times* shortly after the London air had cleared: "My immediate concern [with the fog] is the cost to the housewife. An increasing layer of moist grime on a polished table," as well as "equally begrimed" clothes and linen hangings "blackens" one's "reputation."

But the filth of the past is not my present concern. And what do I care of air pollution? My mission is merely to massacre. I brace my duster in my fist. With rapid fire action take down the sooty residue that besmirches and sullies the moniker "charwoman." I clean and dust and polish and anticipate, with bated breath, our next moment of respite. I dream of the time when Mrs. Newall and I will fire up our fags again, smoking towards victory, that with our greatest persistence and stoicism, awaits us at the end of every working day.

DOGGEREL AND DIRIGIBLES

Oh, Mrs. Newall, Churchill of chambermaids, orator of corridors, bard of bathrooms, declaimer of the lodge. How we smoked and slogged those sullied days away, rapt in mortal combat at that Inn in Ilfracombe. How we sluiced and swabbed and brushed and burnished, how we blasted every board and beam. No bug, nor germ, nor wily worm could endure our duster's thrashings.

As head housekeeper of the Candar Hotel, it was your duty to inspire the charge, as if you were our courageous General, and we, your maids, a light brigade at large. No order met with insolence, no reprimand with cheek. Ours was not to reason why, only to detoxify, and gladly with our rags and mops, and vacuum cleaners rumbling, we set upon our daily tasks, without the slightest grumbling. And you and I, at break time, with our cigarette ash crumbling, frequently discussed life paths I'd trek with the least amount of stumbling.

At least, I recall my time with you in England this way now, in unsophisticated rhyme, with fun and humour, guilelessness and hyperbole. I remember it this way, as I pass the point of mid-life, a time I couldn't anticipate back then. You would have been my age now. So much life had already predeceased you. So much of the world you knew has radically changed.

In the year you were born, just as the year of my birth, the future was veiled and unknowable, a crucible in which time's transformations couldn't be surmised. To live over half a century is to know the fallibility of prophecy. To understand the perpetual motion of human innocence. To realize that the unplanned, the unanticipated, the unimaginable, is what awaits us all.

"Death and taxes" are the only certain things, wrote Benjamin Franklin, long before you and I ever entered this mortal plane, long before the years we worked together, when, according to Margaret Thatcher, taxes were "lethal" and "poison[ing] the business atmosphere of this country." Death, as always, a mainstay of the world, would devour by cancer Conservative politician Anthony Eden, as well as French writer Anaïs Nin, and by a firing squad execution, career criminal Gary Gilmour. As Margaret Thatcher speechified: "The reckoning may be delayed but it comes inexorably in the end."

As we scrubbed and buffed, lit our fags and puffed, and dirty death swirled like smoke above a searing world, I became a hotel resident, while Jimmy Carter was the US president. You may have heard his speech inaugural; yet we included nothing of it in our crafty doggerel, which we wrote for fun with fury, on discarded laundry notes, to win the greatest chortles from our comrades' aching throats.

In the year you were born, poet and musicologist Marion Scott, who would eventually be extolled for advancing and expanding opportunities for women in the arts, joined *The Christian Science Monitor* as their

London correspondent. Two years earlier, in her article "Contemporary British War-Poetry, Music and Patriotism," she wrote that both "genius" and "doggerel" encompassed the "enormous increase in poetic output" during World War I. Poetry, she reflected "is a real, live thing nowadays, and poems are written, not as artistic exercises, but as irresistible impulses towards the expression of thought and emotion," and that "poetry satisfies certain mental needs."

Hardship could drive one to write verse in the year you were born. As poet and critic Laurence Cotterell put it, according to the *Edinburgh Companion to Twentieth-Century British and American War Literature*, "[poetry] 'is what helped to make' the 'immense agony' of the Great War 'just bearable.'" And perhaps the same was true at the Candar Hotel, where the repetitive, mind-numbing tasks of cleaning could squelch the spirit, and the gruesome discoveries of human debris make one ill.

There once was a man from Yorkshire, whose dermatitis and eczema were torture. At the Candar Hotel, he tried to get well, but us maids found his scabs where the doors were.

Whenever he tried to maneuver, his skin dropped like slats from a louver. We're sorry, we said, while sweeping his bed as his flesh had disabled our hoover.

Everyone, both king and commoner, man and woman, soldier and civilian had access to poetry during the Great War. "It acted as both catharsis and commemoration," writes scholar Jane Potter, and continued to be a "prism" through which one could "interpret" and "understand" past events.

In the year of your birth, Mrs. Newall, the *Daily Mail* reports that Private Stanley F. Woodburn of the Liverpool Regiment wrote his will "on a field service form about the size of a post card."

My belongings I leave to my next of kin;/ My purse is empty, there's nothing in./ My uniform, rifle, my pack and kit/ I leave to the next poor devil 'twil fit;/ But if this war I manage to clear/ I'll keep it myself for a souvenir.

Sadly, Woodburn had not been able to clear the war. He was killed in France just before the conflict ended.

In the year you were born, "no fault" divorce was inconceivable. Separations were ugly, increasing in number, and were fodder for the press. Like so much else, in these socially tumultuous and emotional times, divorce was frequently framed by poetry. For example, a "girl-wife," as the *Daily Mail* dubbed her, from the village of Knowle accused her old war damaged husband, Major Sidney George Everitt, of cruelty. He denied the charge, and said she was having an affair with her doctor whom she called "Jimmy." Believing it proof of her inequity, he presented the verse she'd written in her diary at the divorce hearing:

Jimmy, my dear, you're full of fun;/ The folks in Knowle possess just none/ So do hurry up and show them the way/ To be merry and bright and frightfully gay.

There were also "Breach of Promise" cases in the courts in the year you were born. Many a young lady, promised marriage once the guns stopped, found their returning soldier-fiancés less keen on tying the knot than when they'd been in the trenches and the imminence of death was everywhere. The *Daily Mail* reported on the Miss Elsie Pain case under the headline *Girl's Poetry*, and presented the following ditty she had written to her former beau:

Forget me not when you are happy,/ Cast me one little thought;/In the depth of thine affections/ Plant me one sweet forget-me-not./ 'Tis you I love, shall, shall, for ever./ You may change, but I shall never…

For all her passionate avowals, she was ultimately unsuccessful in her case because it was found she'd gone for several walks with a widower and had, damningly, asked him not to reveal this fact.

Poetry was a part of daily life in the year you were born, and so much a part of death that the Buckingham Burial Board was driven to ban tombstone doggerel from its cemeteries. Other graveyards throughout the United Kingdom were also inundated with such epitaphs. In Oxford, for example, a deceased craftsman left instruction that the following be engraved as a memorial:

Here lyeth John Cruker, a maker of bellowes;/ He's craftes-master and king of good fellowes./ Yet when he came to the hour of his death/ He that made bellowes could not make breath.

And sometimes, Mrs. Newall, as we smoke our cigarettes and wheeze, we cannot make breath either, as our lungs begin to seize, and though speech may defy us, and we're brought to our knees, we can still jot down our nonsense, which always seems to please.

Was it you, our noble leader in the battle on filth and disarray, who also led us to savour the sounds of rhyming words and embrace the diversions of doggerel? Verses of victory must have breached your consciousness, as you were born at the close of the Great War, when countless pages of "war poetry" — as it came to be called — were being anthologized.

"Better poetry about it all will, of course, come later," wrote a reviewer who identified himself simply as "A War Poet." He'd contributed to *A Treasury of War Poetry* and *Paths of Glory: War Poems* which although "certainly … largely doggerel," as he claimed, had the distinction of containing "curious doggerel — the doggerel utterance of souls in pain." He predicted that come fifty years, these "sheaves of half-ripe nursery-garden produce" should be as valuable as a postage stamp collection, and that although "the poetic voice positively howls at the unpleasantness of things," future readers may "forgive," remembering "the exceptional incidents" that summoned such utterances as the following:

Our crippled soldiers took the sun,/ Glad that their bloody work was done;/ Being free to feel the morning's charm./They grudged no loss of leg or arm.

When I met you in that seaside hotel, oblivious of the poetry of military personnel, of the soldiers who wrote of missing limbs, and praised World War One with battle hymns, and word was spread both far and near that verse could go with darts and beer, and anyone who owned a pen, could jot a line or maybe ten. And line upon line upon line we jotted, in the stillroom, half besotted, with this unselfconscious language play, unknowing it belonged to yesterday. And with the smoke that we exhaled, our rhymes respired, unassailed, for it was lighter than the air as well, and like our smoke, dispersed our hell.

As well as verse both buoyant and fluffy, the promise of "lighter than air" transatlantic travel was alive in the year you were born. On the very day of your birth, the British airship, R34, landed in Long Island, and was preparing to embark upon its return. Newspaper headlines howled its success, and oceans of ink were spent on its journey.

The R34, built for war, had been completed too late for confrontational calamity. It was used instead, as a headline said, to bring "A message of Amity."

According to the American ambassador, unlike the Germans who used their Zeppelins "to carry disease, destruction, and death among the peaceful population of non-combatants, a message of destruction to quiet, slumbering homes," the airship was being used by Great Britain "to send across the sea...good will and friendship among the nations" and united "people so close in heart and sentiment," as to "afford to the world the best hope and prospect of enduring peace and happiness."

While only a babe at your mother's breast, you wouldn't have known or even guessed, that such a wonderful feat had ever occurred, nor that the patriotism that framed it would continue undeterred. But as the years passed and you became an older child, its likely that you read of airships amazed and beguiled, for what child can resist the charms of flight, especially in picture books with verses so light. You may have read the following, though I can't know it this is factual, only that such books existed, untearable and tactual.

The Children's Airship Book, containing numerous illustrations of dirigibles, presented verse, presumably for the young reader:

Once upon a time one never heard/ of people flying like a bird./ The mode of travelling used to be/ One that would not have suited me./ One drove a coach, or rode a horse,/ But that took a long time, of course;/ Old ladies were alarmed no doubt,/ When trains and steamships first came out./ But how our ancestors would stare/ To see a ship sail through the air,/ Though, I am sure, both you and I/ Hope someday through the air to fly./ Perhaps an airship we may choose,/or else an aeroplane we'll use,/ But there'll be time enough to say/When we are grown up, some fine day.

The book also contained a verse titled *War in the Air*. The writer, it seems, tried to downplay the horrors presented with jangling jolly rhyme as well as a muffled response from the verse's protagonist.

In olden times when soldiers fought/ I'm sure they never never thought/or gazed up into the air/ In search of enemies up there./ But now the foe's on every hand:/ On sea, in air, as well as land;/ No place is safe; it seems indeed/ Two pairs of eyes our soldiers need./ If from the sky a bomb should fall,/ I should not like it, not at all!/ I think, somehow, it's not quite fair/ To shoot poor soldiers from the air.

Dr. Seuss (Theodor Geisel) known best for his rhyming children's books, would have been fifteen in the year you were born. Perhaps he too had been influenced by the outpouring of doggerel, both British and American that, like the R34, transmigrated across the Atlantic. Perhaps, as a lad in Massachusetts, he, like so many of his compatriots, marvelled at the R34's voyage, hoping one day to take a flight in a vehicle that would float among the clouds. Perhaps he'd read *The Boys Book of Airships* and been inspired by Harry H. Kemp's poem:

Brave captains of the ocean of the air,/ Agile the buffets of the winds to dare,/ To dartle upwards on a track oblique/ As eagles fade from peak to mist-wrapt peak.

Little could he imagine that like the R34, he'd travel across the Atlantic or that he'd attend Oxford University, and after failing to achieve a doctorate, encouraged by his wife-to-be, take up the precarious business of professional illustrator and writer.

Little could Dr. Seuss see the future, as it would eventually unfold, with triumph and tragedy, with war and work untold. Internationally, he'd find great success, though Times *reviewer Margaret Drabble would confess, there was "a small," very small "British prejudice." And Michael Church, a reviewer too, found his books somewhat crapuleux. "Vulgarly American," was one of his gibes, as the Brits were used to more genteel kinds of scribes. Yet for all of that, there can be no doubt that the Brits embraced him hale and stout, and bought his books in hordes and droves, consuming them like Hovis loaves.*

The Observer, according to Judith and Neil Morgan, wrote that Dr. Seuss' "rejection of Christian names [gave] him a misleadingly sinister sound," and warned potential readers to "thumb through" his children's works "carefully" so they could "choose the one with the fewest Americanisms." The publicist for Collins, Michael Hyde, claimed that Seuss's rhyming books weren't necessarily seen as children's literature in Britain. They were "often used for teaching adults to read," he's quoted as saying, and many were sold to prisons. "An illiterate old convict would object to be handed a children's book, but he'll settle in with Dr. Seuss."

Horton Hatches an Egg *was rejected by British publishers, seven, when the Secretary of State for Foreign Affairs was none other than Ernest George Bevin, and* The Cat and The Hat, *which in the States sold a million, couldn't for the longest time interest British soldier or civilian. But with ultramodern advertising refrains, influenced by the World War Two propaganda campaigns, Dr. Seuss became a household name, and that cat in the hat did exactly the same.*

But this essay I'm writing is not about that. It is not about doctors or book sales or cats. It's not about Bevin, though prized was his name, it's not about snobbery or haughty disdain. It's not simply about all the fun that was had, making verse out of nothing, as if we'd gone mad, and our uncertain futures we couldn't foretell, as we cleaned, and we scrubbed at the Candar Hotel. But the theme of this piece, if a theme there must be (though thematic divulging is not really for me) is about how one's life unfolds like a rhyme, with surprise and delight and discord over time. We can never predict it, never know the next act, only clean up the messes we're bound to contract, and hope for the best, for the best there must be, along with the bleakest, along with the glee.

"Death and taxes are the only certain things," Benjamin Franklin discovered in the 1700s, and in the 1970s, these two anxiety-producing certainties still plague us. Author, comedian, and doggerel writer Spike Milligan (one of the famous few who has not fled Britain for tax relief) wrote the following letter to the editor of the *Times* shortly after he'd had a nervous breakdown:

Sir, must we continue to suffer the energy-wasting, time-consuming lunacies of [Value Added Tax]. I got a cheque from the BBC for £5 — the cheque arrives in an envelope with a 6 ½ p stamp. My manager then prepares a VAT invoice, this is sent back to the BBC on a 6 ½ p stamp. The BBC then sends me a cheque for 40p with a 6 ½ p stamp on, then we consider the original amount of £5 and the involvement of a BBC clerk, who sends it, the postman who delivers it, my manger who sends back the invoice, thus two postmen are involved, a secretary at the BBC to open it, without working out costs of the envelope, the paper and the printing, the time costs of the people involved, must surely come to more than the original amount of £5. Of course, this doesn't take into account paying it into the bank, where the cashier is involved, and at the end of three months this one cheque is added to all others, then sent to the Customs and Excise. The ultimate was when a 40p VAT cheque arrived from the BBC unstamped — and 13p to pay. I tell you the country is being run by LUNATICS! Sincerely, one of the saner people.

Its hotels are also cleaned by LUNATICS, I don't mind telling you. We're a barmy lot, in our skirts and smocks, flushing soap suds down the loo. And you, Mrs. Newall, our crazy head, while you strip a bed, sing as nutters do. Your voice a pitch of a timbre hitch, as you mimic Jessie Matthews. "At night I creep in bed/ But never sleep in bed/ Just look around in the air/And to my greatest joy/ My boy/ Is there/ He dances overhead." (Jessie, it is said, in the 1930s was of the English cinema, a female "triple-threat.") Down in the stillroom, where our lungs turn grey, you lower the drying rack, where the dusters fray. "We're going to hang out the washing on the Siegfried Line." Your song is an anthem, the World War II kind. "Have you any dirty washing, mother dear? We're going to hang out the washing on the Siegfried Line. 'Cause the washing day is here." You pull the cords, Mrs. Newall, and the drying rack (aka. Siegfried) alights. It hovers above us, like an airship in flight. Although in the year you were born, Mrs. Newall, zeppelins for war were already old school, and thoughts of airships for luxury travel were in, with re-fangled bodies and re-fitted fins. And as you nestled in your mother's

*arms and slumbered, no one could have guessed that the airship's days
were numbered. Even clairvoyants who predicted demise, who foresaw
zeppelins exploding with their innermost eyes, could never have guessed,
despite their attune, that the death of the airship would happen so soon.*

Between 1915 and 1917, 1,500 people were killed by German
wartime zeppelin raids, quotes *The Guardian*. Churchill is said to have
diminished their threat before the war by calling them "enormous
bladders of combustible and explosive gas." However, it took a long
time to figure out how to ignite the gas. Hugh Hunt, a senior lecturer
in engineering at Cambridge University, said an explosive bullet to
rupture the ship, followed by an incendiary one to ignite the ship's
hydrogen, was the method eventually used.

*But airships filled with hydrogen, continued to sail the skies, despite
the many disasters, despite the many carbonized. In the year you were
born, Mrs. Newall, Wikipedia claims there were accidents three, though
this web-source is not always accurate, and not often cited by me. In the
interwar years, as we call them, when you were a growing lass, British
luxury ships developed, despite the flammable gas. Like the race for the
first moon landing and the contest for nuclear arms, the commercially
viable airship was puffed up for all of its charms. In Germany, it had
seemed a winner, as early as 1910, when passengers alighted the LZ-7, to
quench their wanderlust yen. The cabins were most luxurious, with inlay
of mother-of-pearl, with elegant wicker furnishings, and carpets fit for
an earl. Aboard was a classy French restaurant that sold pralines and
liver pâté. It sold lobster and French chestnut chicken, cognac, merlot,
cabernet. But after only two airings, the ship took a terrible dive, the passengers, many reporters, were shaken but all did survive. Yet the zeppelin,
or "airship," as the British preferred, would continue being manufactured
undeterred. "The bigger they are, the harder they fall," boxer Joe Walcot
once spoke, and to this sagacity we may add fugacity, to understand how
airships went up in smoke.*

You would have been a girl of ten, Mrs. Newall, when Britain com-pleted building the R101. It was the world's largest airship at the time, a "mighty symbol of imperial power," and "the pride of the British aviation industry," according to the *Daily Mail*.

Three times longer than a modern jumbo jet, constructed in a hanger so large "that Westminster Abbey could be tucked" in its corner, the ship needed four hundred people to manoeuvre her out of her bunker.

Inside the ship, there was an impressive entrance hall. A stairway, reminiscent of an ocean-going luxury liner led to a sixty-foot white and gold lounge with a brightly polished wooden floor. Pillars, covered in blue velvet, gave the illusion of majesty, while potted palm trees in the corners added warmth and life and a hint of the exotic. On the nautically designed promenade deck, there were folding canvas chairs where passengers could relax, taking in the aerial vistas through cellu-loid windows. The dining room, replete with serenading wireless radio, could seat fifty and the meals served were "as well-cooked" as those "in any West End hotel." The cabins, containing bunks, made up in ergo-nomics practicality what they lacked in luxury. There were aluminum sinks close by for washing up. Toilets, however, were below.

As we puff on our fags at the Candar, and watch the grey smoke bloom, you say nothing of the R 101, Mrs. Newall, or of its "first of a kind" smoking room. You say nothing of its asbestos lining, nothing of its fireproof door, nothing of its electric lighters that were chained to the metal floor. Nothing of the highly flammable hydrogen that filled its gasbags full, nothing of the white-hot smoke, Mrs. Newall, like bales of cotton wool. So much of history, we could have discussed, as we annihilated germs, eradicated dust, as we toked on our cancer sticks, and let them combust, sang songs, wrote poems, the rhymes were a must. So much you had seen in your fifty some years, the good times, the bad times, the laughter and tears, the clichés of life like the last line above, the wisdom, the folly, the hatred, the love. Perhaps if I'd asked, you would have unveiled the past of your childhood, all greatly detailed. Perhaps you'd have taught me, like the best raconteur, about life's continuity and its force majeure. Yet the lessons of your yesteryears arrived without expansion, its verses cut short, with no analysis, no scansion. And at the hotel, where we scrub and we spray, the silt of your past has all burned away, and down in that stillroom, where we puff and we choke, the past disappears; it's nothing but smoke.

The R 101 went up in smoke too, Mrs. Newall, as you may have recalled. It crashed in France on a stormy night, the fifth of October, nine years before the outbreak of World War Two, immediately incinerating forty-six, including Air Minister Lord Christopher Thomson, the Royal Airship Works program initiator, along with virtually every designer who'd had a hand in constructing the ship. Its demise ended the development of airships in Britain.

And yet, what do we care of ships in the air, as we wash the floors, remove the hair from bathtub drains, and stopper chains, and scrub from toilets stubborn stains. What do we care of history, as our bleachy hands grow blistery? Or of following times' trajectory, as we smoke in our stillroom refectory. What do we care about what's come before, when there's twenty guests leaving, all smudging the door, and twenty incoming, with case and with bag, and shoe horns and dentures, and girdles that sag. We clean, and we smoke, and we sing and curse, drink tea, and tell jokes and speak in wry rhyming verse: A fashionable lady from Truro, got her finger stuck in a bureau, dislodge it we tried, but it wouldn't be pried, so convinced her the look was couture-o.

And sometimes, as you must have known, like an awkward limerick, things don't always fit and creative modification is called for. So was the case with the airship shed at Cardington, for example, that had to be extended for the R 101. The airship itself also needed adjustments.

A new bay had to be constructed as the ship's weight was more than desired and its "gross lift" less.

"None of us liked the idea of the new bay being put in the ship," said the widow of Mr. G. W. Short, who had been a charge-hand engineer for the R 101 until its crash. The wives of crew members recalled how the R 38, another doomed airship, had "met with disaster" after it had been enlarged. "We women," Mrs. Short told the *Daily Mail's* special correspondent the day after the disaster, "know a good deal about airships," and none were happy "when we saw R 101 ride sluggishly from her mooring-mast. Seven times she threw out ballast to rise," eventually rising "awkwardly" and "with tremendous effort."

Some eighty-five years after the airship crash, the heavy metal band *Iron Maiden* will include a song on their sixteenth studio album, *The Book of Souls*, that recounts the disastrous flight.

The engines drum, the telegraph sounds/ Release the cords that bind us to the ground/ Said the coxswain, "Sir, she's heavy, she'll never make this flight."/ Said the captain, "Damn the cargo! We'll be on our way tonight."/ Groundlings cheered in wonder, as she backed off from the mast/ Baptizing them her water, from the ballast fore and aft...

But Iron Maiden has not yet released an album, when we clean at the Candar Hotel, let alone found their lead singer, Bruce Dickinson. This rhyming verse about the R 101 is not yet a twinkle in Dickinson's eye. Nor is it a tinkle on his piano keyboard. While we clean toilets in Ilfracombe, North Devon, Dickinson, a working-class boy, just two years my senior, has not too long ago been expelled from the posh Oundle Public School in Northamptonshire for pouring piss on the headmaster's dinner.

Instead, it's the rock band Led Zeppelin — "the world's number one rock attraction" according to biographer, Dave Lewis — who are large and luminous, and soar above the stratosphere. They are, Lewis writes, "so far ahead of whoever might be residing below them at number two as to render it a case of absolute no contest."

Though drug addiction and acts of god had already scorched their skin, no prophet could have foreseen the fall of the mighty Led Zeppelin. As we cleaned, Mrs. Newall, and smoked our fuel, and polished brass handles to shine, the Zep was on tour, an American lure, with no thought of their own decline. But laryngitis and stomach bugs, were only at the tip. Of an iceberg that was large enough to sink their leaden ship. Some claim a curse had fallen, like lightning from the sky, igniting grave misfortunes, the type that horrify. But in our bubble at the Candar Hotel, we were ignorant of trouble, all seemed well. I stood on the stairway, my duster nicely poised and began loudly singing, unselfconscious of the noise: "There's a charwoman who knows all that glitters isn't necessarily clean and she's dusting the stair rail that leads to the latrine, when she gets there she knows, if the door remains closed, she will have to return with the chlorine." Stairway to Heaven, quite popular in the hotels of Ilfracombe, North Devon, could be, for work days, modified, as we battled black moulds with fungicide. For example, we were apt to sing, as mop and rag we'd twist and wring, about the streaks upon the wall, "'Cause you know sometimes streaks have two meanings." And, "there's pee by that book, and a long turd that stinks, sometimes all of our chamber pots need sieving." Ooh, Mrs. Newall, it makes me wonder. Ooh, Mrs. Newall, it makes me wonder. Did such insanity prevent us going under, as we smoked our fags and rhymed like thunder, and cast that wretched filth asunder?

Stairway to Heaven, although never released as a single, and just over eight minutes long, was one of radio's most broadcast tunes. According to the *Encyclopedia of Great Popular Song Recordings*, the "saturation coverage" started slowly. "Building to a peak from mid-1972 through the fall, it was played more relentlessly on radio stations across the board than any chart-topping single." Editor of *Led Zeppelin and*

Philosophy Scott Calef claims the ballad was played over five million times on American radio, and the reason for its popularity among disc Jockeys, biographer Charles R. Cross maintains, had little to do with audience requests.

Yes Mrs. Newall, though "Stairway" was cool, its air time it owed to one factor. According to Cross, though it might all be dross, the length was its prime attractor. While most singles logged in at a three-minute spin, this ballad unique in its making, allowed for all DJs, tobacco addicted, to smoke one whole fag in their breaking. The importance of smoking, besides aiding one's choking, should never be underrated. Though its impact unseen as we dust and we clean, it's still shaping the way the world's weighted. In history's course, the fag is a force, skewing fate's statistical bend, with effect obscure; it is almost sure, its full impact will never be penned. As I write this rhyme, in another time, it gives me pause to think, how cigarettes, like smouldering airships, changed destiny in a wink. Not only through death and destruction, though these are easily exposed, but with invention and research and knowledge, the good and the bad juxtaposed. Without careless cigarette blazes, would fire-retardant be made? And what about the rock band Led Zeppelin, would it have existed without the Hindenburg's aid?

The German airship Hindenburg, which crashed in 1937, was the vessel which Led Zeppelin became associated with. Like the R 101, it had been built for luxury travel and was even more extravagant than the British ship. The iconic photograph, taken by Sam Shere, of the airship exploding graced the band's debut album cover. When asked, many decades later, why the group picked the photo, Jimmy Page said: "It's a dramatic incident…a dramatic album…a dramatic statement."

And please excuse me for being dogmatic, "but a story, ain't a story" unless it's dramatic. "An event or circumstance sudden and striking" (this definition thanks to a dictionary of my liking) is exactly what's called for, exactly the pass, in detailing human foibles and explosions of gas. So many stories, where does one begin? Like an airship in a cyclone, like the records of Zeppelin, they spin and they spin and they spin.

Some years before we emptied chamber pots together, Mrs. Newall, the countess Eva von Zeppelin, granddaughter of the German airship inventor, Ferdinand, threatened to sue Led Zeppelin in Copenhagen. "They may be world-famous," biographer Mick Wall quotes her as saying, "but a couple of shrieking monkeys are not going to use a privileged family name without permission."

The band invited her to a private meeting to convince her of their decency, but before she left, the story goes, she spied the Hindenburg album cover, and like the airship, though not literally, exploded. Consequently, the band changed their name to "The Nobs" for their Copenhagen performance. "And you know sometimes words have two meanings."

"Ambiguity," Robert Plant told *Daily Mail* reporter Geoffrey Hobbs some twenty-eight years after escaping Eva's lawsuit and twenty-seven after *Stairway To Heaven*'s release, is "the only thing that gives [that song] any staying power. I don't think there was ever anything particularly special about it." Hobbs then relates how Plant dismembered the lyrics, presenting them line by line, rendering them "suddenly...as ordinary as the doggerel in the average greeting card," bringing the song "that bewitched rock fans for decades...down to earth like a punctured balloon."

There's a feeling I get, when my wash rag is wet, and my stomach is writhing and heaving. In those pots I have seen rings of piss and feces, and avoid them with sweat glands a-cooking. Ohh, Mrs. Newall, it makes me wonder. Ooh, Mrs. Newall, it really makes me wonder, why don't these folks visit a loo and use its dumper?

Our earthy versions of *Stairway to Heaven* possess no lyrical ambiguities. In the world of chambermaiding, anything abstruse (a smear of lipstick or blood? a splotch of shit or mud?) needs to be eradicated without too much reflection.

"Shoot first and inquire afterwards," Hermann Goering is said to have told Prussian police in 1933, but at the Candar Hotel, inquiry at any point in the operation is discouraged. Disinfectant and bleach always at the ready. Spray chemicals always close at hand. We are like the British Commando, trained in "the school of murder," as the Commando's red-faced roly-poly teacher said. "[Killing is] an art which you have to study, practice and perfect," he is quoted as saying in *The Washington Post* in 1943.

Unlike the "average" English or American World War Two soldier, we maids have no remorse to slow us down. We already know the good major's lesson: "Shoot the Jerry like you're swatting a fly. Get the job done and get away. You'll sleep like a baby even after the bloodiest shamble."

Although, for us, the consequences aren't as dire, we also know not to waste our energy on drama when we clean. Whether ambushing germs or Germans, it never pays to put on a performance. As the major lectured his student commandos: "Never be tempted to say, 'Good evening gentlemen' or anything stupid like that when surprising the enemy. It may look wonderful in print, and may be very British, but it will only get you an obituary."

And finally, when wielding your weapons, be it tommy gun or knife (be it aerosol spray, duster or mop, in our case) you never stab or hack, but play your weapon like a musical instrument. "You have to have rhythm," the major said.

And we do have rhythm, Mrs. Newall, even when we break from the grind, and watch our cigarette smoke entwined; a spiral staircase towards your "Siegfried Line," that drying rack airship you've redefined.

THE TROUBLES

IT WAS A EUPHEMISTIC folk name for the conflict in Northern Ireland, but when my aunt used the label, it inevitably meant tensions at home. I was not a particularly compliant daughter, my mother not a particularly perceptive parent. In fact, in the wake of my father's death and our move from Canada to England, so unmoored and fractious were we that *apocalypse* would have served as a more fitting title.

My aunt found herself on the borderlands of this turbulent relationship, and *The Troubles*, as a moniker, allowed her a humorous sort of neutrality which she used in her peacekeeping role. However, she was far from impartial, and although she'd never state it, her sympathies, I was certain, rested with me.

This may have been because I admired her, or perhaps, because as a teenager, she'd struggled at home herself. It may have been because I was an introvert, and unlike my mother, who badmouthed and backstabbed to win recruits, I was embarrassed to publicly disparage. It may have been because my aunt, nine years my mother's senior, had known her as a spoiled and demanding child, or perhaps because my mother, who'd had a momentary rallying of spirits when we'd first moved to England, had quickly lapsed back into helpless despair.

My aunt, a forward-thinking conservative, didn't have much sympathy for people who wallowed in misery. She approved of the fact I didn't, believed that whatever opportunity she offered me, I'd do my best to make the most of, and consequently spent a great deal of her free time actively seeking people and events she thought might take me away from *The Troubles* and provide, at least, a modicum of respite.

Besides finding me my first-full time job, she got me involved in charitable work, such as selling "ices" at Ilfracombe's ancient, economically endangered *Top of the Town* theatre. It had begun life as a covered market area, called Alexandra Hall in 1901, but quickly evolved into a place where concerts and lectures were held. During the second world war, it was chosen as the "gas decontamination centre" for the town and became known as the "Garrison Theatre" where exiled Jewish actors performed. Over the years, there'd been a host of renovations and name changes. Ilfracombe's tourist industry had experienced a number of booms and busts. As the '70s dawned, however, the resort was well in decline and eventually the money losing theatre became the purview of the Town Council.

My aunt, being a town councillor, who loved her community and zealously advocated preserving the best of Ilfracombe's by-gone years, threw her back into this fiscal crisis and requistioned mine, whenever possible. My social life was another project she oversaw and when Cathy Lyons, the granddaughter of another town councillor, arrived, my aunt envisioned a companion and confidante, who'd act as an emotional buffer for me in the stir of increasing domestic strain, and immediately set to work securing a date for our meeting.

Outside of workmates, I hadn't found many friends. "I expect it would be nice to have a girl-chum," my aunt said, and I agreed. I'd had several "girl-chums" in Ontario, who I occasionally called on before domestic tensions boiled over.

My mother and I battled over many things: my excessive use of hot water, my thoughtless propensity to take the last slice of some particular food, my resentment over babysitting my little brother, to whom I felt inordinately shackled even though I loved him, my bad attitude, my sullen, sulky demeanour that appeared whenever I came through the front door, not to mention the things I did, *only* for myself, and not for her, like laundry and ironing and cleaning my room. But at the crux of it all, I believed, sat the ugly spectre of money. When I had a job, my mother expected that I should "turn something up." This demand, as far as I (a chambermaid earning sixty pence an hour before tax) was concerned seemed totally unreasonable.

Cathy Lyons' grandmother, Millicent, was a rabid Tory with extremely traditional ideas. She'd once met my mother and had heard, on that occasion, all about my shortcomings, and consequently rebuffed my aunt's initial invitation on Cathy's behalf. As a town councillor, with heaps of experience dealing with impassioned people and problematic situations, my aunt reflexively assumed a mollifying stance, but over the course of the next few weeks went about systematically reshaping Millicent's perceptions, and kept me abreast of the progress.

She drew Millicent out, asking questions about her granddaughter, establishing in short order that Cathy, like me, was at war with her mother, and had left Oxfordshire under a cloud of domestic strife. "It's a pity," my aunt said, "but perhaps conflict is the order of things." She made some allusion to the nature of cats, how mother cats tended to turn on their maturing offspring, and how those offspring needed to find caring individuals in the world. I was fortunate to have found an aunt who'd endorse me to strangers, as Cathy was to have found a grandmother to protect her, and eventually my aunt, who unobtrusively sang my praises "committed, hardworking, kind," won Millicent completely over with a decisive declaration of my political persuasion: "Conservative," she'd insisted.

"But I'm not Conservative, Auntie Lena" I objected, once the date of my meeting with Cathy was set. "I don't even really know what Conservative is," I confessed. I'd never followed politics in Canada.

"Nonsense," she said, "of course you're Conservative. You want what's best for the country, don't you? You want to have a job and make a decent wage? You want a happy life?"

Of course, it was all true, except I wasn't Conservative. I was a completely apolitical immigrant, who had grown up with the name "Pierre Trudeau" ringing in my ears. He'd been Canada's Prime Minister even before my family moved to Windsor, Ontario, from the U.S. in 1970. We immigrated then because Nixon, who my father referred to as "Tricky Dicky," was president, and the possibility existed that my eldest brother, now living with his girlfriend in Ontario, would be drafted "as cannon fodder" for the Vietnam war.

I didn't know the difference between Republican and Democrat, Conservative and Liberal, and had never heard of the Labour party, "hostage to the trade unions," which according to my aunt and all her friends had put the country into economic peril. Jim Callaghan's face was not at all familiar to me. I had little idea that England was a sinking ship, plummeting in this strangely politicized land, where the term "sea change" was bandied and I, a relative new comer, was attempting to put my best foot forward, even though I didn't yet have sea legs.

Cathy Lyons, on the other hand, was well equipped to weather any storm, or at least gave that impression. She was beautiful, ginger-haired, as the British say, several years my senior, with a diverse and impressive past. At our first meeting, I discovered she was an ex-police officer, an ex-fiancé, and the ex-nanny of a very prominent politician's family, who had recently been the subject of scandal. The politician wasn't a Tory, and Cathy had no qualms about ridiculing him. "Jumped up twit!" she said in a soft, beautiful, queenly voice when we first met, "And gorgeous, God! You should have seen his wife!" A litany of biting comments about his family followed, everything from hypocrisy, rudeness, and stupidity to foul breath and greasy hair. It made me think that if I should ever accidentally have children and was rich enough to employ a nanny, I would most certainly make her sign a gag order. How horrible to have one's private life made public in such a way. Yet I didn't stop Cathy from her withering rant. I didn't chastise her for telling what I was certain the family wouldn't want told. Instead, I listened intently, fascinated, enjoying all the lovely barbs so beautifully disgorged.

Cathy was different from my Canadian "girl-chums" who generally felt as awkward and alienated as me. She seemed to possess an almost brash self-confidence. But more than this, what struck me as particularly unusual was her eagerness — almost desperation — to have a child. "I'm twenty years old!" she lamented, as if her biological clock had somehow gone haywire and skipped ahead a decade and a half.

As a teenager, my only thought about starting a family was that it wouldn't be happening any time soon. I wanted a career. I wanted to be a writer, and while a lot of lip service was being paid to gender equality, children as a fifty-fifty obligation shared between the men and women who spawned them was unthinkable, even to the most enlightened.

Well into the future, the situation will remain virtually unchanged. "Women will always be grounded by their children to an extent that men aren't," the *Daily Mail* reporter Melanie McDonagh will prophetically write in 2003. I won't be living in England then, but on Canada's West Coast, the mother of two daughters, the eldest Cathy's age. But in Ilfracombe, as the two of us get to know each other, the future isn't mine to see, and Cathy is rhapsodizing about her most heartfelt wish.

"To have a baby! A baby girl!" she cooed, "I'd name her Victoria, after the Queen."

"Isn't the Queen's name Elizabeth?" I asked. I knew little about the monarchy but was certain of this fact.

"Not her," Cathy said with a wave of her hand, "I wouldn't name my child after her." The reigning monarch had no real clout, she explained. "She's a political eunuch, not like Queen Victoria."

Passion brought colour to Cathy's milk white cheeks, and she confessed that true to the fiery-red-head stereotype, anger once ignited could get the better of her, though few things ultimately seemed to make her mad. For example, she rarely got upset about her current job which was horribly regimented. She sewed at a local factory, and unlike my job as hotel chambermaid, which started sometime around the crack of dawn and ended usually at noon, depending on the comings and goings of guests and the number of tea breaks we'd taken, Cathy had to begin work precisely at 9 a.m. for an eight-hour day, with only short well-monitored breaks. I couldn't help but consider my job superior to hers, not only because she had to sit before a sewing machine all day in a dank little hole of a room without any kind of social interaction, but also because of the job's repetitive nature which involved sewing "piece *A* to piece *B*" day after day after day.

Her job was permanent unlike my transient seasonal work, and she got paid much more plus bonuses if she could sew "piece *A* to piece *B*" faster than anyone else in her shop, but despite these extras, I still thought she had much more to lament than me, and was surprised she didn't express red-faced frustration over what to my mind was soul destroying work.

When I live and work in Ilfracombe, *Science* has not yet embraced the study of happiness. The old cliché that asserts money can't buy it is falling out of favour in England. While "relative indifference to wealth for its own sake was widespread," after World War II, according to historian, Tony Judt; in the 1970s the country appears to be moving towards a new materialistic age.

In the North Devon town of Ilfracombe, where Cathy and I reside, Ladbrooks betting shop does a brisk trade as customers dream of great wins on racehorses, greyhounds, football matches and even on political leadership contests. The love of lucre draws mindless swarms of gold-diggers sporting wide-brimmed hats and hauling metal detectors to a nearby beach, after two schoolboys happen upon rare and valuable 18th century Portuguese coins.

The problem, however, is that accumulating wealth in England is like collecting sand in a strainer. Not only is inflation climbing, but "Britain's tax regime in the 1970s," according to *The Telegraph*, is "one of the most punitive in the world" and is responsible for driving big earners, like David Bowie and the Rolling Stones, out of the country. Even I, a small wage earner, find pound for pound, I make more money when I work less. Cathy finds the same, but still tries for bonuses, because there's more job security the faster she works.

She knows much more about the way things are run in the country, and occasionally tries to explain the workings of the British economy. But numbers tend to bore me and the word economic is as grey and un-appealing as a man's flannel suit. I frequently try to change the subject, but when Cathy turns to politics, there's no use trying. She rails against socialism, a term that idles in my mind, along with cooties and boy-germs and other disgusting dangers that invisibly spread. I'm not really sure what it means, though have discovered since living in England that it is akin to Communism and recall my sixth-grade social studies teacher saying that communism "was the evil we were fighting against in Viet-nam."

As a teen who has spent life, up until recently, immersed in North American values, I've learned that accumulating money and posses-sions is the only road to happiness. Yet here in England, where I don't even make a living wage, despite the ongoing war with my mother, I'm happier than I've ever been, and it confuses me.

At times, my work is arduous and there's almost nothing as revolting as discovering that some guest who doesn't have a toilet in his room has availed himself of one of the porcelain chamber pots and left it beside his bed, full of excreta, for me to step in. But I do feel valued and accepted among my co-workers, a collection of women who span the generations, and I relish the unique camaraderie and caring that persists amongst us.

My boss, our head housekeeper, Mrs. Newell, is a former World War Two WREN who speaks in a clipped, precise, aristocratic way. She's as conscientious as she is straightforward, formidable as zany, tough, forgiving, and infinitely wise. She's both our spark and our spur, instilling teamwork and cooperation — two traditional values which diminish existential isolation and promote a cohesive community. It doesn't matter that we make beds, dust rooms, vacuum carpets and clean toilets, jobs which, to objective eyes, might appear ultimately devoid of purpose. With Mrs. Newell at the helm, every job well done is significant in keeping Britain strong, and every working day is an opportunity to engage in a battle against filth and untidiness — two human by-products which she considers malevolent.

"Let us go forward together and conquer," Mrs. Newell solemnly intones at sunrise, evoking wartime speechifying to set the mood for the day, and "Rooms 69, 45, 33, and 26 Need You!" As a North American teenager, a great deal of her World War II humour is lost on me, but when she begins singing in her high-pitched, cut-glass accent "Over my shoulder goes one care" and tossing dirty bed linen and towels out into the corridor as she high kicks her skinny stockinged legs, I can't stop laughing. It makes no difference that I've never heard of Jessie Matthews, England's legendary actress. She made the song popular in a 1930s movie as she divested layers of clothing.

While I can't say that I always look forward to work, I can say that I always look forward to working with Mrs. Newell, who leads her crew of maids with a no-nonsense naval officer's persona, yet paradoxically ascribes to the Mary Poppins' philosophy: "In every job that must be done, there is an element of fun." I'm equally enthusiastic to work with a host of other delightfully eccentric chambermaids, who tell outrageous stories as we clean, or strike up choruses of songs and impromptu poems. I'd like for Cathy to join us. I can envision her, telling the tales of her eventful past. I can imagine her fitting right in.

"Don't you ever find your job boring?" I ask her one day.

"Yes, it's boring," she sighs, "but it's a job...for the time being."

The season is gearing up, and it's becoming increasingly busy at our hotel. I know that Mrs. Newell would snap Cathy up in a second, if she applied.

"Why don't you come and work at The Candar as a chambermaid?" I venture.

"That sort of work wouldn't suit me, I'm afraid," she says apologetically, though offers no elaboration. I'm still so naive about Britain's class system that it never occurs to me that as far as the hierarchy of working-class occupations go, chambermaiding is beneath factory work, and seasonal hotel chambermaiding exists in a place of its own on the bottommost rung of the working-class ladder.

Consciousness of social class is acute in the 70s. Not only does Margaret Thatcher, the grocer's daughter, have yet to come to power, but she also has yet to smash the trade unions and denounce the concept of class as a Communist invention that "groups people as bundles and sets them against one another." Her protégé, John Major — the "modest man with much to be modest about" — according to the *Daily Mail*, has not yet usurped her place, not yet been scorned and dismissed by her as a "silly little man" and not yet become so frustrated by her that he asserts he wants her "isolated" and "destroyed." The phrase a "classless society," which Thatcher first coined, has not yet been espoused by Major, nor has his vision of Britain as "a tapestry of talents in which everyone from child to adult respects achievement." The sharp perceptible runnels of class dividing Britain have not yet in any way been blunted, though I, a newcomer here, cannot yet clearly see them.

Semi-nomadic people with "no fixed address" or "permanent abode" with no care or loyalty or pride of place are thought to become seasonal hotel workers. They are reputed to hang around, long after the holiday makers leave, then go on the dole, vandalize, steal, and frequently become drunk and disorderly. Sometimes they're audacious enough to find their way into vacant dwellings and claim "squatters' rights" as one group has done just down the street from my aunt's and uncle's house. These so-called "rights" date back to the 1300s, and allow people to occupy the dwellings of others, as long as entry occurs "in a peaceable and easy manner."

While the law may have made sense at a time when the catastrophic Black Death had decimated the population and perfectly good houses sat empty, in the 70s, it's the "scroungers" and "freeloaders" who invade rentals that have not yet been let, or worse, the homes of those who are away on holiday.

But the chambermaids at The Candar Hotel, despite their zaniness, are respectable women who have some form of respectable dwelling. Mrs. Newell, the only married member of our cohort, is comfortable enough financially, and doesn't need to work, but, as she explains during a tea break, "I'd go balmy without a job. There's only so much tidying and dusting and cleaning one can do at home, only so many beds to make, so many tubs and toilets to scrub, so many carpets to hoover. It doesn't take long to get things shipshape and Bristol fashion, and then one's faced with the day."

The two younger maids, Jane and Joyce, who only work weekends, don't understand this. They're both students who'd rather be sleeping late than rising before dawn and carting their tired bodies to work. They aspire to a better class of job. One wants to be a shorthand typist, the other, a chef. They work at The Candar because it's not far from their homes, doesn't require long-term commitment, and yields sufficient amounts of spending money.

A survey that will be conducted by *IPC Young Magazines* later this year will identify girls between the ages of 12 and 18 as Britain's "big spenders of the Seventies." Unfettered by adult responsibilities, such as cars and mortgages, this group of 3 million strong possesses an estimated £1,072 million to spend on their treasures. Items to enhance their appearance and/or attractively boost their perceived age, such as fashionable clothing, beauty products, and cigarettes are just some of the purchases these moneyed teens will make. £12 million will go towards eye cosmetics; deodorants will account for £8 million, while £9 million will be spent on nail polishes and lipsticks. Thirty-two percent of the 16-plus group will smoke, and one quarter of these will buy a pack of 20 cigarettes per day. Like Jane and Joyce, I'm a teenager living in Britain and will fall within this survey's parameters. Unlike them, however, I'm a full-time worker, and so my weekly pay of roughly £20 (about $36 Canadian, a quarter of what an Ontario minimum wage job pays at the time) while offering me significantly less than I could have earned at home, affords me comparably more spending opportunities than my two young British co-workers. Unlike them, I'm virtually a chain-smoker, and certainly buy more than twenty cigarettes a day. I like cosmetics, clothes, and grooming products, but when all is said and done, I spend the majority of my money, after cigarettes, on books and magazines, items, I believe, that will assist me on my career path. I also buy the occasional record album and, at Cathy's urgings, frequent the bar at the local Conservative Club. The lager is cheaper than at regular pubs, and although I've not yet reached the legal drinking age, I, like most underage young women, imbibe without consequence.

I still live with my mother, yet defiantly refuse to turn my wages over to her, as she wishes, and allow her to apportion a percentage as an allowance. This is what she and her mother did, and her mother and grandmother before her. In fact, she tells me that all good British daughters have done this since time immemorial, but I am not a British daughter, good or otherwise. I am a child of North America, born in the militant 60s with a rebellious spirit and heart and can keenly remember, mainly because of my mother's fury over it, a song learned in the US, called *Revolutionary Tea* that pitted mother against daughter, and England against colony.

There was an old lady lived over the sea
And she was an Island Queen.
Her daughter lived off in a new countrie,
With an ocean of water between;
The old lady's pockets were full of gold
But never contented was she,
So she called on her daughter to pay her a tax
Of three pence a pound on her tea…

My mother's request for my pay package strikes me as exploitative. In Canada, I reason, most parents take it as a given that they will financially support their teenaged children. I also reason that I wouldn't be in England at all right now if my mother hadn't decided to return to the land of her birth after my father died.

Neither my mother nor I have the distance or detachment to understand that our argument is more about cultural differences than it is about greed and entitlement. From my North American teen's-eye-view, my mother's concern for money demonstrates her avarice and lack of regard for me. I know that she has my father's insurance, also that she collects a number of North American pensions and benefits, including (though this will only later come to light) regular orphan benefits from the Canadian government for me, which is roughly three times my monthly wages. I feel the generous contributions of free childcare I make, looking after my baby brother, are taken for granted, that my mother doesn't appreciate me, that my only value to her exists in my meagre wage. I cannot objectively hear her request, cannot understand that at least part of what she's asking for isn't money, but some connection with her past. This, after all, is why she returned to England.

My stubborn refusal to do what she asks is more than a lack of respect, more than the absence of affection, more than the shirking of duty, from her point of view. Neither of us can see that our conflicts aren't really about money — that money is simply a symbol to which all our tacit insecurities fuse. It will create a rift between us, a rift which will never wholly be repaired, even after she moves back to Canada, even after I move back and put myself through school.

I will graduate and marry and have my first and then second daughter, yet this rift will not be repaired. It will remain unspoken, unexamined, buried beneath the debris of decades, like 18th-century Portuguese coins beneath the ocean's sands. Even after my mother dies, the rift will continue to exist, a testament to the difficulties inherent in communication, a testament that understanding must occur before repair, a testament that money isn't everything, though it somehow serves us to believe it is — serves us to reduce our lives to its worth.

As a teenager, my lack of life experience and the freshness of my wounds makes me incapable of this sort of analysis. Instead, I take my pay package and meet Cathy at the Conservative Club to drink lager and to be consoled. Cathy's soft blue eyes exude compassion; her jaw tightens at the hint of injustice. In the background, ABBA, the Swedish pop group, that will rack up twenty-three British hits by 1983, including "Money, Money, Money" is getting a disproportionate amount of playtime on the jukebox.

It's only after I finish making my case for keeping my pay packet, after ABBA finishes their song, and Cathy finishes her gin and tonic that it occurs to me that she sympathizes with my mother. When she lived at home, she turned her wages over to her mother, and even now, while paying board and lodging to her grandmother and fighting with her mother, she still sends "a quid or two" home. However, she doesn't tell me that my position is wrong, she doesn't berate me for falling short of my duty, doesn't advise, lecture, or scold. Instead, she orders us another round, plonks her hard-earned British Sterling on the table and when the drinks arrive, lifts hers towards mine, and makes a toast to our prosperous futures.

MALOCCLUSION

I SAW NIGEL at a *Young Conservatives* meeting. He was tall and thin with angular features and sandy hair. He wore a dark blue business suit and a sky-blue tie. Unlike most British men I'd met, and unlike Johnny Rotten, lead singer of the newly formed *Sex Pistols* whom I hadn't met, Nigel had perfectly straight white teeth.

His teeth made him look wholesome and boyish, like the all-American pop-star idols who grace the pages of *Tiger Beat*. When I was a prepubescent romantic, I'd attuned myself to the pulse of this magazine, swooning with devoted fervour over each and every bright-toothed star. Now, it's glam rock, and heavy metal I embrace, eschewing my old associations, pretending they never existed, but I can't suppress the truth of my heart: it leaps with aesthetic delight whenever I see a boy with a flawless smile.

In future years, the attraction will fade. In fact, anything perfectly ordered and gleaming will appear artificial to me. But in the 1970s, I'm a product of American social conditioning. Until age ten, I lived in the dental-obsessed United States where bicuspids had to glisten and children's orthodontic head-gear was the norm. Little girls, when asked to describe their ideal future mates, were consistent about only two things: the gender of the mate — male — and the state of his teeth — perfect. I imagine little boys had similar requirements. Crooked-toothed girls with cross bites like mine could look forward to being spurned the moment they opened their mouths. Here in England, things are different, and despite the fact the country is in economic shambles, and the forecast for my future is grim, I can't help but consider myself lucky.

Buck teeth, chipped teeth, rotten green and black teeth are as common in this country as beer-battered cod and chips, and those freaks of nature, like Nigel, who possess perfectly pearly ones, don't consider good teeth a prerequisite to partnership. I know this because within a week of our meeting, Nigel begins courting a young woman whose gums are in the process of receding and who already has lost two visible teeth. Their relationship, however, comes to nothing as Nigel's "old man" eccentricities prove too much for her. He wears "string vests" and "bicycle clips," she complains — objects that distinguish him as decidedly un-hip.

I've never heard of such objects and am as ignorant of their un-hip-ness as the girlfriend seems to be of dental floss. But to be fair, when I meet Nigel, I don't use dental floss either. It hasn't yet been deemed an oral hygiene necessity, and according to *The Times*, next to impos-sible to procure in Britain until recently. *Boots*, the chemist, advertises it along with gum massagers and battery-operated toothbrushes for as little as six pence a roll. Still, it will be years until I buy any, several more before I learn the proper way to use it, years and years before it becomes commonplace in England, and over four decades before the lack of firm evidence calls into question its effectiveness and some hard-bitten flossers stop using it altogether.

But for us, the newly formed Young Conservatives of Ilfracombe North Devon — a group I've stumbled into, like some witless party drunk — there are more important things to focus on than microscopic spirochetes writhing and reproducing in the fissures of our teeth.

Cathy, the founder and Chair of our group, is mad to have a baby and desperate to be a wife. She's recently read Orwell's *1984* and shouts "Victory Gin," as she knocks back a glass of *Mother's Ruin.* This literary reference, while it makes her appear intelligent, is something none of us can figure out.

I'm an apolitical immigrant, with unconscious leftist leanings, yet Cathy, my first non-work friend in England, appoints me to be our chapter's Vice Chairman. She says "chairman" rather than "chairperson," or "chairwoman" even though both these words are commonly used and are more appropriate. She also says "people" when she really means "men." For example, when she first got the brainstorm to start the organization and wanted to convince me to join, she said: "Just think of all the *people* we'll meet!" But there aren't a lot of *people* who attend our meetings. In fact, Nigel, with his sparkling teeth, is the only male.

Less than two decades ago, *The Young Conservatives* was a vibrant national organization, with 2,375 branches and a membership peaking at 160,433. Because of its emphasis on social events, it was lampooned as "the best marriage bureau in the country." Good clean fun was the order of the day, where respectable, like-minded young men and women could mingle.

But times have radically changed. Although our small collective doesn't know it, the organization is presently in a state of decay and its reputation is blackening. In years to come, Sir Julian Critchley, a long serving MP and political columnist, will reflect on its demise: "Social change reduced the *Young Conservative Movement* to a steadily diminishing rump of political extremists and libertarians who flirted with legalizing incest and who, at party conferences, bayed drunkenly at the moon."

Our group — composed of four women and Nigel — doesn't need a party conference to get plastered. There are no extended family

members among us, so incest isn't an issue. In various states of inebriation, however, some members confess their fanaticism. One insists
that although Hitler's methods were shocking and atrocious, he was a
hell of a leader; another demands the return of a 14th century style
capital punishment where criminals not only are hanged, drawn, and
quartered, but their dismembered bits are circulated for public view-
ing. I alone howl at the moon. I do it as a coping strategy, to relieve my
social anxiety, but only when it's dark enough outside to obscure my
crooked teeth.

One evening, after drinking copiously and discussing Margaret
Thatcher's handbag, Nigel asks me, as Dennis Thatcher once asked
Margaret, "How are you getting home?" Like the next to-be Conservative Prime Minister, who missed her train on that historic evening
of 1949, I accept the lift. Because I've lost my front door key and my
mother's not in, Nigel takes us for a spin. He drives to a desolate parking lot, which in daylight and during the holiday season is crammed
packed with tourists. No sooner does his car stop than his arms are
struggling to embrace me. Much to my horror, and later regret, in a
state of complete unpreparedness for these amorous advances, I forcefully defend myself.

My defence is firm rather than vicious, strong rather than fierce.
"You've been hurt," he says, meaning my response is the result of past
emotional injury. I'm only minimally skeptical. Heartache looms large
in my emotional landscape as I still hold a flickering torch for a former
boyfriend. Nigel has exposed what I believe to be my hidden suffering.
It never occurs that he could easily deliver this line to virtually any
teenager with the same effect. As Rousseau once wrote: "The adolescent knows about suffering because he himself has suffered, but he
barely knows that other beings also suffer."

For two days, I mourn what I believe to be the loss of Nigel. On
the third, I confide my misery to Cathy only to be told she's been
speaking with him and he's asked her out. To bastardize the famous

Jane Austen line, "it's a truth universally acknowledged that a single man in possession of one female admirer will rapidly attract another," and so it is with Nigel. Cathy, our Young Conservative Chairman, dates him, even though by this time she's conducting a secret affair with another man. Like Nigel, her lover is politically Conservative, but unlike Nigel he's not a young one. In fact, he's a friend of Cathy's grandmother, and is old enough to be Cathy's much older father. Still, Cathy is attracted to Nigel, and she knows that putting all her eggs into one basket might mean none will hatch, and hatching is foremost in her mind.

Nigel at twenty-three is close in age to Cathy. They're both British, both Anglicans, and both share the same political leaning. It makes sense that they should become a couple, even from a miserable jealous perspective. But for whatever reason, the match doesn't ignite, and at the convening of our next Young Conservative meeting, I detect nothing, particularly in Nigel, that leads me to believe it ever might. I'm surprised, however, when he offers to drive me home again, and not being one to blow a second chance, I suggest we go for an evening stroll in the nearby Bicclescombe Park. This is the park where, not too many weeks before, in a moment of insane and somewhat drunken abandon, I jumped into the duck pond. The young man I was with, a former hotel co-worker and platonic scrumpy drinking companion, simply stated: "You're mad!" It's a reputation I'd been cultivating since childhood, not so much as an act of social rebellion but as a defence against my own reserve. As I stroll with Nigel through the park, I'm all too aware of my shortcomings. I don't scintillate with verbal wit and repartee. I don't believe myself physically attractive. I'm self-conscious of my weight, though I'm not heavy, my lisping "s", though I can't hear it, the smallness of my nose, and my teeth … my god … my teeth! They have become a symbol of the disarray of my existence and for a long time now, I've been convinced that if I could just get them straightened, my entire life would align.

In truth, and from the vantage of time's objective distance, my teeth are not nearly as bad as I perceive them. I'd fallen out of a tree, losing my second central incisor, when I was four. This early loss disrupted the natural spacing, making the right lateral incisor grow crooked. I didn't see a dentist until I was nine, by which time I'd successfully sired a mouth full of cavities. Four had ripened into dangerous abscesses, and it was my grade school teacher, not my parents, who'd insisted I get treatment.

My mother, an immigrant from England, dreaded the dentist's office and didn't believe in sending her children there. She lived by her nation's creed of maintaining a stiff upper lip, even when one's teeth had disintegrated to painful and yielding pulp. I was fortunate that mine had remained stable and decay-free since my tenth birthday, even though the cost of straightening them had been prohibitive.

On this dark, chilly evening as I nervously walk next to Nigel, mentally listing all my shortcomings, my defences rear. Should I howl at the waning moon or cut and run for the duck pond?

Many years from now, when my crazy antics of defence are mostly things of the past, I'll see the movie *Addams Family Values* and re-live these angst-filled days. I'll feel a kindred spirit with the socially inept Uncle Fester, who wedges breadsticks up his nose in an attempt to woo the homicidal nanny, Debbie. Like Fester, I was desperate to appeal, yet had no realistic idea how to do so.

Fortunately, before I decided on either "mad" option, Nigel kissed me. "You'll do," he said.

"What do you mean, 'I'll do?'" I asked. "Do for what?" I punched his shoulder, hard.

"I like you," he said, rubbing his arm. "You're tough."

If I'd been more politically astute, I might have impressed him by quoting Thatcher, the soon to be "Iron Lady," whose rhetoric was always steely, even before she became Prime Minister. But my toughness isn't the metallic kind. I don't possess the stalwart character or uncompromising conviction reputed to Thatcher, only an uncommonly durable and crusty shell that houses a bundle of quivering adolescent insecurities, just as tooth enamel and pulp house raw nerve.

DRIVE

MY MIND TAKES ME back to a sweltering summer day in Windsor, Ontario. Heat rising from asphalt: wavy, kinetic. I think of barbecue charcoal. Of ashy embers in a pit. Of the day I'd kicked my buffalo sandals off in the baking grass and tried to cross an expanse of sizzling tarmac to get to the other side of the street. I could smell my flesh burning on that day and the calluses on my heels melting. They remained on the road like chunks of glue, as I screamed and leapt for shade. This occurred in the early 70s, before my father died, before my mother "went crackers" as the British say and moved us to England, and before I could imagine anything worse ever happening to me than burning the soles off my feet.

I'm frequently flooded with memories when I should be focused. They detonate, like an explosive system, one triggering another. Right now, I should be concentrating on the road ahead. I should be scanning the horizon for potential hazards, checking my mirror and speedometer, reading the roadside signs. But the sizzling heat of bygone times lights the fuse, and my mind takes me back to Windsor, to blistering summer days that don't exist in England. "We had joy, we had fun, we had seasons in the sun." The 1974 Terry Jacks hit plays in my head, and the volatile suction of nostalgia draws me back in time to the Fontainebleau subdivision where one of the many "Mikes" in our neighbourhood had just passed his driver's test.

He was driving his mother's car. There were an assortment of other neighbourhood "Mikes" with him, as well as a Robbie and a Ricky, and my old pal Chuck, who once "had the hots" for me and made his move by rolling on top of me as we lounged and talked on a hill in a park. My father was dead by then and my heart broken, as the boy I'd been dating was seeing someone new. "Get the fuck off me, Chuck!" I'd said and he'd rolled away, as gracefully as a sleek race car after a pit stop. But this memory only arises tangentially. The one that possesses the most emotional leaven, the ball joint to which all these others are attached, is the one of Mike and the boys and me, speeding through our neighbourhood of Fontainebleau on this intensely hot Ontario day.

It's 1978, as my mind makes this journey back to Windsor, its heat, its unmitigated despair, and its carload of teenaged boys, a recipe for disaster, joyriding on an all-too-bright morning of some years past. It's never so bright in this British seaside resort of Ilfracombe, North Devon, the place my mother hoped to accelerate her life but found herself tragically stalled. I know I shouldn't be making comparisons, thinking about the past, recalling my burning feet, or terminated seductions, or even the boys in the car, where I return again and again. I should be paying attention to the undulating road, to the voice of my driving instructor, Mrs. Giles, who smokes a woodbine cigarette and barks an occasional command.

For as long as I can remember, I've wanted to drive, to confidently get behind the wheel of a car and propel myself through space. I've wanted the freedom and control a driver's licence offers, the ability to escape a bad situation and travel somewhere safe. My mother didn't drive at all and had always been staunchly against the idea of girls driving. In Ontario, I dreamed of taking a driver's education course in high school. It was the only promising light I saw. But when I confided my fantasy to my mother, she told me "if wishes were horses then beggars would ride." It was a fighting point that smouldered. It had nothing to do with horses, I insisted, and everything to do with cars. But then I became a high school dropout and the point was moot. Still, there were avenues open to me. Girlfriends whose boyfriends had passed their driving tests. Girlfriends whose boyfriends could be persuaded to teach me how to drive. My girlfriends, themselves, had no great ambitions to become licensed drivers. Still, my joy and hope could not be dampened. Where there was a will, there was always a way, I believed, frequently to my mother's consternation.

As I try to rein in my Windsor memories, Mrs. Giles and I travel up and down the bends and curves of outlying Ilfracombe. We pass miles of ancient dry stacked walls, grey as graphite, persistent and hypnotic. I'm oblivious to the fact that these slate, mortarless walls were erected by property owners in the 1500s, an effort to distinguish boundaries on formerly common land. Windsor, Ontario, was centuries from existing when these walls were ingeniously constructed. Canada itself was not yet a twinkle in mother England's eye. My age as much as my ignorance prevents my guileless wonder. History as well as youth is wasted on the young, though the past, the relatively recent past, with all its triumphs and its foibles, isn't always wasted.

As we motor along a narrow road and my mind sinks back to Windsor, I try to precisely recall events, and how it was I'd ended up in Mike's mother's car. It may have been Chuck who instigated my inclusion, but I'm uncertain. I just remember someone saying, "get in," and dazed, depressed, perhaps even semi-suicidal, I had done exactly as I

was told. There was a case of beer on the floor in the backseat — or
a two-four as we underaged drinkers called it — mimicking the hard-
bitten boozers who wore steel toed boots and made good money working at the local automotive plants.

I was handed a bottle and a cap opener. The car radio blared. CKLW,
the A.M. station that battered our brains with a continuous replay of
its top ten, wasn't as cool as the hard rock FM stations, but the recep-
tion was always less fuzzy. Mike's mother's Ford Galaxie wasn't cool
either, but Mike didn't care. The coolness of chugging bottles of beer
in a speeding car compensated for everything.

All the windows were down, I recall. A warm breeze gusted
through the vehicle. Cigarette packages were removed from t-shirt
sleeves. BiC lighters flared. Smoke poured like grey tributaries above
the rivers of wide, flat, smooth streets.

Unlike Ilfracombe and its surrounds, there were no narrow curva-
ceous roads with blind sharp bends in our Windsor subdivision. There
were no perpendicular hills and valleys, no emergency runaway roads
in case of failing brakes, no laybys, no cattle grids. If there's such a
thing as manual transmission in Windsor, I never experienced it. All
the cars I ever came in contact with were large automatics; all the cars
I ever travelled in were left-hand drive, but Mrs. Giles' car is tiny compared to North American standards. It's a British Leyland vehicle, a
manual, which despite her good instruction, I find incredibly difficult
to operate.

The steering wheel placement is on the wrong side of the car and
traffic beetles past, at seeming breakneck speeds, on the wrong side
of the road. When horsepower came strictly from the beast, driving
on the left was the international norm, but I know nothing of this. I
know nothing of the fact that even in Canada some provinces drove
on the left-hand side and that Newfoundland only changed its driving
practices from left to right in 1947.

There are approximately eighty-one other countries that still drive on the left in the year I take this driving lesson, but I know nothing of them, and even if Mrs. Giles does, she's not here to teach me history or geography or cultural studies. She's here, strictly, to teach me how to drive.

She will not tell me, as the *Daily Mail* newspaper will claim in the 1980s, that driving on the left side of the road "dates back to sword-bearing days when highway travel was a perilous business" and drivers of horses, coaches, and carriages had to keep their right hands free in case of attack. Nor will she apprise me of the fact that the reason why the international norm changed has to do with Napoleon (a southpaw) and his strategic preferences, which he spread with each of his conquests.

Although I'm curious about the whys and wherefores of British driving, I know better than to ask Mrs. Giles. When my mother and I first moved to Ilfracombe and lived with my uncle, I'd made the mistake of asking him why in England they drive on the wrong side of the road. He, generally good natured and calm, bristled: "It's you bloody lot in North America who have it wrong." I imagined Mrs. Giles, not being related and of a temperament that was obviously not accustomed to suffering fools gladly, being even more severe.

Like so many of the older British women I would meet, she was tough, no-nonsense and had served her country during World War II. She may have flown planes, or made explosives, or plotted the course of warships. She may have fought fires, milked cows, drove ambulances, or done a myriad of other jobs that women did to feed the nation and win the war. While the government deemed it unacceptable for women to be directly involved in killing, many British women did "man" anti-aircraft guns and picked off enemy planes and even though prohibited, carried revolvers and learned to shoot.

In the 70s, as Mrs. Giles barks her driving commands — "clutch, gear-down, clutch, gear up, gear up, overtake" — I know nothing of the role British women played in World War II. However, I wouldn't have been surprised to discover an arsenal of weaponry in her trunk — or as the British call it, "boot."

As we motor along the acceptably hazardous roads, I can't stop myself from wondering what she'd think of me if she knew about that day in Windsor when the mercury soared, and Mike's mother's car did too. Flying over wide expanses of black. Our sticky flesh clinging to upholstery. Our hair, for we all wore it long, whipping up in snake-like tendrils, charmed by the danger and audacity of our flight. I believe it happened two years before Ontario made North American history by insisting drivers wear seatbelts. Noncompliance to that law was highest in Windsor, according to behavioural science researcher Dr. Leon Robertson. And as for teenagers, "a group disproportionately involved in severe crashes," Robertson said, "the law had no apparent effect." But even before the law was passed, teens across Ontario eschewed the belt.

What could be more fun than flying, unbelted, in the air, roaring around a suburban neighbourhood in Canada with beer to fuel you and youth to either armour you against any lingering doubt of your immortality, or in my case, strip away any remaining shards of self-preservation. The speed limit in the subdivision may have been 25 miles an hour. Whatever it was, people always drove faster. There was always discussion that the limit should be reduced further, that more law enforcement was required. Yet these discussions meant nothing to us as we bombed around the generous residential streets of Fontainebleau, down Queen Elizabeth, and Rivard, and back again with the velocity of a race car, swilling, whenever we could steady the amber jugs to our lips, frothy beer. The breakneck ride shook the bottles we held between our thighs. Our free hands, the ones without cigarettes, reflexively clasped the tops. There was amazingly no spillage as we sailed along, airborne, with Mike our pilot, laughing hysterically every time he took a bend, and Chuck's or Robby's or one of the other Mikes' heads smashed against a window.

"Can I drive?" I shouted to Mike. Even though I was too young to get a learner's permit, I was confident I was every bit as good a driver as him.

Mike wasn't one of my girlfriend's boyfriends. "No way, Jane Jetson!" he shouted back. I regularly watched *The Jetsons* when I was little and seemed to recall Jane as a nightmare driver. She drove a spaceship, not a car, though Mike's car could easily have passed for a spaceship, the way it flew.

Mrs. Giles' car rarely flies, though sometimes as we descend a steep hill, it feels as though we're hovering. My stomach lurches to my throat and I become weightless. "Floater airtime" is the name for this phenomenon, though I've not heard the term and don't know that it's caused by the reduction in gravity that occurs as one accelerates at the crest of a hill. Mrs. Giles and I wear seatbelts, even though we're not legally obliged to do so. They hold us in place, preventing too much levitation during airtime, and make sense to me here in a way they never did in Ontario. Perhaps it's because I've matured, or maybe because the roads are far more treacherous in Ilfracombe and I've come to value my life a little bit more. Perhaps it's because I'm, at last, taking driving lessons, paying for them myself, and not only can I see light at the end of the tunnel, but soon I imagine, if I play my cards right, I'll be able to legally drive there and meet it.

"Gear up, gear up, gear up, drive along," Mrs. Giles commands, her Woodbine still connected to her lips, her eagle eyes scanning the road ahead.

"Cretin," she intermittently huffs when a driver fails to signal a turn, or signals without turning, or stops without signalling.

In our travels, and we have had many over the course of a year, we never once see a vehicle packed with drunken hooligans burning rubber and scorching tar. We never once see cars exceeding the speed limit or recklessly steering. It makes me wonder what Mrs. Giles might say of me if she had a crystal ball, if she could access my driving past.

I don't even want to think of Windsor with her sitting beside me. I try to stop myself from seeing us plunge through the stratosphere with beer and cigarettes and the radio blaring *B-B-B-Bennie and the Jets*. I don't want to see Mike at the wheel, turning crazily, jumping curbs, making us shriek.

"Gear down. Down! Clutch! Clutch!" Mrs. Giles' voice has become severe.

A truck — a lorry as the British say — perches in a bend on the crest of a hill. I fight to remain present, as the undertow of Fontaine-bleau pulls me back. Some bales of hay have tumbled from the truck, and the vehicle now blocks the twisting precarious road ahead.

According to the *Daily Mail*, despite the three-fold increase of traffic since 1958, people are 70% safer on British roads this year. There are now motorways and better driving instruction than there were twenty years ago, better car designs, and better laws. But none of these things address my malady of inattention. None of these things prevent me from slipping back in time and perceiving a younger, careless, joy-riding me and in so doing, becoming careless once again.

I'm still a teenager when I live in North Devon, though perhaps the trajectory of my life has forced me to be less reckless. I need to get up early every morning for work and would most likely be sacked if I brought shame upon the establishment that pays my wage. I want adults like Mrs. Giles to have a good opinion of me. I want them to believe me worthy of their effort and care, but in this moment, as the lorry driver wrestles the hay back onto his truck, despite my best efforts, I find myself with the carload of Mikes, thoughtlessly racing through a populated thoroughfare.

Risks are higher in crowded areas, there's more likelihood of collision, of killing people, or as the local paper regularly and obliquely reports, of cars hitting telephone poles, as if it were the cars themselves and not their reckless drivers that perpetrate the act. There's more of a likelihood that someone will see us, and "call the cops," as they say in Windsor, yet Mike leads us into this area, perhaps testing his invincibility. He rockets past streaks of startled pedestrians and drivers, tires screeching, CKLW cranked to the max. It's like the game of chicken these boys sometimes play in the park, mounted on each other's shoulders, as horse and rider. Even though they know they will be injured, they grab at shirts, arms, faces, hair and wildly pull. Though they are the best of friends, they behave as if they were mortal enemies. They have no regard for the damage they do and are always guilelessly surprised by the concussions, dislocated shoulders, broken ribs, and chipped vertebrae that follow.

Perhaps I, as the only girl in the car, should assume the role of voice of reason. Stereotypes that will persist over time would have it this way. However, I'm enjoying my beer, enjoying the flight, enjoying the adrenaline rush, as we run a red light, speeding through an intersection.

If Mrs. Giles could see this memory unfolding, I can't imagine what she'd do. Throw me out of the vehicle? Call me "cretin"? Tell me that it would be perfidious to bestow a driving licence on such an unworthy cur? It's the Queen, after all, who confers each licence in the land. Wouldn't assisting one as culpable as me be treasonous?

"Gear up, gear up, gear up, drive along," Mrs. Giles directs, resuming equanimity as I slip back in time again, no longer in the Fontainebleau subdivision, but still with Mike swerving past slow-moving cars on a main Windsor road, as the buzzing noise of the radio, no longer music, sounds like a cardiac monitor flatlining.

In 1974, alcohol impairment is the most common cause of automobile fatalities, though scant research exists that examines the role of the underage drinkers in this finding. *The Globe and Mail* reported that "half of US high school students drank alcohol at least once a month and more than half of those who drank have driven at least

once while intoxicated." Even if I'd been aware of this statistic, it's unlikely that it would conjure the image of Mike at the helm of our
rocket ship laughing manically as we crazily chug beer and fly through
Windsor's busy thoroughfares.

It will be years before such terms that attempt to explain the personality of drunken drivers, such as *sensation seeking* and *reward sensitivity*, find their way into my lexicon. Labels and abstractions will
never sum up the feeling of liberation that travelling in a car, on the
knife edge of life, with beer and the garble of radio tunes on that red-
hot Windsor day produced.

As I follow Mrs. Giles' instructions, curving around bends on the
monotonous, narrow road ahead, observing hills and valleys and the
rusty red soil of the Devonian farmlands' patchwork, my eyes begin to
grow heavy and I feel them wanting to flicker shut. Unlike that fateful
joyride in Windsor, when even sated with beer, I was wide awake, these
driving lessons, despite my excitement to learn, inevitably become
wearying. I rise before the sun each morning to start my working day.
When my chambermaid job ends, I do a two-hour stint working in the
hotel's laundry room, then later in the evening, another two hours
serving tea. Even though income tax sucks back most of it, I need the
extra money for the lessons, but frequently find myself exhausted. I've
tried going to bed earlier, but I toss and turn, remaining alert well past
midnight.

In these years, it's universally assumed that sleepy teens, who cannot easily roust themselves from morning slumber and appear
incapable of going to bed at a decent time, do so because they've
either fallen into bad habits or because they're rebellious. When I
lived in Canada, after I stopped going to school, if my mother didn't
wake me, I'd frequently sleep well into the afternoon. My laziness, as
it was deemed, became yet another arguing point between us. "The
sun's almost set," my mother complained, "and what have you accomplished today?"

On the brilliant, sun-drenched day in Windsor, when Mike, our galactic chauffeur took us beyond the edges of our subdivision, the only thing I'd accomplished that morning was moving, zombie-like, into his car and opening a bottle of beer. Perhaps all of us who'd embarked upon this journey had suffered the harassment of parents, perhaps each of us would have been better off sleeping the day away, instead of taking to the streets in a machine that can be used as a lethal weapon.

I fight to keep my eyes open in Mrs. Giles' car, fight to prevent myself from tumbling back to Windsor, and fight to appear completely present. I wish to convey the image of a responsible, wide-awake person, totally interested and engaged in these relentless miles of curving road. I've never heard the term *circadian rhythm* and even though the term exists in scientific literature, its likely Mrs. Giles has never heard it either.

Well in the future, researchers will discover that teenagers have different sleep-wake cycles than adults, that the slumber-inducing hormone, melatonin, is released later in the day, making late nights and mornings the natural biological norm. But even after science exposes this phenomenon, there will still be no consensus on why the teens who do it perceive joyriding while intoxicated such a glorious way to spend time.

Even though the rock band Kiss' album *Dressed To Kill* has not yet been recorded when we take our joyride, their soon-to-be anthem with the famous lyric: "I want to rock and roll all night, and party every day" is already a refrain among teenagers in the Fontainebleau subdivision. And for some of us, it will remain the chorus we sing for the rest of our lives.

Before I move to England, before the summer beer-fueled joyride, my failed seducer, Chuck, told me of an adventure in which he and Mike piloted a car — not their own — into the projects and through the brick wall of a townhouse. They found themselves in the living room of a woman in curlers, watching TV.

I laughed uproariously, thinking nothing of the trauma the woman in curlers must have experienced or the court date Chuck must inevitably face, but in 1978 it's as if I've taken a detour from party town and I'm no longer travelling that road. In North Devon, my life course has dramatically changed, though I'm not yet cognizant of this fact. As I drive along with Mrs. Giles, I'm mindful only of wanting to be sober and conscientious, wanting to stay awake and alert in the immediate moment, and hoping to unfetter myself from the undertow of Windsor memories which have grasped me so tightly that I'm finding them increasingly difficult to resist.

I can't stop myself from hearing the police siren, of seeing the surprised and frightened look on driver Mike's face as the OPP cruiser pulls out from the flow of traffic, still eating our dust, and begins its valiant chase.

Mike swerves suddenly down a side street that leads to a rural stretch and shouts for us to throw our beer bottles out the window. Reckless driving, driving while impaired, can cost the perpetrator $200 and a three-month licence suspension. What's far more terrifying for Mike and the rest of us, however, is that our parents will be told. Our parents will be hauled down to the police station, humiliated, beyond angry, and we, eventually, will be released to them.

In this year of our joyride, children are regularly thrashed by adults, struck with straps and extension cords, and at the public school we all once attended, the principal Mr. Perry's hard wooden cricket bat. Some of the boys in the car, like Chuck, after elaborate beatings have already been threatened with wilderness camps and military schools, with the spectre of daily discipline served up without the pretence of filial restraint, without one's friends, compatriots, and partners in crime.

"What should I do?" driver Mike shouts, swerving down another country lane, knowing that it's only a matter of minutes before the OPP finds us.

"Stop the car!" I shout, possessed with an authority Jane Jetson never seized. "Turn the radio off."

Mike looks as if he might cry. He's willing to do anything. He snaps the radio's knob and slams on the brakes, the car skids to a stop.

"Put the two-four in the trunk," I command, and Mike does so, as if he no longer has any will. As if he's become an automaton.

Once he's seated again in the car, I tell him to drive along, just as Mrs. Giles is telling me. "Drive along. Drive along," I say. "Don't look scared and don't look guilty."

The police car rounds a bend, its siren singing and its flashing red cherry whirling.

"Pull over," I tell Mike.

"Are you crazy?" one of the other Mikes asks.

"Pull over," I repeat from the back, crushed up against two sweating frightened boys, instinctively knowing, it seems, what we need to do.

Again, Mike does what I say. He pulls over, the cop parks behind us and takes a few minutes to lumber wearily to the car.

"Licence?" he asks, scanning the car's interior.

Mike, suddenly sane, seemingly sober and completely obsequious says, "Yes, sir," and withdraws some paper from his wallet.

"Just got your licence, son?" the cop observes, his gaze moving from boy to boy, then landing and remaining on me.

"Yes, officer. I'm a new driver," Mike says, sounding like the wholesome character John-boy from the television show *The Waltons*.

"You were moving a little fast there, son," the cop says.

"It won't happen again, sir," Mike affirms.

The cop's eyes hold me. I don't know what he's thinking about my inclusion in this car. I don't know if my being here is making things easier for Mike or worse, but then the cop winks at Mike lasciviously. "You boys showing the girl a good time?" he asks.

"Yes, sir," Mike says.

"Okay," the cop says. "Don't let me catch you speeding again."

"You won't, officer," Mike politely responds.

The cop hands the paper back to Mike; he turns towards his vehicle.

"Thank you, sir," Mike shouts after him.

It's as if everyone in Mike's mother's car is holding their breath, until the cop pulls away.

"Thank you, sir," someone breaks the silence with a high-pitched effeminate voice. "Want a blow job, sir?" Everyone but Mike, the driver, laughs.

According to *The Globe and Mail*, in 1974, even though impaired drivers were responsible for most car accident fatalities, the chances of police pulling one over was less than one in 7,500. Slimmer still, the odds they'd be charged. Proportionately, drivers under twenty-four, who made up only one-fifth of the driving population, had thirty-six percent of all deadly car accidents. "And the truly bad news," according to journalist Dick Brown, is that "more young people, more kids, are drinking."

But this is not bad news for us on that summer's day in which we've escaped the police. We feel fortunate we know older people who will supply us with beer, that the homes we live in have well-stocked wet bars or liquor cabinets, and a missing bottle is rarely noticed. In 1974 most of our parents, as is common of parents across the North American continent, purchase alcohol regularly and drink it copiously. We also feel happy that cops, like the one who stopped us, recall their halcyon days and don't interfere with ours.

As I travel along with Mrs. Giles, I force myself awake. I stop myself from thinking of wrong turns and detours, locate myself in the here and now, and cautiously set my sights on the road ahead.

EXPRESSIONS OF THE UNUTTERABLE

MY GRANDMOTHER'S DAY as a domestic servant "of all work" began at sunrise. She would have opened her employers' curtains on her way to their kitchen, where she'd start the fire, laid for the previous night. She'd warm her hands before polishing the range, and once clean, put the kettle on. While the water was boiling, she'd shine the family's boots. She'd clean the dining room before breakfast, which included brushing yesterday's ash from the fireplace, scouring the grate, fire irons and fender, and shaking the hearth rug before setting a new fire ablaze. She'd sprinkle damp tea leaves from yesterday's breakfast onto the carpet, and then with a firm bristled brush, sweep them up, dirt-covered, into a dustpan. Next, she'd clean hallways, whiten the front porch step, and tend to the fireplace in the sitting room. If the employers' baby woke, she'd take him with her while she gave her hands and face a brisk scrub in a basin, changed her apron, and prepared the family's breakfast. She'd feed and clean the baby, in-between serving the family meal, then clear up the dishes to wash, clean and air out bedrooms, turn mattresses, make beds, empty the chamber pots and swill them with water and soda before rushing back to the kitchen to begin preparations for tea.

She'd collapse in bed long after the family had retired for the night. She owned a small black prayer book, which she'd inscribed with her name, and I imagine her praying as sleep drew a veil over her day. I imagine her startled slumber, dream fragments of her falling down the stairs, of dishes and babies tumbling from her hands, of ashes blowing back into her face as a rogue wind turned against her. What I don't imagine my grandmother ever doing is questioning her lot in life, of resisting the social systems that enslaved her.

It was during a particularly bad service, before I'd quit my job at the Molesworth Hotel, in Ilfracombe, North Devon, that I began thinking of my ancestors. My grandmother had died shortly before we moved to England. Her grave was right behind the house my mother, little brother, and I lived in. She shared my name and I imagined the life she must have led. I hoped wherever she might be now, she wasn't working as hard as me and that she wasn't being bullied.

The feisty waitress at the Molesworth, Elaine, had been sacked and the sous chef, Lynne, had walked out in solidarity. Lynne had been so competent that we used to joke she possessed many sets of arms like the Hindu goddesses who battle cosmic forces. No mortal with a single pair of hands could possibly dish up grub like she did. On frantic nights, when the dining room was crammed to overflow and a roast beef dinner with all the trimmings was on the menu, Lynne's performance was a feat to behold. She opened ovens with her ankles, slammed cupboards with her hips, and from way across the kitchen tossed Yorkshire puddings two and sometimes three at a time which never failed to land precisely on the appropriate plates. She could fill a row of ten gravy boats in one continuous motion, without so much as spattering a drip, and then with swift, deft knife swipes, carve slices of rare, medium, and well-done meat, all, seemingly, at once. Her replacement, Edwin Vile, was forty-five, lived with his father and before coming to the Molesworth had never worked a day in his life. In future months his father will be found dead. Edwin will be a murder suspect. However, when he first comes to the Molesworth, the only thing he's suspected of is gross incompetence.

Like Tolstoy's happy families, good services are all alike, but bad services are bad in their own ways, and the service in which I'd evoked the memory of my grandmother was, from the outset, a disaster. Not only couldn't Edwin multitask, he also seemed incapable of processing our requests. Before Lynne left, we'd fly into the kitchen, shouting our orders pell-mell, confident that she or the chef had heard us, but Edwin repeated and repeated what we said, pretending it was for clarification, when in fact it was simply a stalling tactic. The added words befuddled us and made us second guess everything. The kitchen was like an oven, and even when the manager came to help scoop potatoes, we all had the sense that time had been stretched out of shape, that we were walking through molasses. Chris, the chef, who during even the best services would fume and insult everyone, grew beyond irate. Even though he could plainly see that Edwin was at fault for the chaotic service, he began to verbally attack the wait staff as well. "Pull the sticks out of your arses, you cretins," he shouted. He referred to the most senior waitress, Lilian, as an "old whore."

He called Edwin a "bleedin' twit," and then embroidered on that epitaph for everyone: We were "bleedin' bloody arse twits," "bleedin' bloody arse cretin twits," and "bleedin' bloody arse cretin twits who should be taken out into the alley and hanged, drawn and quartered."

I was new to England and hadn't been working long at the Molesworth, but already knew that no matter how vicious Chris's verbal assaults, we were meant to endure them. When I'd first asked Lilian why, she'd said "Because 'ees the chef," and the waitress Janice had chimed in, "You can't run a kitchen wifout a chef."

Later, I'd discover it was also because Chris did a good job for very little money. It was rumoured among the staff that he'd spoiled his chances of a better job through some kind of legal trouble, though no one seemed to know exactly what that was. The owner gave him an extremely low bi-weekly amount to run the kitchen and whatever he was able to save, he could put in his pocket. He'd fish and collect mushrooms and blackberries for the hotel. He'd make deals with all the local merchants. The meals he cooked were far better than the owner expected, and he was adamant that the chef, no matter how he raged and blinded, should stay.

Chris was the king of the kitchen, and his explosions of rage and verbal abuse were perks the owner, for the most part, allowed. "'E don't mean nothin' by it," more than one waitress assured me, but in my first days at the hotel, he'd been so insulting that I'd served most of the meals through tears.

As I listened to him carry on during this particularly bad service, I thought, for the first time, about my poor grandmother, how hard she must have worked as a servant at the turn of the century, and all that she must have endured, and tears pricked my eyes again, not tears of hurt, but tears of fury. The kitchen sweltered like a hot Ontario summer, and my clothes clung to my flesh with perspiration. Everything was out of synch, and by the time the meals got to the tables, they were dry and tasteless, and the guests complained. I was so on edge that I accidently burned my hands and broke a cup, the cost of which would be deducted from my wage. That's why when the hulking Chris shouted over the hotplate, "Stir your stumps you gormless Canadian scrubber," something broke inside of me and I couldn't hold it back.

I felt the blood rush to my face. I pushed my body, threateningly, across the hotplate. "If you can't take the goddamned heat," I shrieked, "get out of the goddamned kitchen you bastard!"

There was a huge collective gasp. It was as if all sound evaporated. Edwin stopped repeating orders, the waitresses stopped clattering plates, the manager stopped scooping potatoes as his worried eyes sought mine. "What have you done?" they seemed to ask. I felt my grandmother's presence, just as surely as if she were standing in the room.

Chris's astonished angry glare was incapable of finding a target to fix to. His face contorted, and I awaited the blast I was certain would follow, but the blast wasn't the vitriolic stream of wounding expletives I imagined; it was an explosion of laughter. "I can't believe you said that," he roared, doubling over, tears filling his eyes. Nervously, tentatively, others began laughing. "If you can't take the goddamned heat…" he repeated, breathlessly, attempting my Midwestern-Canadian accent. "I can't believe you said that." Somehow, following this encounter, Chris seemed to like me better. In fact, even after I left the Molesworth and took a job in another hotel, we remained very good friends and would meet weekly at the local pub to drink lager and to catch up. "I still can't believe you said that," Chris (who by now insisted I call him Uncle Chris) would still occasionally recall, laughing.

He knew that my mother, disillusioned with England, had sold her new home and was packing for Canada, and one night, after knocking back several pints at our favourite pub, Chris became emotional. "You know that when your mum leaves, you won't be alone. You know I'll always watch out for you, just like I was your real uncle." Even though he slurred his words, it was touching. He made me feel safe and cared for, and I valued his friendship more than I valued most things.

One night after a pub crawl, he drove me home and I invited him in to meet my mother. He said he'd always wanted to, and I knew, with her moving back to Canada, there wouldn't be many more opportunities. Because the house had sold much more quickly than she'd expected, she was in a state of being overwhelmed. At first, she was angry that I'd shattered her solitude and brought this drunken stranger in, but Chris took her plump pale hand in his, lifted it to his lips, and kissed it. "I see where your daughter gets her good looks," he said authentically. My mother tittered, "get away with ya," she said and swatted him. I was surprised when she invited him into the living room, that she offered him her chair. I was surprised at the way they talked to each other, like old friends, recalling the old days. They talked about their childhoods and World War II, and I realized for the first time that Chris was of my mother's generation, not of mine.

My mother had a stash of American beer that she kept hidden under her bed with tins of cookies and other items that she feared I might plunder. I was astounded when she retrieved the beer for all of us to drink. I'd never seen my mother so affable, so charmed, so flirtatious. I knew Chris was married, but I wondered from the way he was carrying on if he had romantic intentions and was going to invite her on a date, and then he did, kind of. "Before you go back to Canada, I'd like to show you around Combe Martin."

"Would you?" my mother asked, popping another ring on a can of beer for him. "That would be lovely!"

He stayed until the wee hours of the morning, and just before he staggered out the door, he got all mushy again, and told my mother how she needn't worry about leaving me in England, how he felt like an uncle towards me and would always look out for me. My mother wasn't particularly anxious about leaving me; in fact, it was more likely that she was relieved that I wouldn't be a drain on her anymore, but she accepted Chris's avowal with appropriate sentiment. "It's good to know you're watching over her."

Chris staggered out the door, then tripped, and shouted some unintelligible obscenity before getting into his car and very, very slowly driving away.

I didn't consciously envision them then; in fact, it's only in the last few years that I've been interested in my great-grandmother, Angelina, and her mother, Ann, and have started doing research on their lives. Whenever I think of England and drunkenness now, I see Ann and

Angelina in my mind's eye and imagine them sober in 1878. I see Angelina travelling by train to London with her infant son who will become my grandmother's eldest brother.

Angelina's mother, Ann, like my mother, will become a widow. In 1878, Ann lives in a small run-down dwelling on Colonade, Clare Market, which is west of London's largest public square. She has most probably never seen her grandson, and Angelina, who likely swore off alcohol when she married, may have been feeling particularly parched, although it's unlikely it would have been her conscious intention to come to London to take up drinking again.

The place of Clare Market in 1878, for at least the past hundred years, has had a nefarious reputation. The streets are poorly lit and like the corridors in a maze, narrow with many bulkheads. For the longest time, no police ventured into this area, only watchmen — and these were generally not robust souls, but ancient and impoverished men who gained much more by working with criminals than by attempting to bring them to justice. Things marginally improved when many of the dangerous streets and alleyways were razed for the construction of new Law Courts. The erection of an orphanage, a needlewoman's house, a soup-kitchen and a mission with a chapel also did much to lift at least the feel of villainy that the district exuded. However, the general filth of the streets compounded with pickpockets and blaspheming drunkards conspired to assure that the bad character of the neighbourhood would be preserved.

It was on a Saturday night, just following the pagan festival of Lupercalia, when a full moon rose round and bright into the dome of darkness above Clare Market. The February 17, 1878 edition of *Lloyd's Weekly News* with its sensational opening, "Shocking Depravity and Dissipation," sets the scene. I imagine Angelina and her mother sat indoors on a wooden bench, side by side, at the pub the paper identifies as the *Tailor's Arm*. They'd be fussing over Fred, I imagine. He'd be tired and unable to settle in his mother's lap.

"A bit a gatter will set him right," Ann might say, ordering a beer, twisting and dipping the handkerchief she habitually tucked up her sleeve into the pint glass and pushing the soggy end into his mouth. "'Ere ya go, my little poppet."

Family lore labels both Ann and Angelina as alcoholics, and although the term *alcoholism* was first coined in 1849, the term used to describe substance addictions in this year that Angelina and her mother visit this pub is "inebriety." According to historian Thora Hands, "inebriety" gained popularity as a "disease concept," which allowed for "diagnosing and medically treating" heavy drinkers through the 1870s.

Shortly after this visit, Angelina won't be able to resist the bottle. Eventually she'll succumb to chronic drunkenness, violent outbursts, and *blue devils* as drinkers call delirium tremens. She'll be committed to Whittingham Lunatic Asylum and spend most of the rest of her life there. But on this day in 1878, the unknowable future can't blight the present moment. Rather, it would be her current concerns that cause anxiety, like how she'll resist her persuasive mother who I imagine saying: "Surely, you won't have me taking a drop all on me owny-o."

I imagine Angelina would already know that once she started drinking, it was difficult to stop. I imagine her drinking had already revealed itself as a problem and that she was worried that her husband, Frederick, might find out if she capitulated to her mother's request.

"Blast bleedin' Fredrick," I hear Ann say. "How often is it that you gets to come out to the pub with your mum?"

In 1878, public houses abound in this area of London and temperance recruits claim that the working classes spent more on alcohol than rent. Lexicographer John Camden Hotten points out in his dictionary of slang, that after money, terms that have to do with drink are most plentiful, "from small beer to champagne; and next, as a very natural sequence, intoxication, and fuddlement generally, with some half a hundred vulgar terms, graduating the scale of drunkenness from a slight inebriation, to the soaky state of gutterdom and stretcherdom."

One can be "Berry, Bemused, Boozy, Bosky, Buffy, Corned, Foggy, Fou, Fresh, Hazy, Elevated, Kisky, Lushy, Moony, Muggy, Muzzy, On, Screwed, Stewed, Tight, and Winey." Or when past the point of tipsy, "Podgy, Beargered, Blued, Cut, Primed, Lumpy, Ploughed, Muddled, Obfuscated, Swipey,…and Top Heavy." When one's blind drunk, one "can't see a hole in a ladder" and is all "mops and brooms." They are "off their nut" or have a "main brace well spliced." They have "lapped the gutter," acquired a "gravel rash," and have moved from "chirping merry" to "mauled."

It's likely that Ann is familiar with many of these slang terms in 1878. She makes her living with her needle, hand-sewing shirts for gentlemen, which is especially grueling work at this time of year, when days are growing shorter and natural light scarcer, but drink is relatively cheap. It warms the bones and numbs the mind and makes a body forget all about its aches and pains. It anesthetizes the many who want anesthetization. It becomes their reward at the end of the day.

In my mind's eye, I see both Ann and Angelina feeling brighter for the drink. I see them ordering a second, then a third round. Ordering and emptying tankards of beer.

Little Fred, I imagine, passes out with Ann's handkerchief still in his mouth, and Ann and Angelina continue to drink.

"I'm feeling a bit tiddly," Ann may finally confess, though by now it's turfing out time, and the two rise from their benches. Perhaps Ann can't hold her liquor as well as Angelina and threatens to collapse.

"For pity sake," Angelina might say. "Grab hold of me arm, mum," and Ann might hoist her sodden body up and drape her arm over her daughter.

In my mind's eye, Angelina is able to get Ann out into the night air, but then she reels, like a top, away from her. "Steady on, mum," Angelina calls, unable to grab her because Fred is still sleeping heavily and soundly in her arms. A male patron emerges from the pub. He's a lanky, affable-looking fellow, a stone mason, he later says, and he's obviously quite drunk himself, but he's got hold of Ann and brings her back to Angelina.

"Mind how you go, ole girl," he laughs.

Angelina asks him if he'd help get her mother home. There's no way she could manage on her own, and the man, who introduced himself as Miles, says he'd be happy to oblige. Ann drapes her arm over Miles' shoulder, and the three of them weave through the dim streets, illuminated by the eerie glowing moon. *Lloyd's Weekly News* reports that Miles, who himself is "drunk to a merry pin," assists in getting Ann to bed at the flat. Angelina thanks him, bids him goodbye, goes to a separate room and pushes the door shut. No sooner has she relieved her arms of Fred than her door is flung open violently, and Miles, despite her attempts to shove the door closed, forces his way in.

When my mother moves back to Canada, I don't miss her, nor do I ever plan on visiting her. I go to see Uncle Chris, though, who never did take my mother on the promised excursion to Combe Martin. He and I still meet regularly at the pub, though later than usual, on Fridays, as I've enrolled in an evening English Literature class at the comprehensive school. None of my grade nine Canadian high school credits mean anything, and it's my intention to earn an "O" level. I'm ambitious about education because I want to be a writer. When I first speak with the teacher, Jackie, she comments, "that's very admirable." We're outside and she's smoking cocktail cigarettes, which are pastel pink and mauve. She usually rolls her own, she explains, but these "pretty ones" had been a gift. She doesn't like the fact she's not allowed to smoke inside the college and suggests that because there are only three students (me, Cathy, Cora) that we assemble at her home.

Over the weeks we meet at her house. We read *Brighton Rock* and *The Spy Who Came in from the Cold*, but my favourite book by far is *Tess of the d'Urbervilles*, by Thomas Hardy, and although I find the protagonist Tess embarrassingly naïve, I relate to her, because she's female and because she's a teenager. At Jackie's house, in our self-styled class, we smoke and speak about the ravishment of Tess: Was it seduction or was it rape? This question is one which scholars still debate. All we know is that "darkness and silence ruled everywhere around," and that Tess was sleeping in the forest when Alec found her and warmed his face with her breath.

Cathy doesn't think it was rape, but Cora isn't sure and wants to know how Jackie is using the word seduction. I find it difficult to engage in this discussion because I think that Tess should have appreciated Alec more. He'd been good to her, good to her family, and why, if she didn't care for him in a romantic way, did she let him help her so much? Why did she allow him to ride into the forest with her, and why did she let him put his arms around her waist? Why did it take her so long to realize they'd travelled far from the road, and why when she did finally realize this, did she agree to trust Alec to find their way back again? The fact that this novel was written in the late 1800s and that women — especially young women — had even greater impediments to personal agency than modern women doesn't influence my reading one jot. It will be years before I discover the way human judgment always coalesces around the social mores of the time, years before I hear the term "blame the victim" and understand that I have inculcated the values and viewpoints of the patriarchal society in which I live.

Victorian law defined rape as "the offence of having unlawful and carnal knowledge of a woman by force, against her will," and Mew's *Digest of English Case Law* added, "to constitute rape, it is not necessary that the connection with the woman should be had against her will; it is sufficient if it is without her consent." Among the circumstances in which it's deemed impossible for a woman to give her consent is when she's sleeping, and therefore, Tess is most decidedly raped.

Hardy, however, never spells this out for us because he wants us to feel the ambiguity that Tess herself must have felt. Tess has also inculcated the values and viewpoints of the patriarchal culture, though, significantly, no knowledge of the law. If she hadn't gone with Alec, if she hadn't depended on his protection....But we never hear Tess blame herself in such direct and outright terms. What Tess feels is never stated, though her belief in her own culpability, which mirrors the unspoken belief of her society, is always implied.

Hardy lifts the culpability for Tess's rape into the celestial realm: "Where was Tess's guardian angel? Where was the providence of her simple faith? Perhaps, like that other god of whom the ironical Tishbite spoke, he was talking, or he was pursuing, or he was in a journey, or he was sleeping and not to be awaked."

I didn't believe in guardian angels when discussing this book at Jackie's house. Forces outside our ego consciousness that save us from ruin seemed farfetched to me. It's only after escaping so many potentially damaging situations, over the years, that I've been able to entertain the possibility that something may be present. Perhaps an older us, or an immortal us, who advises from a place of knowing. Perhaps a spirit, or a guide, or an ancestor.

Whatever the case may be, if such things as guardian angels do exist, then on the evening of February 17, 1878, as the newspaper report makes clear, my great grandmother's did not take a little holiday or fall asleep at the wheel. I imagine the scene: adrenaline coursing through Angelina, and suddenly, more lucid and sober than she's ever been, struggling against Miles as he forces her onto the floor, kicking and scratching him, while he punches and restrains her so forcibly that he breaks her collarbone. She must have been in tremendous pain when she fought free of him and struggled to her feet. Fear must have shaken her. Perhaps she was assisted by some ethereal winged one, fluttering like a moth above, giving her energy to persevere.

Clifton, a man who rents a room in the house, is just returning from a night of merrymaking, the newspaper reports. Perhaps he arrives just as the window shatters like a hundred diamonds into the street. He runs up the stairs and into Angelina's room, forces Miles out of the house, and while both Fred and Ann sleep soundly in the drowsy warmth of inebriation, Angelina, pale and numb with shock, allows Clifton to take her to the hospital.

At midnight, and in the absence of Angelina and Clifton, Miles Riley goes back into the house again and enters the room where Ann is sleeping. Ann's angel is not present. Perhaps it had been on a bender and is sleeping it off on some distant cloud. The newspaper article mentions nothing of angels but reports that Ann was asleep in bed when disturbed by Riley, "who struggled with her and overcame her and completed his purpose." The following day, Dr. Mills, the divisional hospital surgeon, examines Ann and details the injuries she's received. "There were bruises on both her legs and hip joints and a portion of hair had been torn away." The doctor presents his deposition at a pre-trial hearing, in which witnesses were also called and asked repeatedly to elaborate on just how drunk the women were. Witnesses say "extremely drunk" and never once need to add "women who get that drunk and bring a male stranger into their dwelling deserve to be raped" because even though the law does not support this view, everyone present in the courtroom, including the now sober Ann and Angelina, must believe it's true.

But I know nothing of Angelina and Ann when Chris takes me on a surprise picnic. He drives us miles and miles away from town. When I ask where he's taking me, he refuses to say. "A special place. A place I think you'll like." I can't read the road signs as we speed past them, as Chris tells me about his wife's ugly aunt Agatha, who doesn't approve of him, and who he says should be working on a Hammer Horror movie set. "She had to have surgery, get a nasty gland removed or something, and Lesley's staying with her for a week."

I've seen his wife, Lesley, only twice. She's petite and blonde and I think quite a bit younger than he is, though it's difficult to tell because she does her hair in a 1950s bouffant and wears lots of makeup. When she came to visit him at the Molesworth, I was surprised he didn't introduce us and more surprised that he pretended he and I hadn't been speaking when she walked into the kitchen. I wondered if he thought it was inappropriate for a chef to be friendly with the wait staff, if he thought the chef was too high and mighty to speak to the underlings in the kitchen. Later, when I asked, he just said, "It's Lesley," and rolled his eyes waving a hand dismissively, like he expected me to know what he was talking about.

He parks his car in a lay-by at the side of a winding road. From the back seat he collects a basket packed with bread, cheese, fruit and wine, all which he's nicked from the hotel. I follow him down a path, through a grove of trees and up a steep grassy slope. All around is beautiful undulating countryside, a patchwork of red soil and green plants. As we ascend the slope, we pass cows and sheep, who watch us with intense and nervous eyes.

It's a warm, sunny day, and I'm feeling lethargic and a little out of breath. Chris is sweating and very much out of breath but continues up this hill, which feels completely removed from the world and with the exception of us, all of the people who inhabit it.

When we reach the summit, where a cluster of ragged trees stand as a camouflage, Chris sets down the basket and removes a bottle of wine. "We made it," he says, "time to celebrate!" He opens the wine and pours two glasses. Before he lays a tablecloth over the ground, he makes a toast and we drink. "I come here sometimes to think," he confesses, "or sometimes when I need to unwind." The wine is rich and potent and after only half a glass, I feel lightheaded and relaxed. I still don't know where we are and would be hard pressed to find my way back to the car alone, but I'm enjoying this excursion and feel untroubled.

Chris makes cheese sandwiches and pours more wine and we both grow effusive, talking about our dreams. "If I ever do write a book," I tell him, "I'll immortalize you," and we laugh.

"If I ever get a boat," he says, "you'll be the first person I invite aboard."

The more we drink, the more a bubble of intimacy grows to contain us. Chris tells me that he has adult children from a previous marriage, but he doesn't speak to them. He says he'd like to see his daughter, but his cow of an ex-wife has poisoned her against him. His son, on the other hand, is a homosexual, and that's something he just can't condone.

I tell Chris about my family, talk about my father's death. It's the first time in my life that I've really spoken to anyone about my father, his cancer, his character, the way even now, sometimes, I don't believe he's really dead.

"I know that no one can replace your Pater," Chris says, getting mushy again, and making tears sting my eyes and a lump form in my throat, "but for what it's worth, I want you to know that I view you as a daughter, and I'll always look out for you."

We drink the heady wine and talk on and on until the sun begins to set; then Chris collects the tablecloth and empty bottles, tosses them into the basket and, staggering, leads us back to his car. He drives slowly and chain smokes on the way to town and mentions in passing some parking ticket that he'd forgotten to pay that he now owes forty pounds on. He won't have the money to take care of it until next week, by which time the fine will be even greater. "If Lesley finds out about the bloody thing, she'll kill me," he says.

"I can lend you the money," I say without hesitation. I know that I have forty pounds in the bank because I've been squirrelling tip money away for a writers' workshop. He pulls over, parks the car, and kisses the crown of my head. "You've saved my life!" he says.

Cora, who is petite and pretty, misses one of Jackie's classes because she'd eaten at a restaurant with a friend and started feeling sick. On the way home, she passed out and someone phoned an ambulance. Later, she tells us she was in a strange state of consciousness when taken into the emergency van. She could see and feel everything, but she couldn't move. She couldn't open her mouth to speak. She wonders what kind of food poisoning this might be, and then she feels the ambulance attendant's hand on her naked thigh. She can't scream, or say anything, but she can see him looking into her face. "Do you know what's happening to you?" he asks. "Do you know what I'm doing?"

None of us believe Cora; Cora says she scarcely believes it herself. She wouldn't believe it at all, she says, if it weren't for the fact that she knew it had happened.

"Were you drunk?" Jackie asks.

"I'd had a bit to drink with dinner, but I wasn't drunk."

"Drugs?" Jackie asks.

"Not that I know of," Cora says.

"Sometimes the mind plays tricks," Jackie offers, and we all accept this vague, trite and comforting thought before we return to our text.

Thirty-three years in the future, a Westcountry paramedic, Robert Steadman, will lose his job for groping an unconscious female in the back of an ambulance. They'll be on the same route to the same hospital that Cora was taken to that night. The paramedic driving will watch the assault occur through her rearview mirror and later say when asked why she didn't call for help: "I was in shock as to what I saw. I was trying to work out and find a reason why Rob Steadman would have his arm in that position."

Cora knew she'd been molested, she knew why her attacker had his arm on her thigh and his hand between her legs, but because there was no witness to corroborate the crime, because everyone she told said she must be mistaken, she didn't go to the police.

Cora left the class early because she still felt sick. As soon as she was gone, Jackie whispered, "I think Cora's a little bit barmy." Cathy and I didn't dispute it, because if a sick and semi-conscious woman can be molested in an ambulance by a paramedic, if a woman can be taken so advantage of by one who has been placed in a position of such trust, then there is no security for anyone and none of us are safe on earth.

A few weeks later, Chris invites me to dinner at his house while Lesley's away. He promises the best steak dinner I've ever had. We drink lots of wine and gossip about all the people we know and at eleven o'clock, after I've finished the small glass of special raspberry liqueur that Chris insists I try, I ask him to drive me home.

"Honestly, I'm too drunk to drive," he says, which is probably true, but it's never stopped him before.

I tell him not to worry, I'll phone a cab, but as I stand, my limbs feel oddly foreign, and then I'm outside my clumsy body watching it collapse to the ground before everything goes black.

Where does my consciousness go in this time of unconsciousness? Does my spirit ascend to heaven in search of my guardian angel? Or does it drop into a hell pit from which I'll never escape? I imagine Chris carrying my body to his and Lesley's room; I imagine the way he must roll it from his shoulder and onto the soft, white double bed. He must straighten it so that it's no longer horizontal, and push it next to the wall. When he looks at that unresponsive body, I wonder what he sees. Does he speak to it? Does he tell it what he's done? How he spiked the liqueur with a drug, maybe? How he'd planned for this night? Does he apologize to that poor insensible body? Does he gloat over its oblivious casing? If this isn't the first time he's done this, does he think of the other bodies? Compare and contrast?

I imagine my spirit high above that inert body shrieking so loudly that it wakes the dead: the angry dust beneath the ground. A cloud of consciousness stirs, and I imagine the rustling wings of angels rousing the living. I imagine the shaking and rumbling of ostrich heads and sour stomachs heaving up bitter bones.

As Chris climbs into the bed and turns me so I face him to make it easier to undo my jeans, the force of fragmented consciousness breaks the spell of the drug and I vomit into his face: wine, liqueur, and the best steak dinner I ever ate. Again, and again, and again, it's all coming back and there's nothing to be done but allow this eloquent intoxicating expression, an expression that will bind me to this past moment, and propel me, wordlessly, into a more ambiguous world.

EMBERS

I ARRIVE AT THE glass doors of the Candar Hotel at 4 a.m., legs jellified, eyes bloodshot, shirt and hair patterned with vomit. A wasted, grizzled man, the night porter whom I first mistake for Charon, the ferryman of the underworld, unbolts the door. "What happened to you?" he asks.

Heavily, my feet drag across the threshold. My mouth isn't working properly. As I hover in and out of the land of the living, I recall his warning the evening before: "Be no later than midnight or you might turn into a pumpkin." It seems particularly ominous in retrospect.

I reside and work in this English seaside hotel. I have a room at the very top. No one else lives up here, and since my mother moved back to Canada and I made the transition to "live-in staff," few have had the curiosity or energy to venture up to this realm. Although there's a lift in the building, it stops short of my floor. The only way up is by steep and narrow stairs that rise to an uncarpeted landing, then twist and rise again to the very summit of the crowning floor. My room is through a heavy white doorway and down a slender corridor. It's the largest of three on this floor, and just beyond, through another door, is a dark and frightening storage area, where dusty, discarded books, an old wardrobe, and a broken chair lodge. When the moon is full, a woman from the town, in love with the hotel's female proprietor, has been found skulking here. The bathroom and toilet are on the other side of this passage, and frequently at night I must embolden myself to make the terrifying trek through. But on this morning, light will already be streaming into the storage area. Seagulls will be shrieking beyond its skylight. There will be no terror in making the crossing, only distress in trying to walk straight.

I rarely stay out past ten in the evening. I know the rules for live-in staff. The night porter says he waited until after midnight, and when he figured I wasn't coming, fell asleep in his chair. "What do you think you're bloody well playing at?" His face swims in and out of my consciousness. His voice is in the process of splitting my head.

"Playin' at?" my mouth clumsily drawls. It won't move as it's supposed to. My throat's raw from throwing up. I'm sure my jaw has fallen away. I squint to take him in, to assure myself that he is, indeed, the night porter. I'm still not completely convinced I've escaped the underworld.

Even if I could process his question, would I be able to tell him what happened last night? He looks so intently at my face. "Are you on drugs?" he asks.

"No … yes … maybe," my mouth forms each word slowly as if my tongue were coated in molasses, but a smouldering voice in my mind, a voice I don't recognize for its sublimated fury, is saying "that bastard dribbled the poison of Lethe into your cup."

This is happening in the 1970s. The term "date rape" has not yet found its way into the popular lexicon, and its formal and more prosaic designation "acquaintance rape" is at least a decade from becoming a classification for this crime. There is no such thing as a "date rape drug" though Rohypnol, GBH, and Ketamine are all available and since time immemorial, drugs have been used to subdue the will of the unwilling.

But the fact that I've been drugged is a laborious revelation as the everyday world buoys under my grasp. I'm unmoored, unanchored, afloat in the archetypal ocean that psychotics inhabit, struggling to make sense of what's occurred.

I usually serve teas, make beds, and clean toilets at this hotel. Sometimes I'm required to dump and clean out chamber pots. I wear a beige skirt and a nylon smock with pockets large enough for dusters and soap, and I use my silver master key to tap, tap, tap on doors before I shout "housekeeping" and enter the rooms of strangers.

The head housekeeper, my boss Mrs. Newall, fixed it with the hotel's owner so I could get lodging for a nominal fee, but as the archetypal waves of Lethe threaten to drown me, I'm aware this situation could abruptly end. I could lose my job. Lose my home. It all depends on the night porter not blabbing. It all depends on the owner never finding out. I slowly make my way up the rubbery, treacherous stairs to my room, slowly cross the great divide to the bathroom to clean myself up, to choke up phlegm. My eyes are frighteningly demonic, the colour of fire. I look away from the old blackening mirror that graces the wall. To behold the flames in them that my friend (who was not a friend) put there, would thrust me again into the terrifying tributaries of Lethe, that anesthetic river of which a single drop dooms one's memories to oblivion.

Years in the future, after George H. W. Bush becomes the 41st president and Ted Bundy meets his end in the electric chair, after British murderer and rapist John Cannan is given three life-sentences and sent to prison, *The Times* will announce "Stereotype of Rapist Badly Flawed," explaining "many rapes are committed by men who have a close relationship with [their] victims." Sexual predators are not how we expect them to be. They're not "mentally deranged strangers, lurking in back alleys," waiting "to attack a woman walking home alone,"

Dr Paul Pollard, of the psychology department of Lancashire Poly-technic, will tell *The Times'* science correspondent. In most cases, they're ordinary men: husbands, and boyfriends, and work mates. They're frequently men who women come to trust and rely upon, men who no one would ever imagine could engage in such a heinous crime.

In the 1970s, a woman rapist is considered an oxymoron, as British law defines the crime as penetration with a penis. Although female sexual predators do exist, and there are also male rape victims, in this decade, few are ready to embrace the reality of these facts.

Even decades in the future, collectively held biases will convolute ideas about sexual predation. According to a 1989 survey that the *Daily Mail* cites, "four out of five women do not think forced sex on a date is necessarily rape," and when, as late as 1991, *Cosmopolitan Magazine* surveyed three hundred of its readers on the topic, it dis-covered not only that such rapes went largely unreported, but that many females surveyed didn't realize they'd been victims of a crime.

In the 1970s, when I divest myself of vomit-spattered clothing at the Candar Hotel, when I stagger into the rushing waters of my bath, which my muddled mind, momentarily perceives as something molten oozing from the orb of the underworld, it's little wonder I'm incapable of considering what happened to me as something that can be pun-ished by law.

I'd gone to have a meal at a former workmate's house. He was a chef. I trusted him implicitly. There had never been anything even mildly flirtatious between us. I was a teenager. He was my mother's age. He'd even once insisted upon me calling him "Uncle Chris." He cooked us steak, gave me alcohol, spiked my drink with something that would knock me out. I woke to find him tugging off my jeans, woke in such confusion, such disorientation and sickness, vomit everywhere, my stomach lurching, impossible to breathe. Somehow, I got away from him. Somehow I made it to his front door, somehow I escaped his house, and made it here, into this cold sobering bath, at the Candar

Hotel, where my muddled, muddied mind starts to clear. Where illumination, at last, begins to flare.

In the 1970s, forensic science is also beginning to illuminate sexual offences, which is considered a "most difficult field of crime." Cedric Stephens, Director-General of Research and Chief Scientist of the Home Office, says "police when confronted with an hysterical girl making allegations" are always uncertain if a "rape [has] actually taken place." Yet advances in science and technology can now "quickly clear the innocent," not to mention help confirm credible allegations.

In this decade, when Susan Brownmiller's book, *Against Our Will: Men, Women and Rape*, sparks international controversy, when feminists predominantly rally, according to scholar Eric Hickey, against both rape and spousal abuse, and when police estimate "that the number of rapes reported...represent only a tenth of those that occur," most women who find themselves in situations like mine are uncertain what to do.

In the 1970s, sexual assault is veiled in myth, cloaked in stereotype, and shrouded in prejudice. Because of this elusiveness it's difficult to understand. What went wrong? How did it happen? How could a person violate another in such an unconscionable way? Even in the future — four decades plus — collective biases will still blind human beings to the nature of this problem, but as a teenager at the Candar Hotel I don't know this. I couldn't even begin to imagine that what has occurred to me exists in a wider social-historical context. In fact, I don't even know, with certainty, what has occurred.

I have yet to hear the phrase "blame the victim," though I've already internalized the concept. The problem isn't rape per se. It isn't sexual assault. It's the way women dress, the way they wear their make-up. "Look at all [the] little girls along Oxford Street with their false lashes and blackened lids," a psychiatrist is quoted as saying in a *Daily Mail* article. "They look like an invitation to rape the lot of them. But not one, I'll bet, intends that."

In this decade, it's not rape that's the problem, but women: their ignorance and unconsciousness, what they wear, the way they behave. Sergeant Harry O'Reily of the New York police's sex crimes analysis unit told *The Times* that the problem is "women are too compliant, too nice.... Their first instinct is to obey and to help." They "open the door to the rapist who uses no force, but a con — a ruse to lower her defenses and make her easy prey for attack."

Back in my room as I ruminate, I don't yet realize I've been conned. I can't quite accept what's happened. I can't quite believe that someone I thought I knew, someone I trusted, someone I'd turn to for help, could possibly do something so despicable. I try to avoid toppling into the underworld, as I plumb the depths of memory searching for damning clues.

I liked the man who drugged me. He was funny and kind when not possessed by his angry work persona. I didn't mind his bawdy jokes, his excessive drinking, or all the minor infractions of the law, mostly car-related, that he amassed. He was forever trying to scrape enough money together to pay off fines, forever borrowing from friends, forever complaining how "skint" he was and how his wife was going to tie him to the bed and flog him, but after the fun was over, he joked, she'd nag him to death.

I didn't have an inside window into his world. There was nothing to make me suspect him of sexual predation. Nothing to make me suspect he was anything but a completely trustworthy friend. There was no documentation of the things he'd said, no public record of crimes he may have committed. There was nothing solid or substantial to pour over, only my memories, only the story I'd constructed with him as my ally and protector. I'd avoided listening to gossip about him. He had many enemies; many women steered clear of him, but this wasn't a red flag to me. My father, who died when I was fourteen, also drank to excess, drove drunk, incurred fines, alienated nice people. He too had a mean side to his personality, a violent temper at times, a denigrating way of speaking. It was a "tragic flaw." I'd learned the term in a Canadian high school English class before I dropped out. A "tragic flaw" was a weakness of character worthy of pity. The term, however, is an "enduring simplification," according to education scholar Peggy O'Brien that "amounts to [an] intellectual bypass, a means of [speedily] proceeding" that "causes us to miss too much."

As I try to piece together the tatters of lost trust, try to come to terms with a revised and horrific reality, I catch sight of the old-fashioned telephone that hangs on my wall and begin to sweat. The phone's only function is to make me accessible to the proprietor and hotel management. Its only purpose is to find me, forever, ready, willing and able to serve. But last night, I wasn't. Last night, if they called, as the proprietor once had done, in the wee hours of the morning, there would have been no answer. Would someone have made the trek up to see where I was? Would the night porter have told them, in passing, that I'd gone out but hadn't returned? Some bright amorphous *Looney Tunes* character from my childhood appears before my flaming drug scarred eyes. "Looks like the jig possibly could be up," it says.

While there's no such thing as a "date rape drug" in this year that hallucinations overwhelm me, it's not unknown for women to be drugged by men they trust and then raped. "Before there was the roofie, before there was the Mickey, or the knockout drop, there was the poppy plant and its storied charms," writes Pamela Donovan. I'm not sure what drug I've been given, not sure exactly when it was administered, only that I have been given a drug, one that did not render me unconscious, as my friend, Chris the predator, had hoped, but one that has left me lethargic and leaden, straddling the boundaries of two incompatible worlds.

As my hallucination ebbs, I re-live the night the proprietor called. She, who never approved of strong emotions or scenes, of unladylike fits or hysterics, wanted me to quiet a sobbing woman. The woman's husband was suffering with chest pains, but the proprietor didn't phone an ambulance. She didn't know how serious the man's malady was, and although she never said so, most probably believed the woman was exaggerating. When it comes to emotionally charged events — the sickness of a loved one, the impropriety of a man — females are thought to be less objective than males in this decade. They tend to catastrophize, make mountains of mole hills, or so collective wisdom tells us.

The distressed woman I went to tend to was slight, perhaps sixty, and was weeping and pacing the corridor when I arrived. She wore a pink housecoat. Her hair was in pin-curls and the only comfort I could offer her was a cup of tea. Later that morning, when she became a widow, she lamented that the hilly terrain of Ilfracombe had killed her husband. She blamed herself for not having realized in this un-dulating region of North Devon the impact of so much sight-seeing on her husband's heart. She reproached herself for not having made him rest, for not taking better care of him, and for "falling to pieces" when he lay dying instead of stoically and silently bearing it.

"Thank you, all, for putting up with my tears…for being so kind," she said that afternoon when her sister from Essex arrived. I hadn't thought of her since that day, or the pale white corpse of her husband who lingered for hours under starched white sheets before a stretcher collected him. Now, however, still drugged from the night before, still teetering between the real and mythic worlds, a small flickering spark, a demon ember, catches my attention as it skips around the room and becomes a fragment of the widow's grieving soul. I'm convinced this renegade spark broke from her spirit, appalled by her meekness, her silence, and self-blame. Why didn't she grab someone by the throat? Why didn't she scream: "Where is the ambulance? For God's sake, call an ambulance." The spark dances over the black phone. It hops across the wall, over my still made bed, and taps on the windowpane, as if exit were its only mission. But it doesn't tap hard enough to break through. It shatters itself, instead, into thousands of embers that pour like rain over the threadbare carpet in my room.

I'm aware that cataclysmic fire is a never-ending worry in a hotel of this age. There have been few improvements or renovations since the 1800s. Electrical wiring is in poor repair. Since 1972, when fire certification became law, owners of old properties like the Candar have been trying to bring their buildings up to code. As with all out-dated constructions, necessary modifications need to be made.

Fire inspectors continually visit. Owners poise on tenterhooks. They hold their breath and tiptoe, as inspectors scribble notes on clip-boards, and breathe a sigh of relief when the assessment comes to an end. I'm unaware, in this decade, that it's easier to renovate a building than a belief system, unaware that physical external hazards are more simply eradicated than a multitude of socially internalized ones.

Fire extinguishers need to be hung on walls, fire alarms installed. While I've grown used to the hotel as a construction zone with the buzz of saws and clank of hammers igniting thoughts of destruction outside every room, I'm oblivious to the intimate and personal destruc-tions and refurbishes that every individual, over time, must face.

Defense mechanisms and the calcification of beliefs are more difficult to negotiate than heavy, troublesome fire doors that thwart speedy passage, add hours to cleaning time, but that can easily be disabled with the use of small wooden stops. As the widow's broken embers transmogrify to blinding sunlight in my room, I consider what I now see as past risks. Dinner alone with a former work friend. Errant sparks in an open corridor. A myriad of small, isolated choices made that have the potential to kindle a holocaust.

I try to move quickly, but I'm trudging through molasses. My throb-bing head won't let me walk. I find a crumpled cigarette and flick my butane lighter which is always close at hand. Back and forth I swim, in and out of delirium. My coordination is compromised, I assume, because of the stinking putrid fumes of underworld bitumen still clinging to my flesh. My stomach reels and roils, protesting the drug — the poisons of Lethe — as I believe my intoxicant to be. Slowly, I cross the threshold, slowly I cross the landing, slowly I traverse the field of shadows through the storage room again, and at the toilet, throw up what appear to be two flaming pomegranate seeds.

"Time is of the essence," though it has somehow stalled for me. I pat my face with water, survey the scarlet lace of veins that still stain my eyes. Work awaits me, and I'm not sure I can make it, not sure I'll be able to physically labour through the day. Yet what is my alternative? Excusing myself on the grounds of sickness would only provoke questions. All I want to do is pull a chameleon veil over my head and disappear for the rest of my life.

In the 1970s, sexual assault is said to be on the rise, though it may just be that assault victims are reporting the crimes with more frequency. As of 1976, with the Sexual Offences (Amendment) Act, rape complainants can retain their anonymity and the media can't publish or broadcast their names. "A reprehensible feature of trials of rape...is that the complainant's prior sexual history...may be brought out in the trial in a [humiliating] way which is rarely so in other criminal trials," the Heilbron Committee, an Advisory Group on the Law of Rape, reports. And even though the crime is registered more frequently, it doesn't necessarily mean it's legally pursued and that the rapist is brought to justice.

In this decade, when I'm introduced to the toxins of Lethe, a woman will flee her British home and make for the United States rather than appear at Norwich Crowned Court and give evidence of her rape. "Judges are overwhelmingly male, elderly, upper-middle class, and public school and Oxbridge educated. They are often appointed on the basis of an excellent record in areas of the law which have nothing to do with rape and have little training or expertise in dealing with rape cases," researcher Mark Cowling writes. It's not unknown "to find the judge joining with the defence counsel in asking the victim prurient questions of dubious relevance to the case in hand. It is not surprising to find that judges are less vigilant than they should be in excluding irrelevant evidence of sexual history."

In this year that I weave in and out of the underworld, fretting over the time it's taking me to find consistent sobriety, and considering my past relationships, two brother predators, Graham and Simon Laskey, are drugging and raping women in Pontypridd, birthplace of Welsh singer Tom Jones, some fifty miles away, across the Bristol Channel. No one is bringing them to justice, and in the 1970s, as Tom Jones' signature song says, "It's not unusual."

The Laskeys lure their victims to their home, offer cups of tainted tea. When the victims wake, they've been sexually violated, but have no memory of the event. Some of the women get away, others are held and subjected to "horrific ordeals."

"Imagine the very worst you can, add some more and then you have some understanding of what they did to these women," Detective Sergeant Sally Burke, who will lead an investigation some twenty years in the future, will tell the *Daily Mail*. The men are "believed to have attacked dozens of victims over 20 years." When assured that the men were in jail and couldn't harm them, two-hundred witnesses made statements; however, the total number of victims "will never be known," police are quoted as saying.

But at the Candar Hotel in the 1970s, it doesn't occur to me that Chris may have drugged other women, nor that it's likely he'll do so again. The reality of rape, of serial sexual assault, of Rohypnol and its sleep-inducing brethren, exists to an extent we, as a society, are far too silent and innocent to conceive. Rape "is a crime which, even today, is still spoken of rarely. A word which — apart from jokes in the bar — is seldom used," according to a 1973 *Daily Mail* article. Two years later, in the same paper a rapist will be flippantly characterized as "a Romeo" and "a Casanova." And a year following this, columnist Jane Gaskell will chide: "haven't those illiterate rapists noticed that it's the Permissive Society these days, and rape is dead un-trendy — unless you want one of those sneering lady feminists to write a book against you?"

Activist Tarana Burke, who will start the grassroots Me Too Movement, is just a three-year-old child in New York when Gaskell's comments are published. The Quaker phrase, "Speak truth to power," used as a title of a pamphlet addressing the cold war in 1955, is decades from becoming a popular slogan associated with sexual assault. It's decades from being defined by writer and professor Lacy M. Johnson as a "struggle against various silences."

Not speaking up, not naming names, not protesting the abuse one has suffered for fear of reprisal or humiliation, or simply because the emotional trauma has muted one's voice, are systemic problems which can't help but affect me, though I'm unaware of them in this decade.

Good news stories of media star cum philanthropist Jimmy Savile inundate the British Isles in this decade. He runs marathons for charities, raises money for worthy causes, and hosts a popular TV show called "Jim'll Fix It" where he makes people's dreams come true. He works as a volunteer "porter extraordinaire" at Leeds Hospital, wheeling drugged patients in and out of the operating rooms and, apparently, has an office in the mortuary. Since 1969 he's also been an unpaid porter at Stoke Mandeville Hospital, doing, he says, "any rotten job that needed doing." At the high security psychiatric institution, Broadmoor, he's a frequent visitor, soon to become a board member, to have his own set of keys and living quarters on the premises. He will even sometimes assist guards capture the occasional escapee. He's involved with youth groups, with disturbed and disadvantaged children, and now and again spends the night at Duncroft Approved School (an institution for wayward, non-compliant, or just plain troublesome girls between the ages of thirteen and sixteen) in Surrey.

When judges make negligent decisions, when there's injustice in the land, it's the Prime Minister, Queen, and Jimmy people write to for assistance, and it's Jimmy, more than anyone, who they trust will bring them aid.

In a *Daily Mail* profile in 1996, journalist and Savile fan Lynda Lee-Potter writes: Jimmy leaves "everyone feeling jolly and special and with a story to tell when they go home." Little could she have suspected the intrinsic irony of this statement or how it would curdle under the future flare of not-so-jolly revelations.

It's only after Savile cozies up to Prince Charles and Margaret Thatcher, after he's knighted by both Pope and Queen, after he becomes an Honorary Royal Marines Green Beret, and receives an Honorary Doctorate of Law, after he dies and some four hundred and fifty people come forward to accuse him of sexual abuse, including thirty-two who say he raped them, will the silence be broken.

One can glance back across an ocean of time and see the damning records and documentations, the things police suspected and investigated, the accusations that were never disclosed. In hindsight, the puzzle pieces fit. The cryptic crossword clues that Savile shed like a viral infection when speaking to the press are manifold, and as Sandy Balfour of *The Guardian* writes, "What no one ever tells you [about cryptic crosswords] is that 'the answer is right in front of you.'"

Cluedo is a British "Who Done It" board game and in 1993 Savile will be one of six celebrities chosen for a special charity edition. "This will be an exercise in seeing if I'm found out," he'll jest. "I have escaped it on the Cluedo board of life, so let's see how I get on with the game." The defrocked clergyman Reverend Green will be the character he chooses to replace. His murder weapon of choice? "[A] shooter — with a silencer," he'll laugh.

Silence is said to be many things. It's said to be golden, it's said to be death, it's said to be complicity. Silence can be thunderous, strategic, or wise. It can be cloaked or veiled or naked. It can exact a price. It can be a private hell. Like a fragile object, it can be broken. It can be a lethal weapon, it can make a noise. It can hide suffering, expose truth, and like a meteorite before it explodes, gain momentum. It can be a conspiracy, a way of shutting conversation down, of keeping people guessing. As Adrienne Rich observes in her poem "Cartographies of Silence," it "is a presence. It has a history, a form." It can sometimes be the only condemnation possible, a remedy for evil, a symbol of solidarity. It can be awful. It can be articulate. It can brood. It can impart a coded message or like a fallen cinder, it can burn.

"The deafening sound of silence" seemed "to permeate the lies and deceit of Jimmy Savile," media studies scholar Simon Cross will write. And in this year that I stagger to the stillroom of the Candar Hotel, hoping I can make it through the workday, hoping that no one will notice my blood-shot eyes, my pallor and trembling, a "deafening sound of silence" will ensconce me. It will provide me with a protective casing, an armour in which I will remain inviolable, a place where I will replay every moment spent with Chris, my friend, my attacker, hunting for retrospective clues to his character. Looking for subtle, telling things. Searching for a flash of insight, a glimmer of understanding, a flicker of enlightenment, or just one small ember to reduce the world of our friendship I'd constructed to something as innocuous as ash.

In the months ahead, I'll move away, escape to a new town and job, and stop searching for the fury to obliterate the past. As the Candar Hotel continues to erect its fire doors, I'll continue constructing my own defences and won't think of Chris again, until three years after I move back to Canada and hear that the Candar Hotel has burned to the ground.

VICTIMS AND VILLAINS

I DON'T RECALL what I was reading the day I took my place as resident domestic at Kiltrasna House, but I remember thinking about Manderley, the manse in Daphne du Maurier's *Rebecca*. I remember thinking about Charlotte Bronte's Thornfield Hall in *Jane Eyre*. Both these novels had already been crossed off my ambitious book list as I attempted to work my way to authorhood through habitual reading.

It was a shadowy day in Bideford, North Devon, when I made my way up the long, curving drive. Sentinel elms obscured the house, and I imagined myself first as Jane and then as the timorous Mrs. de Winter as Kiltrasna gradually came into view.

It was made of grey stone, with large arching windows and turrets. "Secret and silent," as du Maurier described Manderley, "a jewel in the hollow of a hand." Twelve acres of grounds surrounded it, and an ocean of woods lay at its back. The perfect setting for a mystery, I thought, or a ghost story, or a thriller. The perfect setting for a nightmare, I considered, but checked myself. I didn't want to think about that.

Kiltrasna was no longer a private estate. My employer, Edgehill College, had procured it back in 1917 and used it now, along with several other grand edifices in the neighbourhood, as dormitories for their boarders. Approximately fifty-two girls between the ages of ten and seventeen lived at Kiltrasna, and part of my job description included cleaning up after them. Because I was only a teenager myself, younger than several of the girls, I wondered if this might be a problem.

The jovial, broad-faced Mr. Roberts, in charge of all the college's domestic staff, misinterpreted my concern during our interview. He told me that the girls made their own beds and hung up their own clothes. "The housemistress sees to that." There were two other day domestics, he told me, so the heavy cleaning wouldn't be too arduous.

"You get all the school holidays off paid." He watched for my reaction. "Of course, you don't have to leave the house during the holidays if you don't want to. By all means, stay if it suits."

I was trying not to cough. I smoked like a fiend and had chronic bronchitis. It was so bad, in fact, that I'd recently had a chest x-ray for suspected TB. I was afraid that Mr. Roberts might think I was too unhealthy to work, but after he recited my other duties, which included boiling water for tea, and doling out slices of toast and cream cakes twice a day, it began to dawn on me that even if I'd had a virulent plague, Mr. Roberts wouldn't have turned me away. The college was required to have at least two staff members spend the night in each of the hostels, and it was increasingly difficult to find live-in staff, especially, it seemed, at Kiltrasna.

"But please don't misunderstand," Mr. Roberts chuckled lightly, "there's nothing, whatsoever, wrong with the house." It was only that the job required a certain kind of individual, and after asking me a few personal questions involving boyfriends and whether I had one or not (I lied and said I didn't) he proclaimed the job mine.

Even if I'd confessed to having a boyfriend, I suspect he'd have given me the job. It had been advertised in the labour exchange for several weeks, and I was fairly certain that in all that time, I'd been its only applicant.

"We want you to feel comfortable at Kil," he said. "Kil" was the house's nickname. "Let me know if you need anything … anything at all, please don't hesitate."

I stifled a cough and nodded. The following day, I was walking up the winding drive, pretending to be Maximilian de Winter's timid second wife, with a suitcase full of books, a deck of tarot cards, my correspondence lessons from the impressive sounding *London School of Journalism*, and a mini-tape recorder for interviews. I knew that Mrs. de Winter wouldn't have such things in her bag. She was like me in some ways — young and parentless — but mostly she was different. I couldn't relate to her lack of ambition. Before she met Maxim, she had no personal goals. Du Maurier made her unassuming — so much so that throughout the novel, her Christian name is not ever mentioned. Still, in my eyes, she was an admirable heroine, and I pretended to be her — with dull and straight bobbed hair, self-conscious, tense, "shy as a colt." She was an easy character to play, common enough in fiction, a distant relative to Cinderella, who, as a former chambermaid in a hotel, I'd had a lot of practice affecting.

Play acting has, to some extent, replaced calculated madness as my main coping strategy. It's less likely to get me sacked, and so long as no one observes it, less likely to scare people. It allows me tranquil passage through the filth and tedium of a working day, and as I make my way to Kiltrasna's bolted front door and ring the bell, I feel happy that the spirit of Mrs. de Winter is with me — happy that I won't have to go it alone.

Kiltrasna, situated in Bideford, North Devon, is just a short jaunt by car to the county of Cornwall, and although I don't know it, Daphne du Maurier, the maker of my conjured companion, lives in a house there called Kilmarth. The prefix, "Kil," which our houses share, is Gaelic, and could mean any number of things including a cell, a chapel, a brook, a stream, a corner, a grove, or a graveyard. The girls who board there will tell me when I meet them that the name means *House of the Dead.*

Gwen and Lillian, the day cleaners, unbolt the fortress which is Kiltrasna, and drag open its large wooden door. The younger looking cleaner, Gwen, is stout, dark haired, and energetic. She speaks with a Welsh accent and advises me how I might fix up my living quarters. "Ask Mr. Roberts," she tells me. "Last girl yer…," she begins.

"Shush," Lillian, the other cleaner says. She's older, a Londoner. "We in't supposed to say." She wears makeup, lipstick that has somehow found its way into strands of her bleached, Cleopatra-style hair.

"I was only going t'mention," Gwen continues, "how the last girl yer never did fix up that room."

The three of us are sitting at a long kitchen table, smoking cigarettes and drinking tea. "What aren't you supposed to say?" I choke.

The two women look at each other, then at me, and begin to laugh.

It's obvious that Kiltrasna, like Manderley, is a house of secrets. My alter ego, Mrs. de Winter, whispers her concurrence in her mousy way, and now that I walk the hallways of this former mansion, now that I take up residence in what I jokingly refer to as "The Servant's Wing," I can feel the atmosphere of secrets pressing in upon me like the tight cover of a book.

It's the girls I thank partly for this — because I love secrets, and mysteries, and diversions of the mind, and they, particularly the older ones, are in the habit of ferreting out what's unspoken and speaking it — at least to me.

Edgehill College's roots are in the Bible Christian movement, and the school is owned by the Methodist Church. The students who attend, however, aren't necessarily Methodist. Some, in fact, are atheists, but the school and its houses attempt to maintain a godly moral tenor which requires a tight reign, and more often the squelching of any perceived ungodly truths. Thus, secrets at Kiltrasna abound like summer blackberries in bramble.

There are secrets concerning many of the girls, their backgrounds, how and why they ended up at Edgehill College, and the unutterable problems they get into once here. There are furtive nighttime outings, drunkenness, clandestine meetings with the boys at the neighbouring Grenville College, anxious episodes of soul searching, "should one relinquish one's virginity now or wait?" There are pregnancies, threatened lawsuits, quietly managed abortions, fears of venereal disease.

Condoms don't exist at Edgehill College. The hostel's storeroom stocks only sanitary napkins and toothpaste, bars of cheap soap and shampoo. In the year I come to Kil, AIDS is not yet epidemic, and even if it were, it's unlikely that the board of governors, who make decisions about all aspects of the school, would ever consider that these girls could be at risk.

The students at Edgehill come from well-off, middle-class parents or guardians who care enough about their futures (or simply have enough money) to commit them to an establishment which aims at preparing them for sound, socially advantageous marriages. Elocution lessons teach girls how to speak the *Queen's English* even better than the Queen, and edifying Victorian aphorisms, dispersed liberally throughout the hostels, are thought to subliminally reinforce good character. Team sports, healthy competition, instruction in deportment, and physical discipline are all a part of Edgehill's recipe for moulding girls into well brought up young ladies.

Because I've lived in North America most of my life, I know very little about England's extremely delineated class hierarchy and have no clear idea about the place domestic workers are situated in it. What surprises me most in retrospect is that the girls of Kiltrasna, being schooled in social apartheid, chose to embrace me, a Canadian expatriate, an orphan, and a cleaner, as their peer. Whether this occurred through Christian charity, which Edgehill extolled, sheer rebelliousness, or something other, I can't say; I only know that their acceptance was genuine and that almost immediately a backlash began against our nascent friendship.

Sally Hill, Kiltrasna's much loved and easy-going housemistress, was, according to the girls, "cast out." My sister-informers who gathered in my chilly room for a nightly ritual of biscuits and tea, told me that while the official word on Sally was "sick leave," it was the head housemistress who had found her lax and sent her away. The girls feared she might never return and implored me to consult my Tarot cards to put their minds at ease.

I'm only a novice cartomancer, but because I'm hoping to become proficient, never shrink from a divination request. I dim the lights in my room and spread the cards. "Will Sally return to Kil?" I ask. As is the case with most things oracular, answers are rarely direct and always subject to interpretation. The Queen of Wands, reversed, is the outcome card, which according to the book I consult means a woman who is jealous, vengeful, strict to a fault, domineering, and deceitful. We all know Sally Hill is none of these things.

Doreen Kingsley, a retired deputy housemistress, called back into service because of Sally's absence, is presently the other live-in staff member at Kiltrasna. She's slow-moving, addicted to sleeping pills, prone to migraines, memory loss, and exhaustion, but she's wide awake as she scales the stairs to "The Servant's Wing," gently raps on my door, and says, "I don't expect there are any girls in there, but if there are, they'd be wise to get back to their dorms."

We know that all the dorm lights will be turned off in fifteen minutes, and we don't have time to ask the cards a follow-up question. The girls file out of my cold, shabby room, returning to their even colder, shabbier dormitories, leaving me and my alter ego, Mrs. de Winter, to smoke and cough and expectorate and nervously ponder the enigmatic Queen. In the morning, the mousey Mrs. de Winter is still with me, full of timidity and trepidation as I seek an audience with Mr. Roberts to ask for a desk, a bookcase, an electric heater, and some flowery wallpaper to hang on my walls. I return to Kil, half an hour later, after a successful meeting, excited and eager to tell Lillian, and particularly Gwen, that just like Cinderella, all my wishes were granted. Immediately, however, I feel the heavy atmosphere, and see my co-workers' stricken expressions as they introduce a pasty, perfumed interloper — Kil's new housemistress — Cynthia Power.

In my mind, horror music plays a jarring string sforzato. The woman stands like a ghoul, in a circle of shadow, just beyond Kiltrasna's wooden door. Rouge smears her marshmallow cheeks, and her eyes, full of displeasure, scan me. There is something about her of Mrs. Van Hopper, the snob in *Rebecca* who employs the artless narrator before Maxim whisks her away; she also bears some resemblance to the gothic homicidal housekeeper Mrs. Danvers.

She approaches me, eyes narrowed. "Heu doo you doo?" Her mouth as tight as a rat's anus, her face contorted in its struggle to produce an accent that would make any British working-class girl wither. "Would you please see that my rum is in odah."

Gwen lifts an eyebrow. "The housemistress at Kil usually sees to her own room," she explains, not unkindly.

"Ooooew?" Cynthia assumes the expression of one who has just discovered a turd stuck to the bottom of her shoe and minces off.

I didn't need Gwen or Lillian to warn me. I knew it would be best to stay out of Cynthia Power's way. But this resolution is doomed to fail, for before night has fallen, the new house mistress seeks me out. "E would apreeseate et ef you dedn't use this holeway bahthrum," she says. It's considered a staff bathroom and is the closest to my room. It's also the closest to the housemistress' room. Sally and I had agreed to share it. "New one would expect me to shah ah bahthrum with a doemestic," she says, her tight mouth puckered and her great protruding eyes looking down the slim point of her nose.

I'm too stunned not to acquiesce, too stung to argue. I begin to remove my things from the bathroom. Tears prick my eyes, and like *Rebecca*'s nameless narrator, who weeps for different reasons, "I cried that night, bitter youthful tears that could not come from me today. That kind of crying, deep into a pillow, does not happen after we are twenty-one. The throbbing head, the swollen eyes, the tight, contracted throat." But unlike the victim narrator who lives again and again through painful tears, in my weeping that evening, I'm somehow transformed, my feelings of victimhood washed away, and like punk rocker Johnny Rotten am infused with rage, discovering, as he did, that "anger is an energy."

Thirty-six years in the future, the former green-toothed antichrist, once reviled as *the worst threat to our kids since Hitler*, will advise: "You can accept that you are no one or you can fight. That's a part of working-class life – being told that you are no one, know your place, shut up, say nothing. But you've got to stand up and make a noise."

The first noise I make the following morning, after all my tears subside, is the guttural rumble of throat clearing, followed by an angry, gob-producing choking fit. My alter ego, Mrs. de Winter, advises me to be a good girl, to lie low, and as much as I'd like to do this, my rage — now smouldering — won't allow it. I find Cynthia in the kitchen preparing a tray and try to be polite. "Good morning, Cynthia." My voice is trembling. "I've been thinking things over and I'm going to continue using that upstairs bathroom." I feel my face redden. "Sorry," I add, unable to stop myself.

"Mrs. Power to you," she says, in her tense, affected, socially elite accent. "You are a domestic. Domestics do not call housemistresses by their Christian names, and as for the bathroom, we shall see what the college has to say about that." She places her tray on the kitchen table and flounces off to her chamber to make a phone call. She doesn't emerge from her room again, and I'm aware of a volley of communications, the ringing of her telephone, echoing throughout the house.

Rebecca's nameless narrator rears up in terror as I clean. I need this job. I need a place to live. What if Cynthia Power persuades Edgehill College to dump me?

"Don't worry," Gwen comforts. "Housemistresses are two a penny. It's really *your* job that's the hard one to fill."

At lunch time, Cynthia emerges from her room and a message arrives from Mr. Roberts. He wants to speak to me in his office. Inwardly I tremble, but I don't want to give Cynthia the satisfaction of knowing I'm upset.

"Well," Mr. Roberts laughs jovially when I enter his office, "the entire college is in an uproar."

I apologize, though uncertain if I'm the cause.

"No, no, no, nothing whatsoever to apologize for," he says still smiling. "I've met with the head housemistress, and a few others," he chuckles, "and you can go right ahead and use your bathroom." Despite his warm humor, I know what's occurred hasn't amused anyone. "The head housemistress, Mrs. Jones, and I don't always see eye to eye," he says and continues chuckling. He claps his jolly hands. "I do hope you're settling in well."

I nod.

"Good, good, very good," he says, "We're all very glad you're with us," he beams. "And about Mrs. Power," he continues in a more confidential tone, "probably best to just ignore her, don't you agree?"

I nod again, and quickly leave.

It doesn't take the girls at Kiltrasna long to ascertain the enemy. "I heard all about what happened," Janet, a bubbly, extroverted sympathizer offers that evening.

The girls tell me that she's forbidden them to speak to me — forbidden them to speak with any of the domestics.

"She's a megalomaniac, is what she is," a girl, Vicky, says.

"She's the Queen of Wands reversed!" Rachel, another girl, whispers.

But Cynthia Power seems far more unpredictable than any Queen of Wands reversed. Even Lillian, who rarely speaks, comments: "I reckon Cynthia Power is barmy."

The new housemistress has dragged a large armchair and footstool out of the girls' television room and set them up by the front door. She lounges there with tea and biscuits "like Lady Muck," Gwen says, checking girls out in the morning, and checking them back in at the end of the day. In between, she invades dormitories and unceremoniously tips out the contents of drawers. Gwen makes the mistake of asking if she's looking for anything. "This has nothing to do with you," Cynthia says in her tight, artificial voice.

She's been seen reading the girls' personal letters and diaries, and when they come in, she interrogates groups of them in her office. We can't hear exactly what she's saying, but many of the girls emerge in tears. She punishes the younger girls for sloppiness: wrinkled blouses, drooping socks, messy hair. She sends them into solitary confinement if she perceives their body language conveys disrespect. She gates some of the older girls — which means she restricts them to the house. They're not allowed to go outside, to attend extracurricular activities, to travel into the town on the weekend.

"We hate her!" a tiny nervous girl says, defying Cynthia Power's edict of not fraternizing with domestics. Her face is strained with frustration. She pulls up a chair alongside us at the kitchen table. We're on our last break of the day.

"It's a real shame," Gwen says in her singsong voice, "but you don't want her to catch you in here. There'll be hell to pay."

Some fifteen years in the future, Margaret Forster, best known as the author of *Georgy Girl*, will write a controversial biography of the then recently deceased Daphne du Maurier. She will recall a time when du Maurier, living in Egypt and pregnant with her second child, most probably struggling with the inconvenient truth of her sexuality, trying to play "the good wife" to her compulsive, war-damaged husband, began to write *Rebecca*. She felt fearful, ambivalent, and not up to the many tasks she faced. She despised entertaining yet was required to entertain. She felt inadequate particularly in giving orders to the servants. "Her feelings of inferiority in this respect and of being intimidated," according to Forster, "went straight into the character of the second Mrs. de Winter."

"Depression is anger turned inward," the old Freudian adage goes, and women, according to Dr. Teresa Bernardez-Bonnesatti, who spoke at the 1977 American Psychiatric Association's annual meeting, claims women's inability to express their rage lies "at the root of most of their disturbed behaviour." "Self-deprecation," "pathological submissiveness," and "chronic bitter resentment" are just a few of the ways problems manifest: "Women struggle to express justified anger, such as anger against discrimination and injustice, but many cannot or will not protest. Instead they even deny discrimination exists or turn their criticism against other women who dare to complain openly."

It never occurs to me to consider my current alter ego, the second Mrs. de Winter, as pathologically submissive and in denial. Her attempts to protect her murdering, mentally abusive husband by covering up the truth of Rebecca's demise strike me as romantic, not as criminal or insane.

I feel no compassion for Rebecca, the first Mrs. de Winter, see her as heartless and immoral, rather than a silenced victim murdered by an abusive husband. I'm not sure when in my life the balance shifts — when I begin to sympathize with the plight of all voiceless women, not just those who are meek and self-effacing, not just those who are fundamentally "good girls" unwittingly upholding the pillars of a social system that denigrates them.

Perhaps it is now, for in my mind's eye, I notice the second Mrs. de Winter is starting to change. Her mousey bob is cropped and turning the colour of fire, her soft, sensible shoes are swelling to army boots. The homemade blouse and skirt she wears transforms to midnight tatters. Razor blades dangle from her ears, and a legion of safety pins pierce her flesh — safety pins, which do not symbolize safety from xenophobia as they do in a post-Brexit world — but ones that conjure hand grenades and semi-automatic weapons, pins that are only safe so long as they remain undeployed.

As a teenager, however, I seem personally innocent of explosive fury. My anger is a long slow fuse with a quick and terminal blaze. I can't sustain or direct it, and when I don't feel it, I can't will it into being. That's why, when Cynthia Power raps on my door, I politely open it.

As live-in staff at Edgehill College, we're both meant to provide the boarders with clean, healthy, and amicable lodging, but Cynthia has arrived to insist that I confine myself to my room. "I've told them," she sniffs, with deforming superiority, "that they aren't, under any circumstances, to associate with you; and now, I'm telling you," she uses my Christian name, "that you must not, under any circumstances, associate with them."

She tells me it's come to her attention that all these girls are ignorant of distinctions in rank — that she sees it as her duty to alert them. Respectable young ladies do not become friendly with domestic staff. They do not gossip with maids. When they marry, they may have domestic staff of their own and will have no idea how to control them, no idea how to give them orders, no idea how to make them heel. Cynthia fears my ready presence in the house is undermining. She says that she knows I'm "only a domestic" but hopes that I can summon enough intelligence to see that it's all for the best. Everyone, including me, would be better off if I shut myself away, she says, igniting the slow fuse of my rage. I feel it burning up my spine, burning into each vertebra, but before it reaches my mouth with a burst of invectives, she disappears down the hall.

Because I'm a solipsistic teenager, it never dawns on me that my struggles to express and control my anger are more a reflection of my socialization than any personal failings. It never occurs to me that anger, for women, is a double-edged sword. It's two years before I'll take my first psychology course at a community college, three before I'll hear the term "women's studies," and four before I'll learn that girls receive the subliminal message that female anger is both ugly and unfeminine.

I go about my work in a haze, scrubbing floors, scouring toilets, keeping my mind occupied, as I often do, by imagining the pantheon of literary characters who populate my head. I'm surprised to discover Frances Hodgson Burnett's *Sara Crewe*, a childhood fictional entity I met some ten years ago, before I became a voracious reader in the hopes of fostering a writing career. In my memory, I recall her as a *good girl* heroine who lives inside a victim box — a Cinderella-type orphan, left to the tender mercies of an evil-stepmother-type hag.

The details of her story come back slowly: a widower father, an army Captain, and the Select Seminary for Young Ladies, where she's been placed. The Seminary is run by the tall, dull, respectable Miss Minchin, who like Cynthia Power has "fishy" eyes. At first, Minchin is obsequious, but turns vicious when the captain dies. She downgrades Sara's plush living quarters to a damp drafty attic room, feeds her next to nothing, boxes her ears, and works her to the bone, but Sara develops in the process of this humiliation and survives with equanimity until help arrives.

What distinguishes her from the typical *good girl* — and perhaps the reason she's behaving like a sore tooth in my head — is that she's not submissive. Although she must endure Miss Minchin, she makes no pretence of ever respecting her, nor does she attempt to win her over or befriend her. Although she's unable to openly rebel, although her dependency makes her unable to express her fury directly, she's silently subversive.

"When people are insulting you, there is nothing so good for them as not to say a word — just to look at them and THINK," Sara advises. "Miss Minchin turns pale with rage when I do it, Miss Amelia [her sister] looks frightened, and so do the girls. When you will not fly into a passion people know you are stronger than they are, because you are strong enough to hold in your rage, and they are not."

Unlike *good girl* heroines, Sara is not beautiful; she is not conventionally compliant. In fact, in an earlier version of the story, Burnett's narrator tells the reader "she had never been an obedient child." As I recollect Sara, I begin to see inklings of myself. We both share the same coping strategy of embodying the characters we read about. We both fervently believe that "everything is a story — everything in this world," and that "you can make a story out of anything." As I vacuum up Cynthia Power's biscuit crumbs from the common-room carpet, I feel myself become the subversive Sara Crewe, feel the rage rumbling and sense the stirrings of something dangerous.

Passive aggression is a label fraught with negative connotation, one that I would never use to describe the behaviour of non-compliant heroines like Sara Crewe. Neither would I use it for *Pride and Prejudice's* Elizabeth Bennet, who hoped to rankle Mr. Darcy with her biting sarcasm, nor for Tess Durbeyfield who remained silent, sullen, and unresponsive in the face of brutal treatment. Yet to express one's anger covertly, as so many literary heroines seem inclined to do, is nothing short of *passive aggression*. As a teenager, I'm not particularly reflective. It would never occur to me to question the reason we demonize a behaviour which serves the subjugated to seek a sort of equivocal justice — to mete out ambiguous revenge. Women are more likely to be passive aggressive, a future study will determine, though not because they are innately more devious or calculating than men, but rather because, generally, they're less powerful.

The polite young ladies who board at Kiltrasna are expert at passive aggressive behaviour. They abhor Cynthia's tyranny and secure a string of heavy, noisy Christmas bells, ostensibly to hang over the entrance hallway, just outside her bedroom door. Each time a girl passes, she giggles and gives the raucous bells a shake. Other girls take turns knocking on Cynthia's door while she's resting, asking for band-aids, for bars of soap, for sanitary napkins. Asking for thermometers and aspirins, for pens and pencils, for outrageous special permission they know she will never grant. "Come quick, Miss!" various girls shout: "Fiona is having a fit; there's a mouse in the pantry; Gertrude's seen a ghost."

"Enough!" Cynthia shrieks.

"But please, Miss," a little girl persists, "can you sharpen my pencil?"

"You shall all be severely punished!" Cynthia slams her door so hard that stairway railings tremble.

A girl runs past her room, and giggling shakes the bells. Another girl shakes the bells. Another girl shakes the bells. In the entrance hall below, a group of supporters gather. They're turning this torture into a game. They're turning it into a relay race. Another girl shakes the bells. Another girl shakes the bells.

Cynthia emerges from her room in a flowery peignoir, looking like Bette Davis in *Whatever Happened to Baby Jane*. In her hand, she brandishes a pair of razor-sharp scissors. Snip. She slices the string of bells from the wooden railing. They crash into the entrance hall, just missing a group of girls.

"You could have killed us!" one shouts.

"You're mad!" another announces.

Cynthia Power flutters back to her room, seemingly unperturbed, as if she inhabits some other venue, as if she is living some different story. For the rest of the evening, there's an ominous silence in the house, a tension as palpable and oppressive as humidity before a summer storm.

Meekness may be a prerequisite to inheriting the earth, but it doesn't assist in standing against tyranny, or protecting friends, or keeping your job. Because I'm a wanna-be writer, I'd like to think that the pen is mightier than the sword. I weigh the pros and cons of sending off a barrage of letters to the board of governors, of telling them what I've witnessed, of disrupting the complacent assent that allows a bully like Cynthia Power to intimidate and browbeat and despotically rule. But then I realize my position. I'm "only a domestic," as Cynthia continually reminds me — and domestic workers, in England, are not perceived as particularly reliable.

No one would believe me if I told them how Cynthia bullies the girls, how she flies into violent rages, and has forbidden me access to the kitchen and common rooms when I'm off duty. No one would believe the way she speaks to me, the way she belittles, the way she behaves, and suddenly I'm struck with a solution, so simple and obvious that I'd completely overlooked it.

I own a microcassette recorder, a device that will never become wildly popular, but is useful to journalists who can't take shorthand. Mine nestles in a shoebox that I call my writing hope chest, alongside steno pads and pens and all the booklets that comprise my London School of Journalism correspondence course. I've been dreaming of the day I'd get to use it, fantasizing about an interview I'd sell to *Rolling Stone* magazine, and feel a little bit disappointed that its first use will be in the service of something other than writing.

However, the next morning, I load it with batteries, pop in its tiny cassette, and place the compact machine into the large pocket of my work overall. I press play and record, then repeat "the quick brown fox jumped over the lazy dog" several times — I know this is a pangram assessment for touch typists, but it proves to be an equally good test for the tape recorder. When I play it back, my voice is loud and clear as is the sound of girls leaving for school in the hallway outside my door.

I make my way to the kitchen. When I switch on the light, I'm shocked to see dozens of plastic plates and bowls from the pantry dirtied with crumbs, and jam and powdered sugar, stacked in and around the sink. Immediately, I know these have come from Cynthia's room. I've often seen her stealthily spiriting snacks away and have wondered why I've never once witnessed her wash a dish. I've also noticed the diminishing supply of cheap dinnerware in the house — wondered if the girls might be using it as Frisbees, considered walking over to the college cafeteria and asking for some more. But now the missing dishes are a mystery no longer.

I move stacks from the sink to fill the tea kettle. Cynthia arrives, a supercilious expression on her pinched and tired face. She's carrying even more dirty dishware. I slide my hand into the pocket of my overall, click play and record. I'm hoping that she'll say something snobbish and belittling, hoping that she'll incriminate herself.

It's fifteen years since the FBI first wiretapped Reverend Martin Luther King Jr.'s phone, five years since the Watergate scandal, but I'm virtually oblivious to history. Everything I know about bugs, I learned from the popular secret agent shows of my childhood: *James Bond* with recorders hidden in books and cameras, *Honey West* with chewing gum listening devices and powder puff radios. In the show *Get Smart*, microphones could even be found in ice cubes.

I adjust my tape recorder in my pocket. I move closer to Cynthia and the kitchen door. "Wash these," she commands, invisibly enfolding the legion of dirty dishes with a waft of her imperial hand, and although I feel the slow burn of anger in my belly, rising like a geyser to my cheeks, in my mind's eye I see a wry smile on the face of Sara Crewe and realize that I must remain calm — that my wish is in the process of happening.

As I steel myself against abuse, I consider "your word against my word" arguments and how the most marginalized participants tend to lose. George Holliday's viral video of Rodney King's savage police beating lies some thirteen years in the future, and it will be two decades before the word *sousveillance*, which refers to the monitoring of higher authorities by average citizens, is coined. Dashcams will appear in some Texas police cruisers in the next two years, but accessible sound and image technology with Smartphones and broadcasting capabilities for all, not to mention drones that sail through the sky, will remain the stuff of science fiction for many years to come.

"Are these your dirty dishes, Cynthia?" I ask innocently, being passive-aggressive, knowing the use of her name will goad her.

"How dare you call me Cynthia?" she snaps.

"I don't wash other people's dishes, Cynthia," I continue, as if I haven't heard her, allowing the spirit of Sara Crewe to possess me. I'm thrilled when Cynthia's eyes bug, when the crisp, elite mask of her face cracks like an egg, and the crazed demon emerges. "How many times must I tell you, you stupid girl?" she shouts. She slams her arm against a tower of dishes that tumble to the floor and bounce. "Don't you dare call me by my Christian name! You're the domestic, I'm the housemistress. You call me Mrs. Power and you take orders from me!"

"I take orders from no one," I respond.

Her face hardens. She threatens to have me sacked. My legs are shaking when she turns and storms from the room, but I know I've got her. I turn off the tape recorder. All day, I scrub and dust and clean, feeling happy, even when I hear Cynthia on her phone, complaining about me.

At lunchtime, I receive the expected message to report to the college. I leave my tea and my cigarette burning. Even though I have the recording, I still feel nervous when I arrive. "There have been some serious allegations made against you by Mrs. Power," the usually jovial Mr. Roberts says.

She claims, apparently, that I'm continually disrespectful, that I've incited the girls to revolt, that this morning I called her names, threw dirty dishes around the kitchen, and threatened her. Although I've known Mr. Roberts to defend his domestic staff, I'm uncertain how he might respond to my attempts at entrapment, uncertain if he'll see my decision to record Cynthia as audacious, rather than life preserving, but I bite the bullet and play the tape.

His face transforms as he listens. His jaw drops, his brow furrows, but when I turn the tape recorder off, he's chuckling. He politely asks if he might keep it for a while. He tells me he knows a few people who might like to hear it.

In the following days, we receive word that Cynthia Power will be leaving Kiltrasna, that she had only come as an emergency replacement for the former housemistress with no intention of staying. The boarders who listen at keyholes claim to know different. *The college gave her the old heave ho*, they say. *She was mad as a hatter!* Some even go so far as to assert that she arrived at Kiltrasna after a lengthy stay at Exeter's Digby Mental Hospital, which may have been the case. Background checks and psychological assessments weren't routinely done in the 1970s, and even though "seven out of ten people will suffer some form of mental disorder in their lifetime," according to the *Daily Mail*, most will not disclose it, as little sensitivity will be shown toward them or their affliction.

Cynthia Power may have been suffering from a mental illness, yet it would have made little difference to me. My world, as a teenager, is populated with heroes and villains, with sharp delineations between good and evil and darkness and light. The knee-jerk reaction I experience to things that threaten or cause me pain are not met with an effort to understand their origin, or indeed, to understand myself. I'm too caught up with figuring how best to express my emotions in a way that still allows me to survive.

In future years, when I look back upon journal entries and listen to the worn tape recording of my and Cynthia's final ferocious exchange, I'll frame it as a prototypical story — see Cynthia as a classic female anti-hero, like Cinderella's stepmother or Miss Minchin, who through the darkest part of her character, unwittingly taught a would-be victim a permissible way to express her fury, and an unorthodox way to be heard.

REMEMBRANCE

I FIND IT ONLINE, the burned-out husk of a building I once called home. Tall black fingers of ash extend from empty glassless windows, climb towards nonexistent gables, then vanish into stone. For eight years, Kiltrasna House sat derelict before flames scoured her clean, before soot and clouds of rolling smoke blasted her mortar, before she became nothing but debris.

It happened in 2013, on Holy Saturday, the day preceding Easter when, according to the Bible, Christ's soul was said to have descended into hell. On *YouTube*, there are videos of flames, great rhombuses of liquid light, fascia boards dissolving into sparkling tears, and the sound of tortured wood and brick succumbing to its ravages.

When I moved into the house, it was a boarding hostel for Edgehill College in Bideford, North Devon — a British girls' school, that had just, three years prior, taken its first-ever male headmaster, and would in 1992, because of economic pressures, open its doors to students of the opposite sex.

I was given the title of resident domestic there, assigned a room above the kitchen's pantry. During term time, I swept and polished, scrubbed bathtubs and toilets, fumigated slimy shower stalls. On hands and knees, I inched across expanses of linoleum, removing winding black scuff marks with clumps of steel wool. Twice a day I set out flats of baked goods, prepared jugs of hot milk and pots of tea for famished scholars returning from their studies, then cleaned everything up before I went to bed.

I'd burn the midnight oil until dawn, reading, smoking cigarettes, and when the school closed for holidays and I had nowhere to go, I'd lock myself in my tiny room and remain there as much as possible, fearing the cold and darkness that sprawled beyond my door, the unseen energies and loneliness that filled the absence of life in the house and the brooding forest that surrounded it.

To be completely cut off from the world and humanity was still possible in Bideford four decades ago. There was no internet, no cell phones, no mobile devices of any kind. Like Shirley Jackson's haunted mansion Hill House, no one would hear you at Kiltrasna if you screamed in the night, in the dark.

The closest landline I had access to was a pay phone on the main floor at the opposite end of the building, and one late evening, I remember it incessantly ringing. Was it someone calling me? Warning me? I wondered. Was it a trap intended to flush me from my room? A predator, a criminal, a thief, checking out the property? Or was it something other — something supernatural.

Fuelled on adrenalin from chain-smoking and cup after cup of over-brewed tea, I terrorized myself by imagining every conceivable scenario, and never once, in all my sleepless nights, considered limiting the stimulus, thinking happy thoughts, or reading less disturbing books. The gloomy Thomas Hardy and the anxiety producing Graham Greene were a couple of my mainstay companions as were horror writers H.P. Lovecraft and Ambrose Bierce, and during one lonely holiday, Jay Anson, the author of *The Amityville Horror*, became a late-night friend. His book detailing the happenings in a house beset by evil, which sold almost a quarter of a million copies when first published in 1977 and sat for nine months on the best-seller's list, had me cowering beneath bedsheets and hearing every squeak and rustle that emanated beyond my bolted door.

It set me worrying about Kiltrasna, its name, which I'd been told translated to "house of the dead" and its reputation as haunted, which I took with a grain of salt until I was lonely and isolated and stuck inside of its belly. I'd try not to recall the claims of boarders, who swore that after lights out, they'd seen an old man walk the length of the downstairs corridor, then vanish into a wall, or the budding young spiritualists, who'd held a secret séance in the television room, and scared themselves silly alleging a spectre appeared, blotchy limbed, foaming green at the mouth.

I recall one dark and stormy afternoon when I was alone at Kiltrasna, rain lashed the building, and wind like an angry spirit moaned, rattling the windows of my room. A bang and crash drew me from the safety of my bolted sanctuary to the top of the servants' stairwell. There I could take in a portion of the backdoor landing and remain unseen. The toes of two large, man-sized Wellington boots and the sharp chine of a scythe filled my vision. My heart stopped beating, then throbbed with a hard, speeding pulse. The Wellington boots stomped, and a pool of water collected around them, a tributary spread over the sloping floor. "Maddie?" it was a man's voice, and it knew my name. "Maddie? Are you there?" The chine of the scythe tapped the floor twice before its owner stepped forward into view.

It was the groundskeeper, whom I'd met only twice before, checking on me and the house, looking for shelter during the worst of the storm. If I'd been a less impressionable person, I'd have probably offered him tea. As it was, I asked him to leave. I secured all the doors with chairs and tables, then settled back into my cloister to read. Shortly afterwards, my heart stopped again. If there really was some malevolent force in the house, I considered, I had just barricaded it inside.

Kiltrasna, once a massive private residence, sold to Edgehill College for £3,000 in 1917. An advertisement for the property which appeared in *The North Devon Journal* at the time promoted it as an "attractive and valuable freehold...occupying a charming position on high ground, completely secluded...approached by a long winding wooded carriage drive...extending to an area of twelve acres...timbered throughout." According to Richard Pyke, a school historian, "these houses became vacant from the inability of owners or tenants to maintain the domestic staff and to preserve the property with the rising costs of material and labour." But there were also other reasons less impersonal. Reasons that no advertisement would state.

When I lived there, I didn't know Kiltrasna's past. Like other college employees and boarders, the house was simply a dwelling to me, albeit a shadowy, ancient, gothic one, which provided sustenance for the darker side of the imagination. I wasn't old enough to be interested in history, and even if I had been, documents and records were difficult and time-consuming to procure. There were no digital resources, no easy access to antique generations. Anything that might appear unseemly or disreputable had been cut away from the body of time, buried beneath comforting platitudes, and influenced us only as the dead do, by their absence.

Some believe houses are sentient and retain the emotional trauma they witness; others say houses are soulless things. But as I watched my old home, Kiltrasna, burn, I saw more than wood and brick and plaster in its wreckage. Old grand homes, once full of life and promise — full of people who envision future joys. Like most of us, they would have proceeded in the struggles of living without considering the inevitable tragedy of endings. They would have proceeded, luminous, until the small flames that they were burned no longer.

When I research Kiltrasna, I learn it's been demolished. For a long time, it was derelict, a refuge for birds and bats. Edgehill College itself no longer existed. Fiscal problems and blights to its reputation had made it unsustainable. Blazing scandals that in days of old would have burnt out before becoming national news became indelibly accessible and unquenchable. In 2002, one of the college's hungry nine-year-old students was "branded a thief" by a teacher and called "greedy" for taking a second jam sandwich, the *Daily Mail* reported.

In the 1970s, such Dickensian prohibition and censure were commonplace and seen as the sign of good discipline. Children needed to be taught to control their appetites. Teachers, particularly those in public schools like Edgehill, were respected; their judgements, no matter how seemingly inane, were sacrosanct. If, however, a dispute did occur, a "private discussion between college staff and parents" was the normal course of action, as head teacher Elizabeth Burton is reported to have explained. In the 1970s, parents generally didn't make matters public. They didn't take their grievances to the press. They were happy to have their children in expensive private colleges, rather than state schools with "poor standards and crumbling discipline." By the beginning of the new millennium, however, much has changed.

In 2007, a fourteen-year-old Edgehill girl, Charlotte Shaw, died when training for the annual Ten Tors expedition. She was one of ten from the college taking part in this traditional outdoor endurance marathon on Dartmoor, hailed, since its beginnings in the 1960s, as character building and an education in self-reliance. There had been many casualties since its inception. Virtually every year, children would be rescued from the moor, lost, or suffering from hypothermia, scorched by exploding gas cylinders, or brought down by other injuries that required medical care. As a 1983 headline from the *Times* reads, "Ten Tors Tortures Youngsters."

However, the "torture" was seen to have value. As columnist Libby Purves wrote some thirteen years after the *Times* headline, "outdoor adventures" like the Ten Tors were important because "dwellers on this treacherous rock" (meaning Great Britain) "need to be ready for anything." She lamented that the British "grow softer every year, insisting on swimming baths being heated...and windows double-glazed." Though some "voices will be raised in indignation" that such a harrowing and hazardous expedition should exist, "outdoor illiteracy" from her perspective is the greater danger. She also sees Britain as "becoming a horribly litigious nation, quick to blame." But when Purves wrote her column, no Ten Tors deaths had ever been publicly reported. If any lawsuits had resulted specifically from the expedition, unlike Charlotte Shaw's case, they had not gained the attention of the national press.

Newspapers reported that shortly before Shaw's death, cold and bedraggled Edgehill girls "begged" teacher and team manager Chris Fuller to stop the exercise. They were fatigued and drenched from lashing rain and hail, but Fuller told them to carry on. When Shaw fell into a swollen rushing stream, Fuller and two other teachers had already left the moor and were warm and cozy, having breakfast in a café some eight miles away.

Charlotte's mother began legal proceedings and virtually every paper and electronic news source in Great Britain reported on the tragedy. In 2010, the *Times* listed the article "Girl Died on Ten Tors Trek" as the sixth most read story at their website.

After a lengthy court case, Edgehill was vindicated. The damage to its reputation, however, must have been a factor in its decreasing enrolment and ultimate demise. It merged with Grenville College, and in 2009 became Kingsley School, which ten years later was sold to a Hong Kong-based Chinese investment group.

The old gives way to the new; the new, in turn, becomes the thing transcended. As technology advances, it becomes less difficult to follow time's trajectories, to unearth the past from its entombment, to imagine that it's only our presence that breathes life into a space, and that those who come before, or follow, are in some way superfluous.

An electronic document I find online approves the application of The Methodist Independent Trust and Kingsley School to convert the derelict ruin of Kiltrasna into five separate dwellings. The former mansion, I discover, had existed at least one hundred years before I worked there. The sun had risen on her eastern windows and set on her westerly walls. For a century before I called Kiltrasna my home, the sky cast moods, both brooding and merry, above her, and when she was still young, a family consisting of a father, William, a mother, Catherine, twin sons, Hugh and Humphrey, and an elder son, Thomas, had taken up residence inside her walls.

Lieut. Colonel William Lloyd of the 20th Hussars and his wife Catherine (née Garnett) were known for their philanthropy in Bideford. "Many of the aged poor, and children have reason to be grateful for their unostentatious kindness," says William Lloyd's obituary. He was the honorary Secretary of the National Society for the Prevention of Cruelty to Children in the town, also an active member of the church. His sons all followed in their father's military footsteps. All attended the very strict boarding school, Blundells, in Tiverton, and seemed by all accounts to enjoy happy, active lives unmarked by major tragedy until the summer of 1909, when William, unable to be rousted from a bout of depression, consumed a lethal dose of arsenic and ended his life.

At his inquest, Catherine detailed the evening of his suicide. A little after seven, he'd entered Kiltrasna's dining room "not looking well, and complained of feeling sick. He went away and vomited." Five minutes later, when he returned, she noticed a strange green colour on his collar, indicative of poison, and summoned a doctor.

Paris green, a water-insoluble powder made from arsenic trioxide and copper acetate, was frequently purchased as an agricultural insecticide. It was also used for its emerald colour in paints, fabrics and wallpaper and gained notoriety for its accidental, and often obscured, cases of poisoning. In 1861, for example, a nineteen-year-old artificial flower maker in London, Matilda Scheurer, famously succumbed to the dazzling substance after several bouts of illness induced by dusting faux leaves with the toxin. In Italy, in 1890, Paris Green wallpaper that had moulded was found to be responsible for the death of over one thousand children.

When the doctor arrived at Kiltrasna, William was sitting on a sofa with "green stains round his mouth, on his moustache, and down the front of his clothes." Eventually he confessed to ingesting the substance, and although the doctor administered an emetic, the sick man had consumed too much and couldn't be saved. At his inquest, Catherine told the coroner that he'd occasionally threatened suicide, that she'd gone as far as to instruct people not to provide him with firearms, but she never believed he'd actually kill himself. He was, after all, a Christian man.

The following year, while still grieving William's death, Thomas Garnett, Catherine's father, died within the walls of Kiltrasna. Catherine herself followed in 1914, unattended by her sons. Hugh was fighting in France. Humphrey had recently been taken as a prisoner of war in Crefeld, Germany. The eldest, Thomas, the beneficiary of the property, was in a London hospital, invalided home from India and irrevocably paralyzed from the waist down.

In 1916, after being wounded in combat, Hugh died in Boulogne of spotted fever. His belongings were sent to Thomas, who removed the revolver from his kit, put the gun barrel into his mouth, and shot. "There is not the least chance of anyone being accused of shooting me," he wrote in a suicide note, "but to make it quite clear I am writing this to say that I am going to shoot myself. The reason for doing so is obvious."

Kiltrasna passed to Humphrey, still a prisoner of war at Crefeld. In January 1917, however, he made a daring escape in freezing weather to Holland. I wonder if he ever returned to his childhood home in Bideford before selling the lonely edifice to Edgehill College. I wonder if he walked its quiet corridors or stood in the places he'd once played as a boy. As I watch Kiltrasna burn on *YouTube* and think of my own days there, I imagine Humphrey in its emptiness, remembering the past, yet blind, as we all are, to the bright and smoky spirits who haunt the future.

DREAMING

IT BEGINS WITH a dream of music, a ragtime number I'm unable to name, a recurring seven note pattern. My body is falling in darkness. The pit of my stomach, rising ecstatically into the hollow of my throat, the music trilling, high and merry, relaxing me, making me smile. I fall as the mythic Psyche falls, slowly, delightfully, as if the gentle west wind were holding me aloft, as if I were enfolded in the god Zephyrus' wings, dropping through swaths of blackness, dropping, dropping, until the music descends, and its syncopations become less cheerful, more jagged, jarringly relentless.

I try, but find it impossible to stop the falling, to climb up the distant cliffs of consciousness and force open my eyes. The music grows louder, more discordant, the same seven note pattern beating its rhythms into me, pushing me down.

"Go with the flow," "take the path of least resistance": these are phrases not yet popular in the 1970s. I fight against the gravitational pull, and with a sudden jolting cessation, like a bride about to be carried over a threshold, find myself clasped in the arms of an ancient man. But the man isn't really human. His cloven hoofs scrape the ground and I struggle to wake, choking, retching, unable to breathe, fighting to free myself from his demonic crush.

It's morning, I'm living in Kiltrasna, a dorm house for Edgehill College boarders, in Bideford, North Devon, England. My hand instinctively slides beneath my pillow to touch, for luck, a letter that I've buried there. My blue-faced reflection, exhausted and retching, beholds me from a wall mirror. "Cough it up, it might be a gold clock," I hear my absent father's words. I cough painfully, retch and retch, until a wad of thick gummy mucus completely stops my breathing. It's holiday time at the girls' school, and I, the resident cleaner, am the only living person in this massive house. I touch the letter again, trying not to panic. Then, I stick my fingers into the back of my throat, grasp a cord of brown viscid phlegm which I draw from my mouth like a ribbon. Carefully, steadily, methodically, I pull. If I yank too fast or forcefully, it might snap. If it breaks, I know there will be no dislodging it. It's likely that I'll never breathe again.

As I pull the plug from my throat, however, and rack my trembling body with a hawking, hacking chorus, I'm too young and immortal to know that I'm very sick. I retch up another blob of phlegm, tuck my hand under my pillow once more, and collapse, helplessly, into desperate sleep.

Since I first became addicted to cigarettes, I've regularly struggled with bronchitis, each episode growing progressively worse. Before I came to work at Kiltrasna, I was diagnosed with TB, but a chest X-ray and a sputum sample negated this verdict. Instead of being quarantined, I was prescribed shiny yellow pills, large as buttons, that nauseated me and didn't alleviate my retching in any lasting way, and now the retching has returned with vengeance. I wake again from my recurring nightmare, choking, in a house devoid of human occupants, feeling queasy. The only things living here besides me are a gathering of woodlice under a carpet, a mouse in the pantry, a whisper of moths.

Neither I nor the absent boarders of Kiltrasna know when the house
was built. We know nothing of its history, nothing of its prior owner,
a God-fearing, evangelical military man. Some girls would disagree,
but others claim there's an odd energy here. They claim they've witnessed unusual, supernatural things, like the appearance of spectres
wandering through walls, or more frighteningly, in the throes of agony,
disgorging frothy fluids from their phantom mouths. Perhaps they
make these claims because they feel neglected and want attention, or
maybe because they need to believe that something more dramatic
and colourful exists beyond the boring grey of this boarding school.
I'm not sure why they say these things, but sometimes, especially when
I find myself alone, I entertain their claims.

I've seen doors slam shut here for no apparent reason, heard creaking footsteps on unoccupied stairs. But old mansions are prone to
drafts, to uneven floorboards, to weird explosive sounds. After my last
bout of bronchitis and before my health deteriorated for a second
time, a persistent shadow came to hang over my bed, the source of
which I never found. Old houses sometimes defy the physics of light.

As I pass in and out of consciousness, I touch the letter, and the
recurring dream replays. I can't place the jangling ragtime music,
which is so alive that when I stir, it continues playing in my mind for
a minute before I realize it's illusory. How the grooves of this old-time
tune etched themselves into my brain is a mystery. Unlike heavy
metal, glam, or punk, this musical style isn't one I know and certainly
isn't one I'd ever choose to listen to.

Eventually, I'll be able to match this haunting music to this
allegedly haunted house. I'll discover that originally ragtime, just like
the styles of music I enjoyed in the 70s, was considered immoral,
depraved, and evil, that over time it infected the sensibilities of its

detractors. In all likelihood, at some point, between the late 1800s and early 1900s, it filled the rooms of Kiltrasna.

Years in the future, I'll imagine the lady of the house, Catherine (née Garnett), playing my dream song on her pianola, a device that could be purchased by the wealthy at J.T. White's shop in Bideford's High Street. I'll imagine her husband gave it to her with the expectation she'd play only hymns. Approximately 400,000 hymns were composed between 1837-1901 in Britain, and, according to historian and scholar Jeffery Richards, "formed the largest single category of subject matter for pianola rolls." But Catherine, when I learn her name, will come to mind as young and carefree, and not opposed to sneaking harmless guilty pleasures. She'll come to mind some forty years in the future, after the person I was when I lived at Kiltrasna has long ceased to exist.

After slipping back to sleep and falling once again like Alice down the rabbit hole, I open my rheumy eyes and gasp, touch the letter under my pillow, wonder if some malevolent energy beats me down, if it exists only here in this house or if it's been stalking me all my life.

I force myself out of bed, reach for my lighter and cigarettes. The first puff of the day, people say, is the best, yet this first puff tastes like puke, sears my throat, spasms my lungs. I choke and the room twirls. For a moment, everything goes black. As a teenager, my common-sense inevitably gives way to mindless obsession. I'm in what philosopher George Santayana calls the "first-stage of life" where "instinct has learned nothing from experience."

Unthinkingly I traverse the furrows of compulsion, as the world, too, compulsively rotates and revolves. As I choke and gasp for air while I smoke my cigarettes, the world plays out its own suffocating episodes.

Car bombs have been exploding all over the country, but the rumbling I feel is the illness in my throat and chest, an illness exacerbated by Kiltrasna's lonely and potentially tainted surroundings, by its sticky darkness that catches the worst of my worries, and feeds my impulsive mind.

The shadow over my bed is increasing, and I wonder if this is a hallucination or the expansion of some hidden light. If it's a watermark, or fungus. I don't yet know the unhappy history of Kiltrasna, that the evangelical military man imbibed arsenic and died in agony, nor that later his son used a revolver to commit suicide. If I ascribe supernatural forces to the shadow, it's only in passing. What I don't consider is the phantom tar and nicotine of cigarette smoke that escapes in long, grey streams and swirls to the ceiling whenever I, retching and sputtering, exhale.

Demonic possession is a popular theme in books and films in the 1970s. *The Exorcist*, destined to gain the reputation as one of the scariest movies in history, debuted on Boxing Day 1973. Six million US ticket sales, three months later, confirmed its status as a blockbuster. In England, it played for the first time fifty-eight days after its US release. It played to an invited audience at the London West End Cinema, where people fainted and threw up, where, according to manager Oscar Baker, who had to administer smelling salts, one of the lounges "looked like a casualty ward" with "about 20 people tottering around looking green." In future public showings, St John Ambulance Brigade will be on hand to deal with the victims of horror. Religious and consumer groups alike will call for the movie's ban. The collective inability to bridge dichotomies holds the innocent world in its demonic cloven hooves. The Holy War exists everywhere and is destined to persist, though what is deemed as good and what is deemed as evil will perennially change.

The comic book phrase "the evil empire" has not yet been used by Ronald Reagan to describe the USSR. Indeed, Reagan, former movie star, former Governor of California, is not yet a US president. In England, women of a certain age — Margaret Thatcher's age — still swoon for him, as they recall the young and handsome matinee idol, who starred in movies such as *Code of the Secret Service, Two Gun Cupid, Kings Row* and *Juke Girl*. "Oh! to have been his leading lady," these dewy-eyed damsels, past middle age but not yet pensioners, occasionally lament.

This enduring ardour for Reagan is more complicated than a simple passing infatuation that only briefly burns. As long-time British film critic C.A. Lejeune once pointed out, it wasn't just the films themselves, wasn't just the actors, but the conditions that existed outside the movie houses that transmuted the experience for audiences. These still besotted women, adolescent school girls during World War II, fell in love with Reagan as bombs dropped and sirens squealed, as theatre alert signals flashed and enemy planes soared above. Hearts palpitated, sweat varnished hands, the nervous stomach rumbled with fear's tingling delight. Love, or something like it, kept them riveted to their cinema seats, and unless the theatre copped a blast, the movies continued to play despite the overhead battles. Trauma, as a great fixative, should not be underestimated.

Film projection is how a celluloid image is cast upon a screen in the war years, and 35 mm movies will remain the industry standard for the next seven decades until the advent of digital technologies. Psychological projection, on the other hand, a defense mechanism that facilitates the displacement of usually unsavoury, unconscious content, is destined to endure.

In psychological projection, it's mostly human evil that is said to split away from its carrier and find harbour elsewhere. Demons and enemies, rapscallions and rivals, nations and neighbours often become targets. Unconscious evil may remain personified in others, frightening and challenging its sender, forcing her to bolt her front door, don a crucifix, build a bomb shelter, harness military might. Forcing her to misinterpret and abhor, to see wickedness as existing only outside of herself until, like Prospero in *The Tempest*, she acknowledges the "thing of darkness" as her own.

Collectively favourable qualities and aptitudes can also be projected. Things like intelligence, talent and beauty may remain undeveloped or too heavy to bear. Romantic love can result in such cases, analytical psychologists tell us, and reclaiming projections, both good and evil, they say, releases creative energy and transforms that which is exiled into wisdom.

At Kiltrasna, as I cough and retch and smoke cigarettes, if I possess any wisdom, it remains in embryo. The world is basically black and white to me. Good and evil are opposites which, like oil and water, are impossible to mix. My projections are many, my consciousness slim, and I don't yet realize the dangers in this.

My self-esteem is so low and my ability to realistically examine so nonexistent that I can't value my life. I sincerely believe I'm of less consequence than any of the people I know, that given an ultimatum by a murderer, to live or save the life of one Edgehill girl, for example, I'd gladly and without any reservation sacrifice myself. I don't realize that this doesn't make me noble and Christ-like, that because I'm blind to my own worth, it simply makes me self-destructive. I can't yet discern the differences between feelings of insignificance and actions of humility, nor will I be able to do so for many years to come.

I mindlessly smoke and retch and reach beneath my smoke-infused pillow to touch the lucky letter before I succumb to sleep. Circling, like a vine maple samara, twirling to earth. Giddily dropping into the unknown. What fertile loam my demon-bridegroom may provide is a question beyond my ken.

The letter is a totem. It was penned by an old ghost, a boy I dated for three months, when I was fourteen years old and lived in Canada, though dating, which implies events like dinners and movies, isn't the right word. All we ever seemed to do was make out in his father's car, or in his bedroom when his parents were away.

Though bombs didn't drop and there were no air raid sirens, the incendiary odours of hell were riveting. I was at war with my father. My father, in the end stages of terminal cancer, was at war with death. The boy, four years my senior, tall, quiet, self-absorbed, was someone I thought "cool," someone able to assuage the inferno's heat. He was mad about the band *Black Sabbath*. He dressed, as one would expect of an emissary from the underworld, entirely in black. He even had a pair of black leather platform boots, the kind that rock stars wear, custom made.

In the 70s, when a rock concert ended, audiences lit butane lighters to call the musicians back to the stage, and when the cool boy who dressed like a rock star drew the final curtain on our relationship, the traumatized girl that I was stole a little fire from perdition, and lit a torch, unaware of the magnitude of the shadow it would cast.

Although my father died, I dreamt he was still alive, that someone had given him "the gift of eternal life." I wanted to know who, and as a grin was breaking on his sallow deadened face, revealing two elongated, pointed canine teeth, he gestured to the shadows and the boy. Predictably, the boy was clad in black. He was cool. He met my father's grin with an impish smirk, baring fangs of his own that glinted in inscrutable light. These two monsters, I thought, were creatures I loved, and although embryonic wisdom counselled me to run, the fear of losing them impaled me.

But dreams in the 70s, though terrifying, hold little I consider meaningful. They may be caused, to quote Scrooge's rationalization of Jacob Marley's ghost, from "an undigested bit of beef, a blot of mustard, a crumb of cheese, a fragment of underdone potato." They may be caused by the random firings of the brain, or as a way of clearing the head of accumulated haphazard debris. Although I'm a wanna-be writer and an avid reader, who now appreciates the power of a well-crafted metaphor, I'm years from discovering that symbols are the language of dreams, years from understanding that these enigmatic missives, like the best literature, can reveal objective truths.

Instead, it's the letter from my ex-boyfriend, potent as a relic, where I search for understanding. I re-read it several times a day and tuck it beneath my pillow when I sleep, hoping to conjure, from all he doesn't say, the truth of his feelings. Although we've only been corresponding for a short while and I've only received three letters, I'm already considering quitting my job and returning to Canada. "Love always and forever" has been his valediction, followed by a long series of x's and o's.

As I choke and smoke and try to divine what my ex-boyfriend in Canada feels for me, my present boyfriend in England, Nigel, a general accountant who is studying in Wales to become chartered, doesn't even enter my mind. Like Jonathon Harker (solicitor) and Mina Murray (teacher) in Bram Stoker's novel *Dracula*, our occupations keep us apart. We only see each other twice a month, though we exchange letters frequently. Nigel's letters are always fun and friendly, jokey and newsy. I look forward to receiving them, and like hearing all about his busy life and ambitious plans. When we date — and we do date — we enjoy each other's company, though recently, since receiving the first letter from my ex-boyfriend, I've noticed my enjoyment waning.

Although I've not seen or heard from my ex-boyfriend in years, his presence not only has remained with me, but has miraculously evolved. His character has morphed from cool to composite, with an abundance of intelligence and compassion, good judgement and sensitivity — gifts that I admire and which I wish I could cultivate in myself. In my mind, he is deep, analytical and lucid. A man, no longer a boy, with a genius's brain and a poet's soul. When I left Canada, he was just beginning a university degree, and now, he writes, he is almost finished. He writes that he is much in demand. He's landed a part-time job as a researcher. His employer finds him indispensable. His teachers adore him and have encouraged him to pursue graduate work. His vistas have opened through education. He's even learning German, he tells me, "at the Universität."

In response to my letter, in which I outlined my failures and short-comings, spoke of my chronic cough, my terribly crooked teeth, and propensity to run to fat, he wrote, generously: "You will never be fat! Fat-bottomed girls don't turn me on, even if *Queen* does sing about them, hubba hubba."

I'm not a fat-bottomed girl, although I don't realize it, and my teeth aren't so terribly crooked, though I'm wearing braces to correct the positioning of one nonconforming renegade. The cough, however, is a fact. My compulsive chain-smoking makes it worse, but some obstacle of insight or flaw of perception prevents me from under-standing this. I smoke and rasp and choke, as my flooding eyes swim over my ex's letter: "Remember, there is always someone here who cares about you," he has written. My palpitating, nicotine-activated heart melts each time I read these words and will melt even more later after I receive his next letter and the Edgehill girls return from their holidays. "Liebe kam da verlobt, jetzt war es wieder gekommen," he will write, offering no translation, knowing I can't read it. A boarder at Kiltrasna who knows German will translate: "Love came as engaged, now it has come again."

This larger-than-life love hangs like a cloud of dark smoke or a stain in my brain, sucking the energy from ordinary pleasures, insidiously eclipsing relationships, making all that I live feel anemic. Even the upcoming writers' workshop I plan on attending dims in the dark shadow of this exalted love.

Like Mina Murray, I've "been practising shorthand very assidu-ously," travelling to a nearby business college through the chillingly black Belvoir woods that extend behind Kiltrasna. Although I've never been religious, I always wear a crucifix when I tear through the long tree-lined paths and have memorized the 23rd Psalm to recite on these tense journeys. "Yea, though I walk through the valley of the shadow of death, I will fear no evil" is the passage with the greatest resonance, and I say it both to myself and aloud whenever I negotiate the woods or generally feel my safety is in peril.

Mina, like me, is ambitious. We might both be considered modern women of our times. She rides the crest of first-wave feminism, and I flail in the trough of the second. She learns shorthand to become the helpmeet of the man she loves. I learn it, for all intents and purposes, to pursue a journalistic career, though still, in the 1970s, without a man's affection, without his approval and approbation; any profession a woman may pursue offers less than partial fulfillment.

The phrase "the woman who has it all" is popular this year and uncomplicated by the later rejoinder, "but wants to give some of it back." As an adolescent, the Superwoman myth frames my expectations of a future, even though the realities of cooking and cleaning and serving a man are lost beneath broad vocational aspirations and the promise of undying love.

Nigel and I have spoken of cohabiting once he completes his course. We've looked at old, rundown cottages, imagined how we might remake them, talked about wallpaper and carpets, gardens and chicken coops. Early in our relationship, Nigel secretly dated the secretary from his former office. He confessed that it was my occupation as a cleaner that made him second-guess his feelings. He couldn't see a girl with such a lowly job gelling with the image he had of himself. But the date with the secretary was memorably uninspiring. He felt awkward and was unable to relax. "She didn't laugh at any of my jokes," he joked, trying to deflect my distress. "She didn't find me suave and witty," he persisted, hoping for at least a chuckle. "It was stupid of me," he finally acknowledged. When I didn't respond, he said, "At least I'm telling you what happened!"

Gradually, I forgave him. Gradually, his transgression faded, and our relationship resumed, almost as if nothing had happened, but as soon as I got the letter from my ex-boyfriend in Canada, I recalled Nigel's offence. How could I be sure he wasn't dating another woman in Wales, a woman who he deemed a classier accessory than me?

I told him about the letter and my intention of writing back. What I didn't tell him was the compulsive late-night visitations of thoughts, misty, ethereal, shapeshifting. Chimeras, who sucked the vitality from my everyday world as I sucked on my coffin nails, leaving me torpid and depleted, a sleepwalker, languid, in the sickness of sleep, yet also anxious and on edge.

I didn't tell Nigel that like Mina, I'd been bitten by something uncanny, something incorporeal that like the white mist she reports pouring through windows and door joinings, getting thicker and thicker, was materializing into something beyond my rational control. Like a cough, like a dream, like a fevered slumber, pleasure and oblivion kept me mute. Nigel, friendly, jokey, innocent, could not divine the cause of my silence, nor the source of my temperamental pallor.

As I smoke and retch and re-read my sacred letter, thinking nothing of Nigel, before I swoon back into deathly sleep, I try to glimpse hope. I imagine I will find it in the embers of preternatural undead love, clean and untarnished, like a beacon of light projecting salvation into an empty, starless night.

WHITE

WHITE, LIKE THE porcelain toilet bowls I clean, the blinding snow unfolds; it rolls across the land, up knolls, beyond the globe of sight, beyond the white sclera where vision stops and snow, bulky gems of white, recommence their falling.

It's "the winter of discontent," according to the British media. Temperatures have plummeted to lows not seen since '63, and widespread strikes, in response to Labour Prime Minister James Callaghan's pay freeze, are making the country even chillier.

The girls' college where I work as a resident domestic is closed for the Christmas holidays, so I have an opportunity to come to the Arvon Foundation's Totleigh Barton, a medieval farmhouse turned writing retreat. I've saved for this holiday for two years and feel rather triumphant, having achieved my goal in spite of my meagre wages.

The house is situated two miles east of the village of Sheepwash in rural Devon. John Fairfax and John Moat, poet and poet-artist, founded the Arvon Foundation in 1968, and Ted Hughes, friend of the founders and soon to be poet laureate of England, has maintained his loyal and consistent support. Although I've been diligently attempting to dispel my literary ignorance, I've never heard of any of these poets, never read a line of anything they've written. I have only one old volume of poetry, *Poems That Live Forever*, a legacy from my deceased father, who, unlike the poems in this volume, did not endure.

One of my favourites in this collection, and one my father paid me to learn by heart, is a ballad by Robert Service, *The Cremation of Sam McGee*. As I sit, pen in hand, steno pad open and watch the blizzard swirl alfresco, I think of the following lines: "Talk of your cold! through the parka's fold it stabbed like a driven nail./ If our eyes we'd close, then the lashes froze till sometimes we couldn't see;/ It wasn't much fun, but the only one to whimper was Sam McGee."

Associations are strange things, and I can't figure out if this poem, imprinted in the chemical traces of my brain, arises from the curious weather or from the fact that one of the poetry tutors, Wes Magee, shares a somewhat similar surname to Service's unfortunate Sam.

Wes is the first tutor I speak to. He's thin, tall, dark-haired, and strikes me as extremely urbane. His first book of poetry came out with Faber & Faber six years ago, and his latest work, *No Man's Land*, which may already be a *Poetry Book Society Recommendation* this year, will be available at the retreat and become the first volume of poetry I ever buy. I won't know that in his alternate life, Wes is a primary school teacher nor that in years to come he'll quit teaching, become a full-time writer, and gain fame and recognition as a children's author. After this retreat I will not think of him for over a decade. Then, sometime in the late 1980s, I'll buy a book for my six-year-old daughter called *The Witch's Brew and Other Poems*, see his name on the dust jacket, and read about the trajectory of his life.

George MacBeth is another tutor at the retreat, and I purchase his hardcover volume, *My Scotland*, to add to my suddenly burgeoning poetry library. He lets us know that he worked for the BBC, that he produced poetry programs, and then packed it all in to take up novel writing. He announces in the forward of *My Scotland* that his work is "the nearest I shall come to writing an autobiography." But if autobiography had been his calling, there is no doubt that his life adventures, even up to this point, were remarkable enough to merit public interest. In the 1950s, he joined weekly with a gathering of poets who sought to erect a new movement in Britain, one that would liberate poems from the anti-romantic and formalist trends of the time. The members, many of them internationally renowned, collectively would become known as "The Group." Its impact would be far-reaching, though, needless to say, not far enough to stretch to me.

I am at a loss when an *in-the-know* retreat participant whispers this affiliation. All that comes to mind are rock bands and those Canadian painters, "The Group of Seven," whom I recall were frequently mentioned in my high school art classes when I lived in Windsor, Ontario. Had George MacBeth been one of those artists? While I still could recite every line of Robert Service's poem that I memorized at age eight, I drew a complete blank on The Group of Seven and thought it best not to share my query. George was a writer, after all, and his accent was clearly British.

The *in-the-know* participant, a woman named Fiona, was a workshop aficionado and a literary gossip. She proceeded to tell me that George MacBeth had once had an affair with the famous American Pulitzer Prize winning poet Anne Sexton.

I didn't know who Anne Sexton was, but thought her name fitting for tales of lax moral conduct, and following the advice of *Writer's Digest*, a magazine I subscribed to in spite of the outrageous overseas postal costs, noted it down in the back of my steno pad as a potential name I might appropriate for some future character. Because I was unaware of the poet, I was also unaware of her mental illness and of her suicide four years previously. Fiona didn't enlighten me, but moved to speak to another, less ignorant arrival.

In years to come, I'll think both of Fiona and George MacBeth while reading Diane Middlebrook's controversial biography in which she gives details of Sexton's numerous affairs. I'll read how George, in 1967, after interviewing and dining with Sexton, went back to her hotel and slept with her, while her friend and biographer, Lois Ames, snored in the bed beside. George will be quoted as saying, "there was nothing particularly louche or Sixties about it, no crowds of people sitting about smoking pot."

I will recall George using that word "louche" several times over the course of the retreat, though the context in which he used it will be lost to me. I will remember jotting down the unfamiliar word and feeling disconsolate because it was only composed of one syllable, and still, I didn't know its meaning. That evening, when George is reading to our group, he will articulate other words, words embedded in his latest poems, which will elicit similar feelings of discomfort. I've never heard of England's most ridiculed moral campaigner, Mary Whitehouse, who two months hence will win a libel battle over what she, and obviously the courts of England, considers "a blasphemous poem." The losers will be the pioneering paper *Gay News* and the poet, James Kirkup, whose poem "The Love that Dares to Speak its Name" renders a sex scene between a Roman centurion and Christ. But undoubtedly George has heard of Mary, who for years has been considered "the bane of the BBC." George, himself, has been called to give opinions in censorship cases. In 1968, he shocked a court when asked for his opinion about J.G. Ballard's booklet *Why I Want to Fuck Ronald Reagan*. When asked, "Is this not the meanderings of a dirty and diseased mind…?" his response included his offer to broadcast the work if it ever became available to the medium.

I, of course, know none of this. I have never heard a four-letter word publicly performed until today, and am certain, that while Robert Service probably used such words in his rough and tumble life in the Yukon, he would never think to sully a poem with one. I'm completely out of touch with contemporary poetry, with Philip Larkin's "They fuck you up, your mum and dad./ They may not mean to, but they do." I have never read the *New Humanist*, where this poem first appeared seven years before nor Larkin's volume, *High Windows*, where it was subsequently published.

Some thirty years from now, this verse of Larkin's will have become so much a part of British culture that a Bedfordshire divorce court judge will quote it as the preamble to a custody battle ruling, and *The Sun* newspaper, under the headline "His lewdship," will report on this innovative proceeding. But to me at this time, "dirty words" no matter how powerful or appropriate, seem out of place in poetry, and I colour to the roots of my hair at George's reading.

It's likely that George is still married to his first wife, though he mentions nothing of a marriage partner or appears in anyway shackled by matrimony's constraints. It's also likely that he's already met the young writer, Lisa St. Aubin de Teran, whom he will marry in 1982, the same year she wins the Somerset Maugham Award for her first novel, a semi-autobiographical rendering of her tumultuous seven-year marriage to a Venezuelan land owner. In the future these writers will purchase a sprawling isolated castle in Scotland, responding to an advertisement in *The Sunday Times* that reads, "remotest lodge in the UK, would suit an eccentric." But in spite of their purchase and shared unconventionality, their five-year marriage will be unhappy. When their divorce is finalized, George will marry another younger woman. Shortly afterwards, he'll be diagnosed with motor neuron disease and become paralyzed before dying in 1992.

But it is "the winter of discontent," three days after Christmas and, according to the Church of England, the feast day of the "Holy Innocents," and none of us know what lies in store for us. The snow, white and sparkling, flutters from the sky like a miniature dole of doves and we fifteen strangers, who have braved the elements to attend this five-day workshop, mix and mingle and drink cheap red wine.

Of the thirteen students, eight are women. A few are on the other side of mid-life, but to me, a teenager, everyone is older. There is Casey, the forty-something artist's model with bleached blonde hair, who speaks in a soft well-modulated semi-whisper and Patricia, the fashion model, who is half Casey's age, though substantially taller. Her voice is deeper, more resonant, but when she talks about her "operation" (apparently some sort of foot surgery that restored her self-esteem and changed her life forever), her voice becomes trance-like. There's a kindly, homespun, maternal woman named Daphne, who, in future years, I'll learn propositioned Wes on New Year's Eve and led him to a room in the renovated Piggery after issuing the directive, "Come with me."

And then there is Judith. Feisty, gregarious, "in-your-face" Judith, Judith the journalist who has come to Totleigh Barton in a dual capacity, as a learner to absorb anything worthwhile the tutors may impart and as a freelance writer for a national magazine that has commissioned her to produce a story. Within minutes of meeting her, I fall madly in love. Judith of the sheep-skin vest and hiking boots looks nothing like these other women, who although quite outgoing and self-assured, even to my immature eyes radiate insecurity about their writing talents. Judith appears to have no insecurities whatsoever. She appears not to need any kind of validation. Her notepad is open and she's scribbling conversation in shorthand which she'll later use in a two-page glossy article for which she's already been paid a lot of money. I'm in love with her curiosity and her direct and honest questions which many shrink from. I'm in love with her ability to straddle the conventional world of women and the professional world of men. I form an attachment to Judith, a crush, but one devoid of eroticism; I've been well indoctrinated as a heterosexual. The love I feel for Judith leads me not into lustful fantasies of the two of us, but rather into hopeful fantasies of my future self.

Judith's journalist husband, Mike, who runs a news service in Swindon, and her cameraman, Brian, who has his own business as a portrait photographer, have come with her on this assignment. Both men respect her judgment, and I observe a collegiality between them that I've never observed between women and men before. Judith doesn't feel inclined to sugar coat anything she says to them, she isn't into propping egos, and what seems even more remarkable to me is that she doesn't appear to fear their censure. As a teenager, I'm terrified of male disapproval, though not introspective enough to consciously analyze my fear.

While I've never seen or heard it, the statement "a woman needs a man like a fish needs a bicycle" has already been coined by Australian activist Irina Dunn, modified by Gloria Steinem, and printed on t-shirts. But the world I know is not one in which men could ever be superfluous to women. From all I've learned through observation and personal experience, it is better for a woman to be dead than despised by men. Judith obviously doesn't share this opinion, which is both refreshing and empowering, and I make a point to hang around her to understand this new-found perspective and maybe even absorb a little bit of it whenever I get the chance.

It's four years since the British parliament passed the Sex Discrim-ination Act, fifty since the "Famous Five" got Britain's Privy Council to declare women "persons" under the law. The Women's Liberation Movement in America, which, according to journalist Anthea Disney, is "sweeping all before it," is different from The Women's Liberation Movement here. In England, in the 1970s, I have no idea what the dif-ference is, only that even women like Judith, whose occupations and intellect challenge gender stereotypes, prefer not to identify as "libbers." They prefer not to identify with women's groups at all.

Margaret Thatcher, poised to become the United Kingdom's first female leader and who, according to the *Daily Mail*, will "have scored the biggest triumph yet for sexual equality" if she wins the upcoming election, also dismisses feminists. "The vocal and fanatical element in that faction," she is quoted as saying, "[are] strident women. And I don't like strident women," she adds, even though there's no question that she herself is considered one of them.

I've only ever heard the adjective *strident* used in relation to women. It means unpleasantly forceful, loud, and grating. I always think of "stride" when people use this word and see expansive footsteps and ugly water insects skidding across swimming pools. I don't consider that the term is used as a social mechanism to silence the marginalized, that any expression of force in a woman is deemed unfeminine and therefore unpleasant.

Women's libbers "seem to hate men" and "are contemptuous of any woman content to be a wife and mother," Thatcher is quoted as saying. Such sweeping and unsubstantiated generalizations are a matter of course this decade. They make women fearful of joining beneath a common banner and demanding social change, though I'm completely unaware of this, as I am to the many debates that rage over gender equality.

I've never heard of Fritz Spiegl, the well-known English writer and broadcaster, nor of the lively Radio Four program in which he asks Betty Friedan if she's ever looked the word "libber" up in the Oxford English Dictionary. He tells her it means "to castrate, to emasculate, and Scottish school boys even to this day, when they talk about a very sharp knife, they say my cast-libber."

Friedan, in reply, chastises the entire country as "terribly given to clichés" that the US has long outgrown, and then upbraids the program's host, Sue Lawley, for referring to the actress Ann Baxter, another guest on this show, as a "female female."

Lawley explains, in a voice she's worked hard to posh-up and polish clean of any organic trace of her common Black Country dialect, that she described Ann Baxter as a female female "because she came up against a real male chauvinist and she adored him. She had to give in to him, because she loved him, and in the end don't we all have to give in when we love? Surely that is being a very female female."

Even before I began consciously questioning woman's place in society and how that influenced her relations with men, such a response would have made me reflexively retch, and despite the negative press libbers receive, I'd have quietly sided with Friedan.

"I think that love is much more complex than that," she'd said, "and being a woman is much more complex than that, and anything that tries to deny that complexity in clichés is nothing that interests me and isn't related to the woman's movement." If I'd heard this Radio Four broadcast, I might have thought of Judith as a woman not conscribed by clichés. As it is, however, I just see her as a strong woman, a writer, a woman I'd like to emulate.

"Women have been cut off from their capacity for action," Germaine Greer told *The New York Times* in 1971. She was commenting on her book, *The Female Eunuch*, which, according to *The New York Times* reviewer Sally Kempton, was "brilliantly written, quirky and sensible, full of bile and insight." Even though Greer, an Australian, resided in England, the book sold much better in the United States. In Bideford, where I lived, I'd seen it in the local bookstore and was curious, but not curious enough to overcome my fear of buying it. I knew that in some circles, Greer had become an object of ridicule. There were some very unflattering big-mouthed caricatures of her, and I'd witnessed television comedians ripping her to shreds. If I'd bought the book, I imagined the store clerk would judge me. I imagined he'd think I was a libber too, and the contempt which would ooze from his eyes would most certainly penetrate my thin skin and singe my enquiring soul. It seemed safest to stay clear of the book, so I did. Its content was mentioned occasionally in the media, though greatly distorted I realized later when as a university student in a women's history course, I finally did read it.

In England in the 1970s, as the snow falls at Totleigh Barton, there is misunderstanding about feminism, righteous indignation, and backlash, but I don't know it. In a BBC Radio exchange, a Mrs.

Brander-Dunbar asked Greer: "From what do you wish to emancipate women?" Brander-Dunbar is an eighty-year-old retired district councillor who claims she has "never experienced any disadvantage in being a woman." She says perhaps this is because she's lived by her good father's edict: "Always try to look like a woman," but "act like a man."

I've heard British women refer to their own sex as "feeble" and "crippled" men. Some of my female friends and co-workers label women as "bitchy" and "untrustworthy." I make the assumption that neither I nor they are included in this observation. It's an observation so commonplace that I never question it. I know nothing of the ancient misogynistic poisons we ingest, nothing of the diminishment and demonizing of women and how that shapes our society and limits its horizons.

Three years after Greer's book debuts, twenty-three-year-old, Greek-born Arianna Stassinopoulos, third woman president of the Union at Cambridge, will, according to the *Daily Mail*, put "herself at the head of what she sees as a…massive anti-Women's Lib movement." Stassinopoulos, who will one day move to America, marry Republican Michael Huffington, start the *Huffington Post*, run for governor of California, and be called "the most upwardly mobile Greek since Icarus," comes from a wealthy family and is described as "glamorous with lots of charm." She's always "stunningly" dressed, "impeccably" made-up, and is quoted as finding women's liberation "repulsive." When Greer's publisher challenged her to write a 50,000 word reply to *The Female Eunuch*, she embraced the proposal, producing "a modest bestseller," *The Female Woman*. Her book, by no means as popular or enduring as Greer's, is both praised and derided by a variety of reviewers. Joseph McCulloch, for example, writer and rector of St. Mary-Le-Bow church finds it "eminently sane," putting right "the contemporary confusion of ideas about the sexes which the Libbers have so conspicuously worse confounded." The reviewer of the *Times*

Literary Supplement is put off by Stassinopoulos' spurious proposal that "women are genetically different in their outlook and talents."

I know nothing of Stassinopoulos' thesis, that she fears liberation will "compel women into male roles by devaluing female ones." I'm several years her junior, a cleaner in a girls' school and unlike her will never own a sporty Alfa-Romeo car. There are no male cleaners where I work, and if there were, they'd be paid extra and likely assume more professional-sounding titles. I know this, though I've never given much thought to traditional female roles and occupations. My sights are set on writing. I want to be a journalist, like Judith. I want to make a living with my pen. Judith assures me that this is not only possible, but probable, that my dreams are sound and reasonable, that I'm not just pissing in the wind. I can't believe my good fortune when she offers to help me, when she invites me to her place during the spring holidays for an unpaid apprenticeship, when she tells me that she and her husband will give me writing work to do.

I want to be a journalist like Judith but have no realistic vision about what's required in attaining this goal. I've no idea that female journalists are by far a minority, nor that they'll remain so indefinitely over time. I don't know that in the 1970s, women employed by media organizations are generally relegated to women's news, which consists predominantly of fashion, recipes, and celebrity gossip, and that more worldly news is covered by men.

Judith is a freelance journalist, which seems to mean she has the freedom to pick and choose the stories that interest her. She travels to far off exotic lands like China and Russia, and has recently been in Belfast, reporting on "The Troubles" from a woman's eye view for a monthly woman's magazine.

I'm blind to the discrimination that exists in the media, blind to the fact that males dominate management and trade unions. I don't realize that most women stand a snowball's chance in hell of securing permanent full-time work as mainstream journalists, and that if Judith wasn't partnered in the writing business with her husband Mike, her freelancing career wouldn't economically sustain her.

There are only a few female journalists in England, mostly contract workers, not relegated to "women's news," though I don't know it. Joan Bakewell, for example, whom I've never heard of, dubbed "a thinking man's crumpet," is, according to *The Observer*, a "shining light among grey men." She's worked in broadcast journalism for at least fourteen years and will become a news item herself when she quits the BBC's arts programme *Mainstream* because the "major, current affairs-type pieces on the arts" that she was promised never materialized. But this won't be the first or last time Bakewell finds the happenings in her life newsworthy. Unlike a male reporter, the personal life and appearance of a female journalist is frequently considered a newsworthy topic. In 1971, after sixteen years of marriage to a BBC producer, their parting will be seen as "a lesson in modern marriage and divorce." In 1973, interested readers will be told there's "a new love in [her] life … actor and writer Jack Emery, who is ten years younger than her." In 1976, Joan's "alluring bosom in a bikini with the rest of her hidden discreetly under-water in the swimming pool," will become the subject of speculation. But "later in a frock" it will be revealed that the reason for the hidden nether regions must be because "the dishy Ms. Bakewell has become really rather portly round the middle." In future years, reports about her subsequent divorce from Emery will make the headlines, and the bombshell of bombshells, which will echo like thunder virtually any time the lightning that is Bakewell appears, is the secret seven-year affair she had with Harold Pinter between 1962 and 1969.

While sexual biases shape my life, as they shape the lives of all women, they do so invisibly, camouflaged. My ignorance of this fact may be a blessing, for if I'd been in possession of the troubling details, disillusionment would have derailed me before I'd learned how to properly spell.

I believe I'm an individual who acts upon my own personal preferences, yet I can only prefer what I feel I'm entitled to choosing. Like most women, moments of low self-esteem assist me in rationalizing bias. I'm not good enough, smart enough, skilled enough, there must be something wrong with me. I want to believe what Margaret Thatcher says: "It's not because of your sex that you get anywhere, it's because of your ability as a person." As a person I have a chance. I can work hard and make myself able. Sexism, on the other hand, is like a concrete wall across the highways of accomplishment. There are methods of scaling it, but before this is possible, one must first acknowledge that it's there, and I don't.

There's a dearth of female role models in the '70s, and while there's discussion about the importance of male and racial minority mentors, as late as 1973 there's still academic debate over whether girls really need women to help them negotiate career hurdles. As Greer Litton Fox writes: "The importance of role models for … career aspirations … is well documented. However, whether the sex of the role models is a critical factor in career aspirations and career choice is still at issue."

In 1975, academic Marion Woods ascertained ten critical characteristics necessary for women to succeed in management positions. None included female role models. "Femininity," however, made the list, along with "support of an influential male." These two criteria for advancement appear virtually universal in most occupations and are most likely linked.

In the 1970s, although I don't know it, there are many examples that support Woods' research. Ultra feminine Arianna Stassinopoulos, for example, became the lover of famous journalist Bernard Levin, twenty-one years her senior, who helped establish her writing career. Besides being "the big love of my life, he was a mentor as a writer and a role model as a thinker," she's quoted as saying. Her books were written "with editorial help from Levin." Later, she married Texas oil heir Michael Huffington, who became, according to some accounts, "a vehicle for [her] considerable ambition."

Joan Bakewell, too, who in the '60s was known for her miniskirts and her feminine physical charms, had the guidance and assistance of a man. Her first husband, Michael, whom she met as a student at Cambridge, was a well-respected producer at the BBC when she was offered her big break at the station.

Even exceptionally able Margaret Thatcher, who claims ability is everything and discounts arguments of privilege and discrimination in the careers of women, had an abundance of male help. She married an older, wealthy, Tory divorcee, who paid her way through law school and then, according to his obituary, "encouraged her to shine." She won over other men in her party, rising to leader of the opposition by chance, and then by another twist of fate, toppled Callaghan's Labour government with a single vote. Labour MP for Batley Alfred Broughton was recuperating from a heart attack, and Callaghan was loath to ask him to make a trek to the commons and cast his ballot. Fate, rather than Thatcher's obvious talent, was the deciding factor in Callaghan's defeat, while her feminine charms, both flirtatious and maternal, were most definitely in evidence as she blazed her political trail into the '80s and beyond.

"Any woman who understands the problems of running a home will be nearer to understanding the problems of running a country," she's famously quoted as saying, and "I've got a woman's ability to stick to a job and get on with it when everyone else walks off and leaves it."

The women's liberation movement didn't help her advancement, and she was always vocal on this point. No woman deserved her gratitude, not even her mother whom she claimed to love dearly even though after Margaret turned fifteen, they "had nothing more to say to each other." It was her father, Alfred Roberts, whom she followed: "I just owe almost everything [to him]," she said.

Strong, attractive, influential men, "proper men," military men, became her friends, like Keith Joseph and William Whitelaw, who once said, "I shall stand by her to the end."

"Every Prime Minister should have a Willie," Thatcher purportedly said about the indispensable Whitelaw, when for health reasons, he was forced to stand down. She was unaware of double entendre, some suggest, while others claim her innocence, like Marilyn Monroe's, was feminine and calculated.

"Jim Callaghan couldn't organize pussy!" she is quoted as saying, and once at a Putney training centre, when leaning over a well-endowed, wrench-wielding apprentice, she exclaimed, "Goodness! I've never seen a tool as big as that!"

Margaret Thatcher was born eight months after Marilyn Monroe, and both, according to Sarah Churchwell, "tactically deployed traditional ideas of femininity ... to reach the pinnacle of male-dominated professions." They "emerged from a process of 'makeover', ruthlessly transforming themselves into the type of woman (they thought) their culture would recognise and reward."

"Great men" interested both women, and both women surrounded themselves with men. Besides Margaret Thatcher's all male cabinet, she adored Ronald Reagan, and found the charming Soviet leader Mikhail Gorbachev someone she could do business with. Even France's socialist, François Mitterrand, who once is purported to have said she has "the eyes of Caligula and the lips of Marilyn Monroe," was a man whose strength and courtliness won her over, despite their political differences.

But as a winter storm engulfs Totleigh Barton, I thrill in thinking that a writing career can at last be mine, that my strong woman mentor, Judith, will help me make it so. I know nothing of the obstacles or roadblocks I face, nothing of potential discriminations. Fate, although its icy fingers have already tampered with my life, already shaken its foundations, and like a snow globe, turned it upside down, show only glistening particles of hope swirling now.

I'm aware that there are only three male students at this writers' retreat, besides Judith's husband and her photographer. One is an older married man, the other two are self-proclaimed bachelors in their twenties. I suspect that at least one of them, Calvin, who's been stalled on his novel for over a decade, came to Totleigh Barton looking for some action, and not solely the sort that improves stagnant plot lines.

When he hits on me, I'm both flattered and frightened. I don't understand why he hasn't set his cap for Patricia. She's closer to his age, more sophisticated than I, and a much more eloquent conversationalist. I'm unconscious of the fact that my occupation as a cleaner — or "charwoman" as some call it in England — could possibly be a draw. Though I've frequently heard the British slang word "scrubber" used synonymously for slut, I know nothing of its historical roots and will not, for many years, understand the socioeconomics of sexism and why this word has come to be connected to my occupation.

What Calvin doesn't know and what will take me years to comprehend, though I've already accumulated enough evidence of this fact, is that I only really want fraternal relationships with men. While it's thrilling to be desired sexually, which, according to the subtext of society is the pinnacle of achievement for a woman, it's far more satisfying to be desired for the sisterly qualities that I possess in abundance.

I'm companionable, a good problem solver, and would know better than to be lured to a gingerbread house if we should ever become lost in an enchanted forest. On the other hand, I'm not happy to forfeit a game, say of basketball or chess, in order to assuage male pride. If I compete with a man and he wins, I'm OK with that, but I become paralyzed in the face of his pouts and tantrums. If a man comes to despise me, particularly for an achievement, I'm desolate. The downside of being a sister to a man is in wanting him to take as much pleasure in my successes as I do in his and, so far, this has rarely been my experience.

Even if Calvin had known this, I imagine that it wouldn't have made the slightest bit of difference. Not only was there nothing I could prove myself successful at here, but Calvin wasn't interested in the inner workings of my psyche. My North American accent, however, was another matter. British men, he tells me, find such accents sexy.

"Why so?" I ask, not realizing I'm supposed to say "thank you" or more aggressively, "not half as sexy as North American women find the accents of British men."

Calvin puffs a laugh. He doesn't know what to say. There's an awkward silence. "Maybe because it's different?" I offer.

"Perhaps," he says, relieved.

Later, instead of writing, he, I, and the other young man, Bernard, go outside to play in the snow. The hilly terrain is dense with driven white and despite my good fortune meeting Judith and the trajectory of career success I imagine, I become homesick for Ontario, for the two marzipan knolls of the Fontainebleau subdivision in Windsor, where I once naively tobogganed with my school friends, having no clue what the future held.

The snow is falling and it feels like a shower of embers. None of us are attired for it. I'm wearing my mother's thin hound's-tooth coat that she abandoned when she grew sick of England and returned to Ontario. The men are even less warmly clothed, but this doesn't stop us from having a snowball fight, or later, using metal platters that we borrow from Totleigh's well equipped kitchen, to sled down the hills. It's fun! We're having childish fun and nothing sexual or "louche" blights our innocent pleasure. Our bodies are numb to the freezing cold and our beings oblivious of the tainted human complexities which, eventually, we'll again be forced to confront.

HINDSIGHT

TWO NIGHTS BEFORE an avalanche of snow falls and the water pipes freeze at Totleigh Barton, the writing retreat in South Devon, England, the famed author Colin Wilson arrives at dusk. He carries heavy bags into a small self-contained building a few feet from the 16th century manor house where workshop instructors and participants are preparing dinner and getting drunk. He shuts himself away, choosing not to join the festivities, which compels attending revellers to speculate. The less sympathetic say he's arrogant. The awestruck excuse his social misdemeanour as the product of incontestable genius. I'm the youngest person attending this workshop, and I make no judgements at all because I'm ignorant and fearful of being exposed.

I dread the thought of being rejected and long for social inclusion. I carry tarot cards in my purse partly for this reason. There is never a shortage of people who welcome my fortune telling, even when they consider me personally a few cards shy a deck, and once speculation about Wilson begins, a few tipsy revellers concur that I ought to try my tarot reading on him. He's written a book called *The Occult*, but I only know of his novel *The Mind Parasites*, which is set in a Lovecraftian horror universe.

I've read many of H.P. Lovecraft's stories because Jack, my former Windsor, Ontario, boyfriend, whom I still carry a torch for and who's recently begun exchanging letters with me, admires this author. His admiration has imbued the name "Lovecraft" with paranormal significance, for the torch I carry is fuelled, I'm convinced, with inextinguishable and selfless love. When I wrote that Colin Wilson was slotted to be a special guest reader at this workshop, Jack wrote back almost immediately, rhapsodizing over Wilson's coolness. Not only did this catapult the author to the top of my reading list, but it also made me determined to get his autograph to send to my lover who was, as the official marching anthem of the US cavalry says, "far, far, away." Unbeknownst to me, and certainly to Jack, is the fact that Wilson's imitation of Lovecraft doesn't represent admiration. In truth, Wilson once disparaged the author, and only wrote like him when August Dereleth, Lovecraft's friend and longtime supporter, challenged him to see if he could produce something better in a Lovecraftian style.

It could be my yawning vacuity as much as my interest in fortune telling that moves Totleigh Barton's roisterers to elect me Wilson's tea and biscuit bearer. His room is in a renovated shed beyond the main building. I'm ignorant of the irony that Wilson's most famous book, published in 1956, is called *The Outsider*. It's a study of the social outcast in literature and was praised by critics as "the seminal work on alienation, creativity and the modern mind-set."

Wilson wrote it when he was just twenty-four after realizing that his existence paralleled many of his favourite literary characters and authors. When it debuted, he was lauded as "England's answer to Albert Camus," according to Lynn Barber of *The Observer*. This status, however, was short lived. Twenty-six years after I take Wilson his tea, he'll lament that for half a century, the literary establishment forgot him, but "forgot" is not quite the word, Harry Ritchie, of the *The Guardian*, would use.

"The literary establishment looked on in horror" at the discovery that "their wunderkind was a nincompoop," Ritchie declared in his 2006 article, *Look Back in Wonder*. The condemnation, according to Ritchie, occurred almost immediately following Wilson's meteoric rise to fame. He was asked to write a series of reviews for *The Sunday Times*, "but three strange pieces later, the series came to an abrupt end." Wilson was further disgraced after abandoning his wife and child for another woman. The woman's father came after him with a horsewhip on discovering some pornographic fictions in Wilson's notebooks, which he'd mistaken as fact. The woman's mother beat him with her umbrella. To add insult to injury, the *Daily Mail* published excerpts of his journal: "I must live on, longer than anyone else has ever lived…to be eventually Plato's ideal sage and king…" and "The day must come when I'm hailed as a major prophet."

But much time has passed since these early jottings, and the future, evolving in the belly of the present, is not yet available to lament. If Wilson, dressed in rumpled tweed and signature black turtleneck, feels slighted by the literary establishment, he doesn't show it. His portable typewriter is already warm on the table, and books, bigger than breadboxes, splay open on the bed. He wears a pair of heavy-duty Wellington boots, which would be incongruous with the scene if it weren't for the fact he appears so completely driven to write as to be oblivious to footwear.

I know nothing of his prodigious output as an author, that, in his own words, he writes "as a dog with fleas scratches," that in some circles, due to the esoteric variety of his topics and the diversity of their discipline, he's considered something of a magi. To me, he looks a bit disheveled, but besides this, nothing out of the ordinary. Still, I tremble in his wake.

"Hypergraphia" — the overwhelming urge to write — is a term not known to me, nor is the name of the behavioural neurologist Norman Geschwind, who just a few short years before linked the phenomenon, along with three others, to temporal lobe changes in epilepsy.

While it's likely Wilson has never been diagnosed with this disorder, all four of the "Geschwind Syndrome" behaviours could be applied to him. His preoccupation with philosophical and spiritual concerns is consistent with Geschwind's findings of hyper-religiosity. His panty-fetishism, which he'll write about in future years, might be considered "atypical sexuality," and his long-winded, circuitous, non-linear explanations about his theories of human consciousness — which some interpret as erudite — certainly could be viewed as "circumstantiality," which is the "often tangential, elaborate, and irrelevant" speech that demonstrates disturbances in thought.

Like epileptic saints and mystics, Wilson is no stranger to the transcendent moment. In fact, part of his philosophy considers that these heightened states of awareness — moments in which "everything" looks and seems "deeply interesting, as if twice as real as normal" — can be attained by anyone. A trick he proffers to "get the mind into a state of intensity approaching a sexual orgasm" is to vigorously concentrate — to focus upon an object until completely fatigued, then exert one final burst of mental effort and abracadabra, presto changeo, the mundane falls away and the numinous is revealed.

But, of course, I know nothing of this philosophy when I meet the man, nor have I ever heard of the deceased American psychologist Abraham Maslow and his ideas about the "peak experience," which Wilson draws on liberally. I know nothing of the "spots of time" of William Wordsworth, or the "moments of vision" of Thomas Hardy, or the "epiphanies" of James Joyce. If I have had transcendent moments, I have not yet read enough and do not yet have a vocabulary to describe them, nor can I induce them at will, à la Wilson, for if I could, I would surely have transformed this moment and with heightened consciousness observed something more intense than this rumpled, boot-clad man, smiling curtly and saying "Ta."

Instead, as I hand Wilson his tea, I think of my ex-boyfriend, and how completely gobsmacked he'll be when I write to him. I wonder if he'll like me better, knowing I shared the same air as Wilson, if in his eyes, my proximity to this "cool" writer will confer a certain coolness on me.

I don't ask Wilson for his autograph, however, or make the offer of a card reading, as I'm too nervous and feel guilty for having interrupted his work. Instead, I retreat to the wine-fuelled ebullience of the main house, shuffle my cards, and lay them out.

I frequently read my own cards, always feeling a little uneasy because the tarot book that guides me considers the practice taboo. Mary K. Greer has not yet written her ground-breaking metaphysical classic *Tarot for Yourself*, so I, like most itinerant card users, still await sanctioned permission to breach what feels like a most unnatural rule. Unlike Greer, who studied English literature at university, I'm unfamiliar with *archetypal symbolism*, and don't yet recognize the collective patterns rendered in the cards, nor do I see them as psychotherapeutic tools, a way to explore inner worlds or a method of facilitating individuation. I see them simply as predictive — as a means of gaining information about the future. Therefore, my questions tend to focus around Jack: *"If I send him Wilson's autograph, will he write sooner? Will he care for me more?"* Often, when I ask these kinds of questions, I don't get the happy cards I'm hoping for: the lovers, the two of cups. In fact, frequently, when I ask *Jack* questions, I get the opposite.

The Devil is a card in the tarot deck that turns up regularly for me when I'm doing "Jack" readings. It means obsession, addiction, bondage, but I'm too obsessed, addicted, and bound to apply this card to myself. When it appears as the answer to my question, I simply swipe it up, reshuffle the deck, and ask my question again. Reading for oneself may be taboo but reading the same question on the same day is strictly prohibited. I know this, but I do it anyway — as an alcoholic drinks, as a hypergraphic writes, "as a dog with fleas scratches."

What I need is for someone to break the circuit, close the valve, divert my attention, and eventually this happens. Judith, the journalist, who has unbelievably offered to mentor me, and is writing an article about the workshop at the behest of a national magazine and whom I already idolize, takes a seat beside me and asks me to explain the deck.

Because I'm a novice reader and not particularly interested in the history of cartomancy, I don't have a lot to say. I know there are seventy-eight cards and that they're divided into twenty-two major and fifty-six minor arcana, but when Judith asks specifically what an "arcana" is, I become embarrassed because I'm unable to answer.

Judith is a strong woman, a writer, who, from my perspective, appears to have her life more than together. She and her husband run an agency in Swindon which delivers news, advertising, and feature articles to local, national, and international publications.

When she quizzes me on my method of interpreting the cards, which, at this stage of my evolution as a reader, can be summed up as rote memorization, I'm unaware that any other method exists. I know nothing about psychics who use the cards simply as a place to focus, or interpreters who dispense with standard meaning and rely on the symbolism inherent in each card. I know nothing of the oracular reader who will get a strong feeling or a direct message, though this will become my path with the tarot, as it will with my pen, until I discover less jarring ways to work with repressed unconscious energy.

I don't yet see any connections between writing and tarot reading, though, unbeknownst to me, writers abound who do. Canadian poet George Bowering in a future memoir will note this affinity and cite Margaret Atwood, Robert Duncan, Jack Spicer, Robin Blaser, and others who worked with cards in the sixties and seventies. He'll even own to using them himself and give a point by point accounting of how they came to inspire his book-length poem, *Geneve*.

I haven't yet heard of T.S. Eliot or read *The Wasteland* which features *a wicked pack of cards*. Nor do I remember ever coming across the work of the tarot-wise W.B. Yeats, who, in his autobiography, *The*

Trembling of the Veil, explains how "images well up before the mind's eye from a deeper source than conscious or subconscious memory."

"Every weirdo in the world" might be on the same "wavelength" as Thomas Pynchon, but it will be years before I read the works of this reclusive writer, who shares my astrological sun sign and self-consciousness over ugly, crooked teeth. I've never heard of his "monstrously long and overpopulated" novel *Gravity's Rainbow*, which uses the cards as a fictional device.

Italo Calvino has already freed himself through publication of his experimental work *The Castle of Crossed Destinies*, which he claims had "obsessed" him "for years." In his introduction to the work, he says he'd been "tempted by the diabolical idea of conjuring up all the stories that could be contained in a tarot deck," but I know nothing of this; I'm a virtual literary tabula rasa, my mind a vast and empty slate to be filled.

Some seven years in the future, Cormac McCarthy will publish his epic anti-western novel, *Blood Meridian*, where tarot symbolism is ubiquitous, and when Anthony Burgess dies in 1993, more than half a dozen tarot decks, including one he designed himself, will be among his recovered possessions, along with an unpublished work about two gambling women and their fortune-telling cards. The story *Chance Would Be a Fine Thing*, written in the early 60s, was rejected by publishers who couldn't foretell Burgess would eventually be lauded as one of Britain's most important writers.

Although I'm an amateur cartomancer, I'm unaware of the multifarious dimensions of prophecy, and have done little assessment of the human condition. The fact that there may exist a collective survival reflex, honed through the ages, which impels people to predict, is a thought I don't yet have the educational infrastructure to entertain.

I rarely read newspapers or watch television in this decade, so remain unaware of all the fashion forecasting and political prospect prophesizing, the picking of winners, and the divining of celebrity dramas. I don't know, for example, that style writer Susannah Kent foresees the end of "grubby" make-up bags with the advent of pencils "for lips, eyes, and cheeks." I don't know that John Whitney, a rival broadcaster, sees BBC's Radio One as an "ageing Gaiety Girl who is losing her attraction" and predicts the station "will fade away" in the eighties. I don't know of the prophesy that race car champion James Hunt will be re-signed to his team, despite his disastrous season, nor that forecasters recently predicted the Queen would confer a title on Princess Anne before the birth of her first child to prevent it from becoming a commoner. Lager beer is prophesied to climb and climb in sales, and Sarah Miles, the actress who played Anne Osborne in *The Sailor Who Fell from Grace with the Sea*, is forecasted to marry actor-director Harris Yulin. I don't know about any of these predictions, nor the fact that not one of them is destined to come true.

Prescience is an extremely imprecise phenomenon, no matter who is doing the forecasting, though I don't know this. Five months before Colin Wilson and I breathe the same air and Judith and I discuss my portending deck of cards, the *Daily Mail* will ask an astrologer, a tarot reader, a clairvoyant, a pendulum vaticinator, and an I Ching cleromancer when the world's most eligible bachelor, Prince Charles, will pack away his playboy antics, find himself a bride, and settle down. "This year," "not this year," "sometime in the future" comes the dissonant chorus of readers, who with greater or lesser detail outline the rosy future of the man they all believe will one day be king.

"Please forget all the old nonsense you've heard about cruel, vindictive, and over-sexed Scorpio subjects," begins the astrologer, referring to Charles's sun sign. "The modern breed...are brainy, dynamic and powerful." Mercury, in the Prince's chart, facilitates him "gliding from one inconsequential romance to another," she says. However, we can rest assured that "he'll choose his wife with discrimination" because he "realizes that this relationship must last."

Needless to say, although Prince Charles met her the year before this prophecy, Diana Spencer is not even a twinkle in a crystal gazer's orbuculum. The fact that she will one day be said to have written a letter accusing the Prince of cruelty and mental abuse, of "planning 'an accident'" in her car, a "brake failure and serious head injury in order to make the path clear for [him] to marry," is not something anyone would want to foretell.

"Hindsight is 20/20" as American author Richard Armour is said to have observed, and considering the *Daily Mail*'s tarot reading from a "four decades in the future" perspective, the *hinds* one *sights* are ample. Future conditions are "not so good" the reader owns, though "self-reliance" will see Charles through. The prince is "a man who loves two women," a younger one, his destined bride, and an older one, Charles' mother, the reader assumes. Although he will face "a time of decision, a choice in which…intuition should overrule somber reasoning…all's well that ends well," the pithy cartomancer concludes.

The problem with predictions is not that most fail to come true, but rather the fact we are creatures of the moment, filled with present preconceptions, our minds unwittingly moulded by our culture's cherished touchstones and illusions of intransience. We are storied creatures whose narratives of the future arise from a constructed past — whose brains only know the language of a certain moment and believe in the veracity of the here and now. The Delphi Oracle may speak, yet it's our entrenched reality that interprets the words.

"'Future' is the key word in considering Colin Wilson," critic Nicolas Tredell wrote in 1982. "He looks both at existence — at man as he is now — and at evolution — at man's movement towards the future; a movement which is occurring all the time." Here at Totleigh Barton, as I spread my tarot deck out face up on the table and Judith studies it, I can't correctly anticipate what the future holds for me.

I'm surprised the following evening after Wilson's workshop talk when Judith herds us into the dining room, away from boisterous revellers, so that I might read his cards. This is not a selfless act. If her article should take a turn towards Wilson's book, she wants to make sure she gets more than a boring head and shoulder photo of the author. Wax pillars blaze in antique candelabras. The air is electric with my angst. I forget everything I've memorized about the cards, so blather mindlessly, while Wilson contemplative, quizzical, mysterious, poses for the camera, intermittently nodding his head.

When the reading and the photo-shoot ends, he obliges me with an autograph for Jack, offers to send me a book, and tells me if I'm ever in Cornwall, I ought to drop in for a visit. He could be a genius, or an arrogant git, a wunderkind or a nincompoop. It could be, as Tredell will write, that people of "[t]he twenty-first century may look back on [him] as one of the novelists who foresaw the future of fiction, and something, perhaps, of the future of man," but none of it matters to me as we sit in the dining room of Totleigh Barton, the glow from the candelabras illuminating our faces. I think only of the letter I plan on writing Jack and let my mind wander forward into machinations of speculative destinies.

DEAD EWES

DISORIENTED, WE WAKE under white eiderdowns, dreaming that we've tumbled into soft graves, that the world has swallowed us in glacial purity. Our bodies feel leaden as we attempt to rise, throw off the heavy layers of sleep, throw off the failures of a dying year.

Through pane-crossed windows, the frozen, blinding world bleats. It cries for us to see the newness it anticipates: its fine paper smoothness, its sparkle, a million microscopic stars. All the tracks we made the night before, all of our constructions, buried. The owl-like wind has swept the land, grasping yesterday in talons, erasing its existence.

Our tutor, Wes Magee, wakes to pounding on the goose shed door. "Get up! All the pipes are frozen."

We're sluggish, moving past thick walls, over creaking stairs, in this pre-doomsday manor house, Totleigh Barton, where we've come to learn and write, to socialize, to leave our ordinary lives and shave off the fleece of our perpetual routines. We're moving to the threshold of a new year, moving numerologically from consciousness to sacrifice. Although it will not happen for several weeks, astrologers tell us that we're already feeling the effects of Pluto's crossing into Neptune's orbit, and Neptune usurping Pluto as the farthest planet from the sun. For twenty years, the planet, named for the god of the underworld, will trace this aberrant path, while mysterious Neptune embraces its new position as an outcast of the solar system. For twenty years, astrologers tell us, we can expect transformative energies to be complicated. We can expect the obvious to be obscured.

Outside, the mantel of glistening snow extends beyond the yard and hills, beyond the fields. Drifts climb everywhere like phantoms who weren't wise or swift enough to disappear. At breakfast, we all castigate the cold, but there's something to be said for it, especially as we sit before a roaring fire that blazes and snaps and spits its sparks up into the fireplace hood. Especially when cold remains the enemy without, the excluded one, the one we furtively watch and curse: our social lubricator, our poultice for all collective ills.

And although there are thirteen of us enjoying this writing workshop at Totleigh Barton, there are many ills in Britain this year. Approximately 1.4 million are unemployed and that number daily climbs. The Labour government, in an effort to control inflation, refuses to melt a pay freeze it has imposed on the public sector, and consequently the public sector moves in mad revolt. Garbage collectors illegally strike and local recreation grounds pile with refuse. Rats have a field day in Leicester Square, which has become a communal dumping place for rubbish. Hospital workers block hospital doors, and those who are capable of getting inside make do without clean sheets or hot food. In some areas of the country, cancer patients go without treatment as supplies of chemotherapy drugs are withheld.

The Guardian reports that eighty gravediggers were on strike in January of this year, that one hundred and fifty corpses accumulated for storage at a factory in Liverpool, and that each day twenty-five more were added to this sum. It was a delicate situation for the government because it involved taboos around unions, family grieving, and death. Plastic heat-sealed bags could be used to preserve bodies for close to two months, but this was found to be "totally unacceptable for aesthetic reasons." The suggestion that soldiers might dig the graves was abandoned as the Ministry of Defence demurred. Who could tell what ill effects such macabre employment might have on young recruits?

In November, 26,000 Bakers' Union members went on strike, reducing the country's supply of bread by seventy per cent. In some parts of the country, consumer panic-buying led to rationing, but the word of the moment everywhere is "queue." Queue, like the "tail of a beast"; queue like a "braid of hair"; to use Winston Churchill's neologism, Great Britain has become a "Queuetopia."

The British have always had a penchant for queuing. George Mikes, the Hungarian-British author, writes that queuing is "the national passion of [this] otherwise dispassionate race" and that "an Englishman, even if he is alone, forms an orderly queue of one."

But there are grave political ramifications to the queue, memories of post-World War II deprivation. Snaking lines of people await fruits and vegetables as tomatoes from the Canary Islands rot on Liverpool docks.

An industrial dispute stops the publication of *The Times* newspaper for nearly a year. Ford car workers go on strike, miners go on strike, and tanker drivers, who deliver fuel, go on strike asking for a sixty percent pay raise. It's the largest workers insurgency since the general strike of 1926 when the working classes shut the country down, though in this year, the country is still limping along.

The situation inspires poet Philip Larkin to observe: "The lower-class bastards can no more stop going on strike now than a laboratory rat with an electrode in its brain can stop jumping on a switch to give itself an orgasm."

Despite the discontent, there's still humour. We can still laugh. And we do laugh as we sit before the roaring fire at Totleigh Barton, not only because we're giddily hung over, but because these collective ills as they motion about us, like stars and planets in their celestial realm, do not appear to have any orchestrated effect upon our inner worlds. We are each a solitary bubble in the murky sea of humanity, a single tree in the global forest, a grain of sand in the universal desert. We do not recognize the way we merge with what surrounds us; indeed, at this time, it's impossible to contemplate. We rub up against isolated events, feel the prickle of momentary frustration. The larger picture lies beyond our present vistas, and laughter — malicious, mirthful, wry, sounding like a donkey's bray or the bawl of a lost lamb — compensates for our blindness.

Beyond these walls and windows, the snow has made a mockery of man, hiding beneath its deluge all his progress, his entire livelihood, all the scrapes and scars it pleases him to suppress and disremember. The snow, like some enchanted veil, has fallen solid as a sheet of steel in the fields and all is quiet, all is hush, as if this noiselessness were echoing back upon itself — until a resounding knock breaks the silent spell.

I distinctly recall three firm strikes, like a spirit responding to the summons of a medium. "Who's there? Who can it be?" The door was in the kitchen, and I recall a chill as some iron bolt slid innocently over wood, and a blast of that despicable winter weaselled in. Totleigh Barton is reputed to have ghosts, a servant girl whom several poets have claimed to see, as well as an old monk who appears in the dining room from time to time. But ghosts reside everywhere in Britain, ectoplasm runs amok, and a ghost could never have caused the stir that the shivering, hawk-faced man — a veritable giant, who needed to stoop to negotiate the door frame — caused upon entering our temporary abode. I didn't catch his name, but the kitchen swelled with sweat and the palpitation of frantic hearts thrashed with discernible unease. "Dead ewes, dead ewes, dead ewes," a chorus whispered, as the giant of a man stood outcast between the back door and the refrigerator's shadow, looking like some sort of British Boo Radley.

I knew there had been sheep in the fields. I'd seen them on my arrival. I looked out of the window for them. The white expanse of snow burned my eyes and made me squint. I couldn't see the sheep at all. Had this imposing man brought news of the sheep's demise? Might this be why everything had turned to electric discomfort, to uncertain and hesitant reserve? The laughter we'd shared just moments before still reverberated in my head as a buried childhood joke materialized: "Why did the cows fall off the cliff? Because they didn't see the ewe turn." I knew it was inappropriate to broadcast. I knew it was best to quietly blend with the curious flock and try to make sense of their whispered anxious bleating, and finally, it came to me, and I understood that the mantra they uttered wasn't "dead ewes," but "Ted Hughes" and that Ted Hughes was this imposing, awkward-looking man of whom all, but myself, it seemed, appeared to have some knowledge.

Hughes was, in the 1970s, considered "a poet of the first importance," and had, the year before this workshop, received the OBE. But it wasn't his literary renown to which my awe-struck, dumbfounded workshop colleagues were responding. Their fear of approaching him, of saying "hello," had to do instead with his personal repute. He'd been married to writer Sylvia Plath, who'd committed suicide shortly after he'd left her for another woman. The identity of the other woman, Assia Wevill, was not widely known nor the fact that six years after Plath's death, Wevill also committed suicide and took with her the child of her union with Hughes. In the future, mistress upon mistress upon mistress will come to light, but on this snow swept day, it's the spirits of Sylvia Plath, Assia Wevill, and his forever four-year-old daughter, Shura, that hang around his neck — like three spectral albatrosses he can neither digest nor purge.

"Dead ewes," the Totleigh Barton gaggle continued to whisper, and it's only now that I can appreciate the unintentional meaning of my mishearing. I discreetly tried to examine the man who stood by the door looking nothing like my conception of a famous poet. He was too large, too rough, too muscular and not in any way flamboyant. His face was weathered and carried no animation. Combined with the high rubber boots that he wore, this convinced me he must be a sea captain or a farmer, and when it was finally muttered that he'd trekked over here from his nearby farm to make sure we were surviving the snow, I was too ignorant to even consider that a farmer, immersed in the nitty-gritty of earthly toil, might also be inclined to write poetry.

There was a noticeable solitariness about this man, a kind of invincible cloak. In retrospect, perhaps he'd manufactured this appearance as a defence against invaders, but in the kitchen at Totleigh Barton, I didn't think that way. "Stoical farmer" was the label I'd reduced him to, and when I learned there were sheep buried in snow drifts and that he intended to go out to the fields to unearth them, I thought "dead ewes!" and offered to tag along. It wasn't that I expected I'd be much help. I knew nothing whatsoever about livestock. However, I wanted to be a writer and was a devout adherent of *Writer's Digest*. I'd read on more than one occasion about the importance of writers gathering grist for their mills — and although I wasn't completely sure what "grist" literally was or how it could be advantageous to a mill — I did understand that an abundance of life experience was thought to be beneficial for writers.

I flung on my coat and boots, and enthusiastic for adventure traipsed after farmer Ted, whose long-legged strides were each equivalent to about three of my own. A handful of curious students followed at a distance animated and buzzing. I couldn't make out what they said, though in years to come I'd discover that Sylvia Plath's life, as well as who should be blamed for her suicide, was very much a subject of public speculation. Many of Ted's close friends hadn't liked her, some considered her a bitch; his sister Olwen considered her "straight up poison," and several believed that her taking her own life was the most lethal strike she could deliver against Ted. But such malevolent judgement only weighted the scales against those who expressed them, for by far the greater public sympathy coalesced around Sylvia. She was seen as a young mother abandoned by a faithless husband with two small children and no domestic support. She'd been a good wife and homemaker, relentlessly ambitious about her husband's career, taking charge of submitting and, when rejected, resubmitting his poems for publication. She'd been a brilliant poet in her own right, but always extolled Ted as the greater genius.

After Sylvia ended her life, Ted destroyed her last journal. He'd done so, he'd explained, because he didn't want his children to ever see it. He didn't reveal the content of the journal, and so people assumed it contained rebukes and evidence against him. He never publicly grieved Sylvia's death, and so people assumed he didn't care. He was silent and didn't refute all of the stories concocted, and so people concocted more and accepted all that went un-refuted as truth, and yet the rickety scales of justice would not rest here: they clinked and clanked, like the shackles on Jacob Marley's ghost, the disproportionate weight of allegations, always succumbing to their opposites — an enantiodromia, as Swiss psychoanalyst Carl Jung would call this phenomena — the natural tendency of any "teeter" to eventually "totter" and so on ad infinitum.

The year before we wander out to that snowy inhospitable field in search of sheep, Ted in a letter to a friend wrote: "Much of the atmosphere of this last year has been decided by the latest wave of publications about Sylvia. I'm not at all sure how much that is affecting me.... Sometimes I think I ought really to try and write it all out, as I've occasionally started doing, and then other times I ought to forget it, vanish, and start again somehow. I met a healer/ spiritualist last week who told me to lie flat on the earth, splay out my arms and legs, and let it all go — release it into the astral. I feel she might be right. But then I feel you have to deal with it, too — if only to put an end to 'evasion'. What's certainly wrong is staggering along year after year, neither dealing with it nor letting go, just getting older."

In this fierce winter of discontent, though we may not notice it, we're all, to some extent, staggering along, clinging to wafers of undigested past and growing older. We're all, to some extent, constrained by this feature of memory, of suffering, and the condition of being human, that resists the finality of death. Perhaps this is why we write and perhaps this is why we move towards the snowy field to free what living beasts we find there. Perhaps it's a symbolic attempt to liberate ourselves — reclaim the long lost shards of splintered wholeness — re-collect and set free the memory of a once Edenic past.

"Dead ewes," I faintly hear a voice rise like a stream of cold and dusty smoke behind me.

Nothing in the field moves. It's as still and stagnant as stone.

Farmer Ted's voice is deep and rough and quiet, and I have no notion that his instruction on how to find and free sheep will become, for me, a bardic initiation. It will begin by acknowledging the heat of breath, the spirit that escapes the body, the life force, the pneuma, the essence that melts the matter where Wisdom is entombed, and when he points them out, I'll see the paired holes, round as tiny peas, *spiritus* which has streamed from the sheep's nostrils, chiselling the petrified whiteness, like words on an open page.

The sheep are buried not because they are unthinking and illogical creatures, who in panic have scattered from the safety of the field's centre, but because I, the neophyte, need to hone my scattered attention, to focus "patient concentration" on the natural, physical world.

If I had access to the story of Ted and Sylvia, as no one here at Totleigh Barton does, I'd discover that Sylvia considered herself Ted's pupil, that Ted considered himself a master bard, a seer-poet of the ancient Celtic kind. I'd discover that daily, he'd set exercises for her, training in concentration and observation, so that she might overcome the wild distractions and aimless inattentions of her busy brain. I'd learn that Ted plotted astrological charts, that using this arcane science, he insisted on certain works being published on certain days, that he foretold Sylvia's great fame as a poet, and told her in a letter that it would come about through her marriage partner. "You will see all this for yourself when you learn to prognostic."

Ted worked with the Kabala, Tarot cards, and the Quija board. His friend, Daniel Weissbort, recalled Ted teaching him the principles of Feng Shui. "There was much of the pedagogue in Ted," Weissbort wrote, and the pedagogue in Ted was tutor to Sylvia.

Al Alverez, friend to both poets, argued in his autobiography that Ted had given Sylvia the keys to the underworld, and after he left her, she used the magic he'd taught to unlock its doors. If Sylvia were alive and in this field, it's likely that she'd spot those holes right away, likely that she'd move, unflinching, to take the long broken tree branch, the wand, Ted extends. She'd know if it were oak or apple, know the proper place to tamp the snow to find the living treasure. I, on the other hand, have not yet exhumed even my fundamental instincts and am caught marvelling at creatures who, even while buried alive, remain placid.

Who could guess that sheep can exist concealed in snow for weeks? That their precise mouths will burrow to the earth, and nibble on the shoots of grass around them, and once the grass is gone, they'll eat their own wool, balding themselves, and then devour the fleece of their neighbours. But these lucky sheep will never face such extremes, and there will be no casualties, no "dead ewes"; for farmer Ted and his small astounded entourage will pull them from their snowy sarcophagi just as if they were dormant poems awaiting excavation from the under-world, and their bleating will ring above the snowy fields, a lesson in writing and an education of death and resurrection for any who listen and are moved to take up their pens and write.

ACKNOWLEDGMENTS

I wish to thank all the people, past and present, who have supported me in the development of this book.

These include my life partner and always first reader, Eric Henderson; my children and grandchildren, who supply a steady stream of memory triggers with their own life experiences; my emotionally intelligent cat, Pye, who although technically not a person, was an encouraging and warm presence, particularly during revisions.

I also wish to thank Pat O'Brien, Pam Verhagen, Anne Wood, and Heather Owen, who read early portions of this work and offered valuable responses.

Further, I'm indebted to Andreas Schroeder and Anthony Barrett, who gave insightful suggestions on early drafts.

Bill Owen added to my understanding of World War II Britain with firsthand accounts of his time stationed abroad in the Canadian Air Force while Dorothy Livesey gave me a civilian's eye view of the war years.

I am also grateful for the support of the Canada Council for the Arts, which funded several of the pieces in this work and continues to fund many of the literary magazines which publish Canadian writers.

Early versions of these essays and memoirs appeared in the following magazines: *Room; The Malahat Review, The Antigonish Review, The New Quarterly, Event, subTerrain,* and *The Fiddlehead.* I thank the editors and editorial boards of these publications for giving my writing a place to be showcased.

And last, but not least, thanks are due to Brian Kaufman and Karen Green at Anvil Press for their care and competence in publishing.

ABOUT THE AUTHOR

Madeline Sonik is a teacher, writer, and editor. Her work has been published extensively in journals, magazines, and academic anthologies. Her literary nonfiction title, *Afflictions & Departures* (memoir/essays), won the City of Victoria Butler Book Prize, was a Finalist for the Charles Taylor Prize for literary non-fiction, and was nominated for the BC National Award for Canadian Non-Fiction. Her other books include *Stone Sightings* (poetry), *The Book of Changes* (poetry), *Arms* (a novel), *Drying the Bones* (stories) and *Belinda and the Dustbunnys* (children's novel) and, most recently, *Fontainebleau* (stories). She has a MFA in Creative Writing and a PhD in Education, both from UBC. She has also been the recipient of numerous awards, prizes and fellowships for her writing.